ACCOUNTING AND FINANCIAL MANAGEMENT

For I.T. Professionals

ACCOUNTING AND FINANCIAL MANAGEMENT

For I.T. Professionals

Y.P. SINGH
Assistant Professor and Management Consultant
(Financial Management and Accounting)
IISE Business & I.T. School
Lucknow (INDIA)
(www.iiseindia.com)

PUBLISHING FOR ONE WORLD

NEW AGE INTERNATIONAL (P) LIMITED, PUBLISHERS
New Delhi • Bangalore • Chennai • Cochin • Guwahati • Hyderabad
Jalandhar • Kolkata • Lucknow • Mumbai • Ranchi
Visit us at www.newagepublishers.com

Published by New Age International (P) Ltd., Publishers
First Edition: 2007
Reprint: 2008

Branches:

- 36, Malikarjuna Temple Street, Opp. ICWA, Basavanagudi, **Bangalore**. © (080) 26677815
- 26, Damodaran Street, T. Nagar, **Chennai**. © (044) 24353401
- Hemsen Complex, Mohd. Shah Road, Paltan Bazar, Near Starline Hotel, **Guwahati**. © (0361) 2543669
- No. 105, 1st Floor, Madhiray Kaveri Tower, 3-2-19, Azam Jahi Road, Nimboliadda, **Hyderabad**. © (040) 24652456
- RDB Chambers (Formerly Lotus Cinema) 106A, Ist Floor, S.N. Banerjee Road, **Kolkata**. © (033) 22275247
- 18, Madan Mohan Malviya Marg, **Lucknow**. © (0522) 2209578
- 142C, Victor House, Ground Floor, N.M. Joshi Marg, Lower Parel, **Mumbai**. © (022) 24927869
- 22, Golden House, Daryaganj, **New Delhi**. © (011) 23262370, 23262368

ISBN : 978-81-224-2153-8

Rs. 150.00

C-08-10-3185

Printed in India at Mehra Offset, Delhi.
Typeset at River-edge Graphics, Delhi.

PUBLISHING FOR ONE WORLD
NEW AGE INTERNATIONAL (P) LIMITED, PUBLISHERS
4835/24, Ansari Road, Daryaganj, New Delhi-110002
Visit us at **www.newagepublishers.com**

Dedicated to

Almighty :

LORD SHIVA, ALLAH & PRABHU YISHU MASIH

with whose blessings

this book is published

Preface

Management in India increasingly realises the use of accounting information for efficient management of business enterprises. Accounting is the science of measurement, analysis and communication. The designing of accounting systems, generating information and transmitting it to the management has expanded the scope of accounting and financial management.

This book has been written with a specific aim i.e., to cater to the needs of I.T. professionals (especially MCA students) of U.P. Technical University as well as other universities also.

I.T. comprises of Hardware part, Software part, and Information part. When we talk of business application software, we need to recognize and understand business information because problem recognition is the first step of software development. Accounting and Financial management are said to be the language of business because it enables the user to recognize and understand complexities associated with business information. This generates the need for study of Accounting and Financial management for I.T. professionals. This book has been written from system's point of view to facilitate I.T. professionals. A system comprises of three components as shown below:

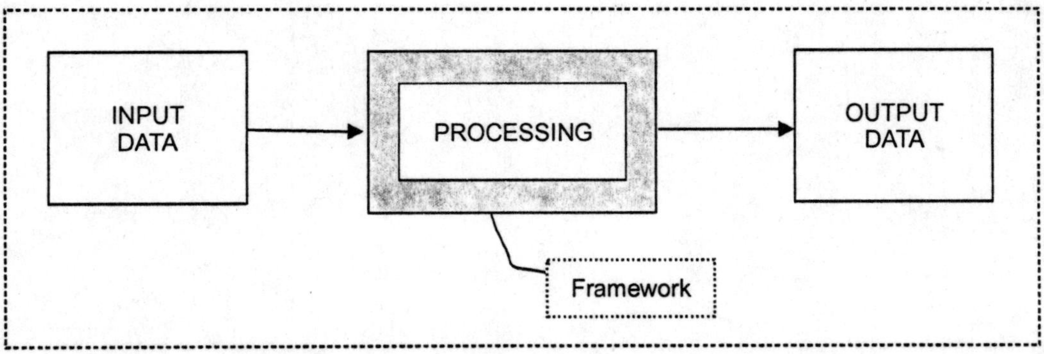

Accounting as system takes business transactions/events as input data and process it within the framework of accounting principles and theories leading to generation of a number of reports (output data) which in turn acts as input data for financial management. **Financial management as system** process it within the framework of external environment and takes financial decisions (output data) viz. financing decisions, investment decisions and dividend decisions.

This book is also intended to assist beginners of management courses like B.B.A., B.Com. etc. and non-finance executives at work enabling them to understand business information (published in form of annual reports) and complexities associated with business organization. Furthermore, I am extremely grateful to my godfather Dr. Girish Bihari (Ex-DGP, UP), CMD–IISE for his kind support and to New Age International Publishers, New Delhi for publishing this book so nicely and elegantly.

I convey my sincere thanks to my parents, my younger brother 'Raju' and my lovely friend for their support and encouragement.

Last but not least, I shall appreciate receiving comments and suggestions from readers for the improvement of the book.

Dr. Y.P. Singh
Lucknow (India)
Email: doctorypsing@rediffmail.com

Contents

Part-I: Financial Accounting

Part-II: Management & Cost Accounting

Part-III: Financial Mangement

Part – I

Financial Accounting

Chapter–1

Accounting and Financial Management A Conceptual Framework

LEARNING OBJECTIVES

In this chapter we will study:

Introduction

Need for Accounting and Role of Accountant

❑ *Important terms*

Defining Accounting—Traditional and Modern View

Accounting Information

Branches of Accounting

Difference between Financial Accounting, Management Accounting and Cost Accounting

Accounting Information System—Information flow chart

Users of Accounting Information

Steps in Accounting Process

Limitations of Accounting

Accounting and Financial Management—Inter-relationship

Organisation Structure for Accounting and Finance Activity

Utility of Accounting and Financial Management for Information Technology Professionals.

1.1 INTRODUCTION

- Organizations play an important role towards economic development.
- There are different types of organizations engaged in trading and manufacturing of goods/services.
- On the basis of motive, there may be two categories of organizations.

Organizations

Profit motive → All business organizations have profit motive (*The intention is to earn profit (profit = revenue – cost)*)

Non-profit motive → Social organizations like club, trust, church, government hospital, and government schools have non-profit motive *(The intention is to earn revenue just to meet the cost of meeting the objectives i.e., no profit no loss.)*

- Both category of organizations (stated above) need money to fulfil their objectives *i.e.,* **to sustain and to grow.**
- There are two aspects of money (Fund).

Measurement of money | **Management of money**

- In a very limited sense **measurement of money** means how much money has been invested and where *i.e.,* record-keeping whereas, **management of money** means from where the money will come in and where it will go *i.e.,* procurement of fund (Financing decision) and utilization of fund (Investment decision).

  Thus,

- ***Accounting*** **is concerned with measurement of money.**

  Financial Management **is concerned with management of money.**

'Measurement of money' in a broad sense means systematic record-keeping *i.e.,* maintaining books of accounts popularly known as book-keeping to generate such information which helps the interested groups/individuals in decision-making process *i.e.,* planning and controlling future activities.

'Management of money' in a broad sense includes all the financial decisions starting from planning to controlling financial activities under external/environmental factors (micro and macro both).

Thus, in a nutshell, **Accounting** is information-generating system whose objective is to collect, process and report financial data of an organization to all the interested parties (internal and external both) for decision-making *i.e.,* planning and controlling financial activities.

Thus, in a nutshell **Financial Management** is a decision-making system whose objective is planning, analysis and controlling financial decisions under external environmental factors (micro level and macro level both).

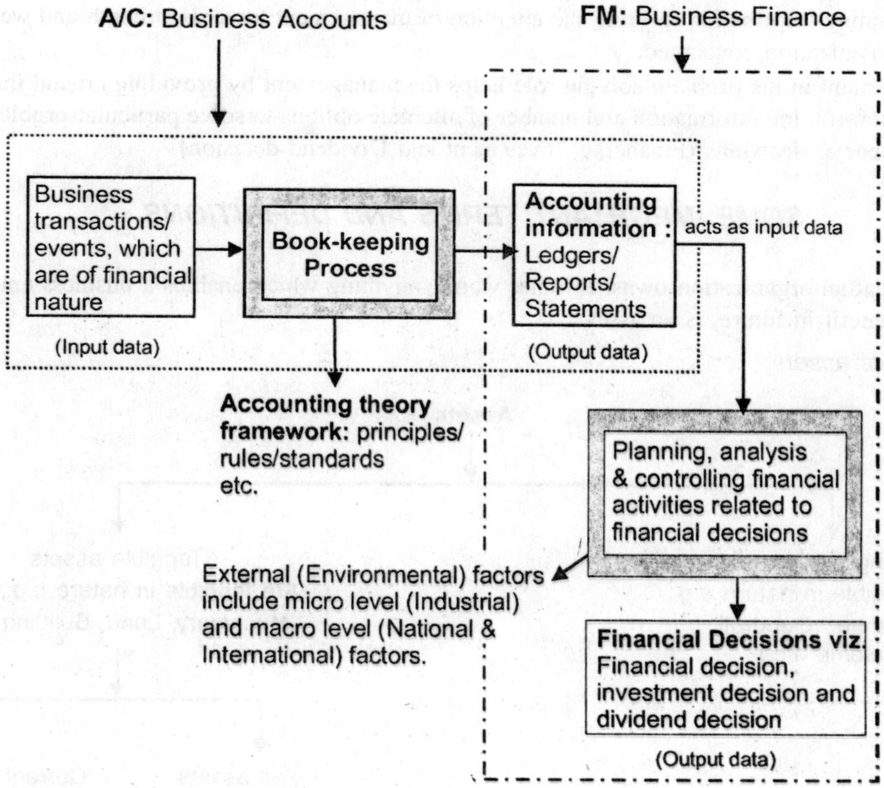

1.2 NEED FOR ACCOUNTING AND ROLE OF ACCOUNTANT

1.2.1 Need for Accounting

Accounting helps in knowing:

- What is the result of business operation after a certain interval *i.e.,* profit/loss?
- Financial health: Will the organization be able to meet commitments/obligations in the near future?
- What is fund/cash position?
- What the organization owns *i.e.,* assets to the organization.
- What the organization owes *i.e.,* liabilities of the organization.

and many more things, which help in decision-making process. This creates need for accounting.

Now, before going into details of accounting, first have a look on important terms frequently used in accounting. This will help in clear understanding of accounting concept and process.

1.2.2 Role of Accountant

With the help of proper accounting system, accountant helps the management in three ways:

- Record-keeping/book-keeping
- Attention-directing
- Problem-solving
  - Accountant in his record-keeping role maintains books of account.
  - Accountant in his attention-directing role generates different statutory and non-statutory routine accounting information to bring the attention of management towards strength and weakness of the organization concerned.
  - Accountant in his problem-solving role helps the management by providing crucial information *i.e.,* non-routine information and number of alternate options to solve particular problem related to financial decisions (Financing, Investment and Dividend decision).

SOME IMPORTANT TERMS AND DEFINITIONS

Assets

Assets mean what an organization owns. In other words, anything which enables a business enterprise to get cash or a benefit in future, is an asset.

Classification of assets

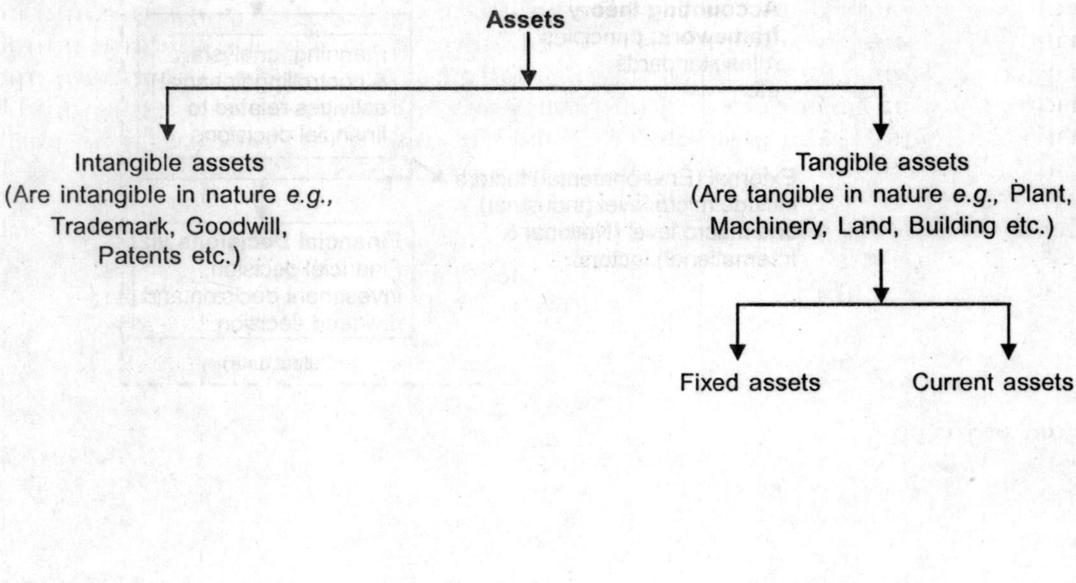

- **Fixed Assets:** Assets that are acquired for relatively long periods for carrying on the business of the enterprise and not meant for resale, *e.g.,* land, building, plant, and machinery etc.
- **Current Assets (CA):** Assets which are either in the form of cash or can be converted into cash within one year/short period *i.e.,* get converted into cash within one operating cycle of business *e.g.,* Cash, Inventories, Debtors, Bills Receivable, etc.
- **Liquid/Quick Assets:** Assets, which are immediately convertible into cash without much loss, *e.g.,* debtors, marketable securities, stamps etc. *i.e.,* except stock, all CA are liquid assets.

Liabilities

Liabilities mean what the organization owes. In other words, it is an amount, which a business owes and has to return or account for. For example, loan from banks, trade creditors, etc.

Classification of liabilities

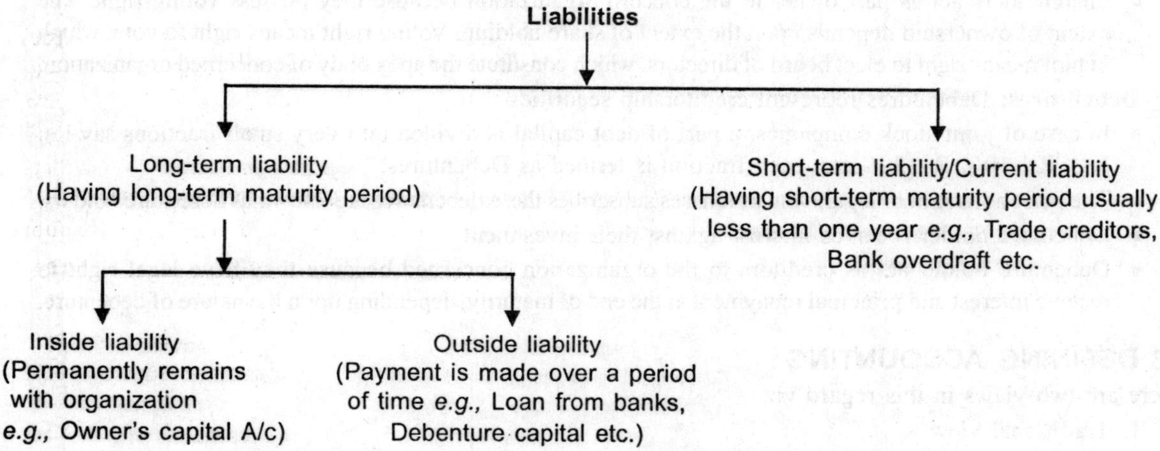

Capital: It refers to the amount invested by the proprietor in business enterprises.

Revenue: It means income of a recurring nature from any source related to business.

Capital Expenditure: An expenditure, which has been incurred for the purpose of obtaining a long-term advantage for the business, *e.g.* expenditure incurred for purchase of fixed assets.

Revenue Expenditure: It denotes the cost of services and things used for generating revenue. In other words, all items of expenditure, whose benefit expires within a year or which have been incurred merely to maintain the business or to keep the assets in good working condition, is taken as revenue expenditure. For example, salaries and wages paid to employees, depreciation of business assets, maintenance expenses of motor vehicle, etc. Revenue expense is different from loss. An expense is supposed to bring some benefit to the firm, whereas a loss brings no benefit to the firm. For example, loss by theft, loss by fire, etc. While calculating the income or the profit of a business for a particular period, the revenue earned during that period is to be matched with the expense incurred in earning that revenue (matching concept).

Deferred Revenue Expenses: A revenue expenditure whose benefit is to continue for period of two or more years. Such expenditure is written off not in one year but over a period of two or three years. For example, expenditure incurred on heavy advertisement, preliminary expenditure, etc.

Creditor: Any person who gives credit is a creditor. The supplier supplying goods on credit is creditor. Creditor is one to whom the business owes. Owner is a creditor under 'Separate Entity Concept'.

Debtor: A person who owes money to the business is called a debtor. He is a customer to whom goods are sold on credit.

Solvent: A person who is in a position to pay his debts as they become due.

Insolvent: A person who is not in a position to pay his debts as they become due. The dues from an insolvent debtor are known as Bad Debts.

Reserve for Bad Debt: A reserve from the profit of the organization is created for bad and doubtful debts. It is a buffer for anticipated loss (under conservatism).

Shares: Shares represent ownership securities.

- In case of joint stock companies, owner's capital is divided into very small fractions say Rs. 5/-, Rs. 10/-, Rs. 20/- etc. each fraction is termed as Shares.
- The person (natural or legal) who purchases/subscribes these shares are known as shareholders.
- Whatever shareholder receives against their investment is known as dividend. This may be in form of cash or kind.
- Shareholders act as part owner to the concern organization because they possess voting right. The extent of ownership depends upon the extent of share holding. Voting right means right to vote, which in turn means right to elect board of directors, which constitute the apex body of concerned organization.

Debentures: Debentures represent creditorship securities.

- In case of joint stock companies, a part of debt capital is divided into very small fractions say Rs. 5/-, Rs. 10/-, Rs. 20/- etc. each fraction is termed as Debentures.
- The person (natural or legal) who purchases/subscribes these debentures are known as debenture holders.
- Debenture holder receives interest against their investment.
- Debenture holder act as creditors to the organization concerned because they have legal right to receive interest and principal repayment at the end of maturity, depending upon the nature of debenture.

1.3 DEFINING ACCOUNTING

There are two views in this regard viz.

1. Traditional view
2. Modern view

1.3.1 Traditional View

Traditionally *i.e.,* up to first decade of 20th century, accounting was merely restricted to book-keeping leading to preparation of income statement and balance sheet only, referred as financial statements (Audited financial statements are statutory requirement demanded by government for the purpose of income tax liability).

- Income statement presents summary of all the expenses and incomes during the financial year (1st April to 31st March).
- Balance sheet presents what the organization owns *i.e.* assets and what the organization owes *i.e.* liabilities at a particular point of time, usually at the end of financial year *i.e.* on 31st March.

1.3.1.1 Book-keeping

- Book-keeping means systematic recording of all the financial transactions/events in the book of accounts. ***Book-keeping is not concerned with disclosing or interpreting the results of the business.***
- Systematic recording means identifying, measuring, recording, classifying and summarizing (trial balance only) financial transactions/events, under accounting theory framework. ***Note: Accounting theory framework will be discussed later in the book.***
- Transaction means exchange of money with money's worth *e.g.* sale of goods for Rs 10,000.
- Event means happenings *e.g.* loss of stock due to fire worth Rs. 5000.
- Books of accounts are the place where financial transaction/events are recorded.

1.3.1.2 Evolution of Modern Accounting

With the passage of time the role of accounting has changed significantly and in present stage it is accepted as an information system, which helps the management in economic decision-making. In other words, modern Accounting is book-keeping plus much more. The following definition of accounting arranged in chronological order are evidences regarding changing role of accounting over a period of time:

(*i*) **1941:** The American Institute of Certified Public Accountants (AICPA) defined accounting as: "The arts of recording, classifying and summarizing in a significant manner and in terms of money transactions and events, which are in part, at least, of a financial character and interpreting the result thereof."

(*ii*) **1966:** The American Accounting Association (AAA) defined accounting as: "The process of identifying, measuring and communicating economic information to permit informed judgements and decisions by uses of the information."

(*iii*) **1970:** Accounting Principles Board (APB) and AICPA states: "The function of accounting is to provide quantitative information, primarily financial in nature, about economic entities, that is intended to be useful in making economic decisions."

1.3.2 Modern View of Accounting

According to this view, accounting is an information generating system. It takes business transactions/events as input data, process it which is popularly known as book-keeping process which includes identifying, recording, classifying and summarizing business transactions and events under accounting theory framework and generates output data in the form of statements and reports which helps all the interested parties (internal and external both) in economic decision-making *i.e.* planning and controlling financial activities.

In other words, accounting is book-keeping process which generates information known as accounting information to help all the interested parties (internal and external both) in decision-making *i.e.* planning and controlling financial activities.

Thus, the role of accounting is, information system hereafter referred to Accounting Information System (AIS).

Accounting as information system can be presented as shown below:

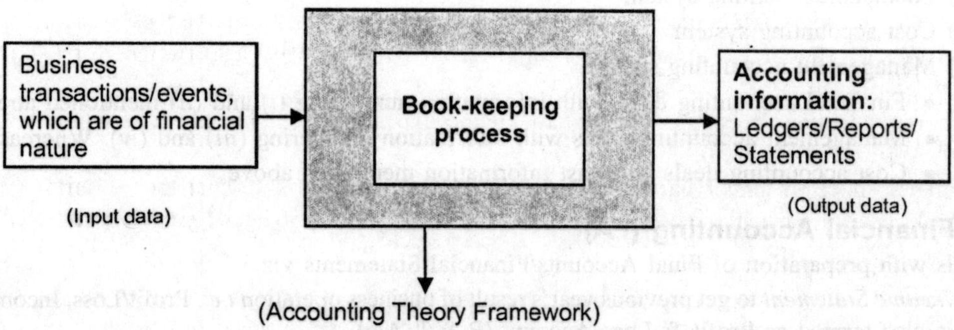

Both the views on accounting have one thing common *i.e.*, book-keeping. In other words, book-keeping is an essential part of accounting process. But before going into the mechanism involved in various stages of book-keeping process, let us have a look on information generated by accounting system known as Accounting Information.

1.4. ACCOUNTING INFORMATION

The information generated through accounting system can be categorized in two parts.

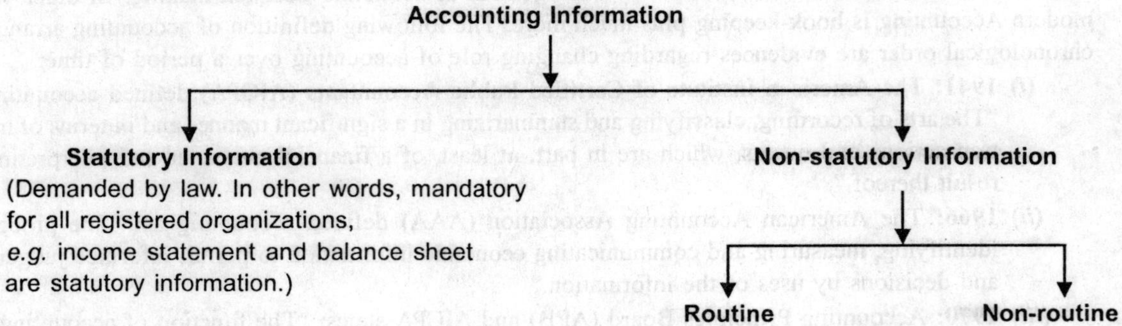

- Routine information is generated after certain intervals. Examples of routine information are fund flow statement/cash flow statement, annual budget, performance reports, cost sheet etc.
- Non-routine information is need-based information generated by accounting system to help in solving specific problem, *e.g.*, marginal cost sheet, zero-based budgeting etc.

Thus, accounting helps in knowing (say):

(*i*) The result of business operation *i.e.* profit/loss through income statement.

(*ii*) The financial position *i.e.* picture of assets and liabilities through balance sheet.

(*iii*) Fund position/cash position through fund flow statement/cash flow statement.

(*iv*) Resource utilization position/financial health through ratio analysis.

(*v*) Cost records for different cost centers through cost sheet.

And many more things that are required for decision-making process.

1.5. BRANCHES OF ACCOUNTING

On the basis of information generated by accounting system, there are three main branches of accounting:

(*i*) Financial accounting system

(*ii*) Cost accounting system

(*iii*) Management accounting system.

- Financial accounting deals with information numbering (*i*) and (*ii*) mentioned above.
- Management accounting deals with information numbering (*iii*) and (*iv*). Whereas
- Cost accounting deals with last information mentioned above.

1.5.1 Financial Accounting (FA)

FA deals with preparation of Final Accounts/Financial Statements viz.

(*i*) *Income Statement* to get previous year's result of business operation *i.e.*, Profit/Loss. Income statement is also termed as Profit & Loss Account (P & L A/c).

(*ii*) *Balance Sheet* (B/S) to get previous year's financial position *i.e.*, picture of Assets and Liabilities.

1.5.2 Cost Accounting (CA)

Cost accounting deals with present information *i.e.*, determining unit cost at different levels (known as cost centers) of ongoing production. Cost accounting process includes:

(*i*) Cost determination *i.e.* costing

(*ii*) Cost analysis *i.e.* studying behavior of profit with respect to cost and volume.

(*iii*) Cost control *i.e.* comparison of actual cost with predetermined cost/standard cost.

For above-mentioned information, CA system generates:

(*i*) *Cost sheet* for cost determination.

(*ii*) *Report on CVP (Cost-Volume-Profit) analysis/BE (Break-Even) analysis* for analyzing behaviour of profits with respect to cost and volume.

(*iii*) *Report on variance analysis* for determining variances and to take corrective action whenever needed and hence cost control.

Note:

- Both FA and CA takes input data for further processing from book-keeping system.
- In an organization book-keeping system functions as a part of FA system. In other words, it is not in isolation.

1.5.3 Management Accounting (MA)

MA deals with all those information, which helps in decision-making process *i.e.* planning and controlling financial activities. In an organization, MA is common to both FA and CA because all those information, which are generated by FA and CA system are useful in decision-making process and comes under the preview of MA system *e.g.*

- CVP analysis and variance analysis of CA system also form part of MA system.
- Fund Flow Statement (FFS) of FA system also form part of MA system. Because it presents the flow of fund through business organization during financial year and is of great help in assessing fund position.

Apart from above information which are common to both FA system and CA system, there are some information exclusively generated by management accountants *e.g.*

(*i*) Projected statements like:

A-Projected income statement to estimate coming year's target profit.

B-Projected balance sheet to estimate coming year's target financial position. (*i.e.* assets and liabilities).

C-Projected FFS/CFS to estimate coming year's target fund/cash position.

(*ii*) *Developing budget and budgetary control system* for the purpose of budgeting.

(*iii*) *Marginal costing techniques* for short-term decision-making purposes.

1.6 DIFFERENCE BETWEEN FA, MA AND CA SYSTEM

Financial Accounting (FA)	*Management Accounting (MA)*	*Cost Accounting (CA)*
1. Financial accounting is concerned with preparation of financial statement *i.e.* income statement and balance sheet.	1. Management accounting is concerned with accounting done by management itself that help the top-level management in decision-making.	1. Cost accounting is concerned with cost determination *i.e.* costing, cost analysis and cost control.
2. Financial accounting is governed by certain accounting principles, concepts and accounting standards etc.	2. Management accounting has no such restrictions. The management as per its requirement prepares it. The tools used for	2. Cost accounting is also regulated by certain rules and formats. The techniques used for cost control is standard

Contd...

Financial Accounting (FA)	*Management Accounting (MA)*	*Cost Accounting (CA)*
	management accounting are–ratio analysis, cash flow and funds flow analysis etc.	costing/variance analysis.
3. Financial accounting takes raw information from book-keeping system.	3. Management accounting takes input data from financial accounting as well as cost accounting system.	3. Cost accounting takes input data from book-keeping system *i.e.* from the various vouchers.
4. The auditing power of financial statement rests with public accountant *e.g.* C.A. in India.	4. Management accounting does not require auditing but can be reviewed by a senior executive.	4. Cost accountants, audit cost accounting information.

Note: **Position of MA system with respect to FA and CA system:** MA system is common to both FA and CA system.

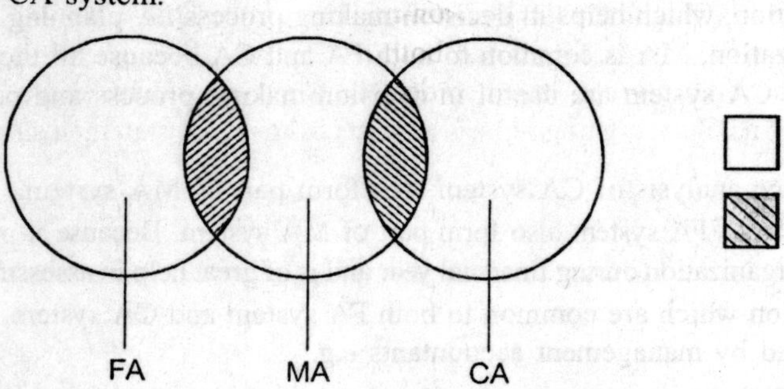

1.7 ACCOUNTING INFORMATION SYSTEM (AIS)

1.7.1 Information Flow Chart (Level 1)

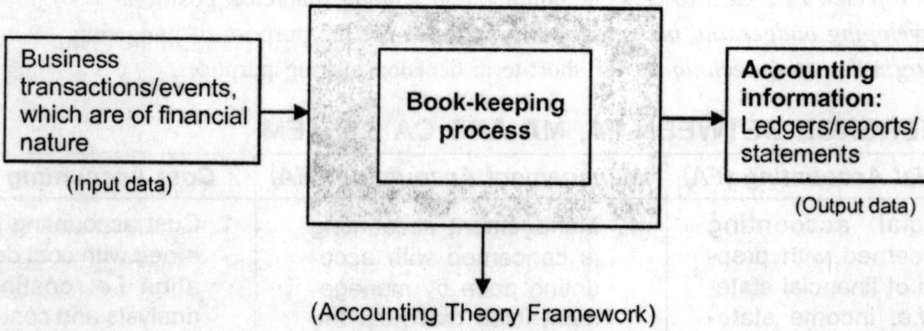

1.7.2 Information Flow Chart (Level 2)

There are 4 sub-fields/components of accounting:

(*i*) Book-keeping system
(*ii*) FA system
(*iii*) CA system
(*iv*) MA system

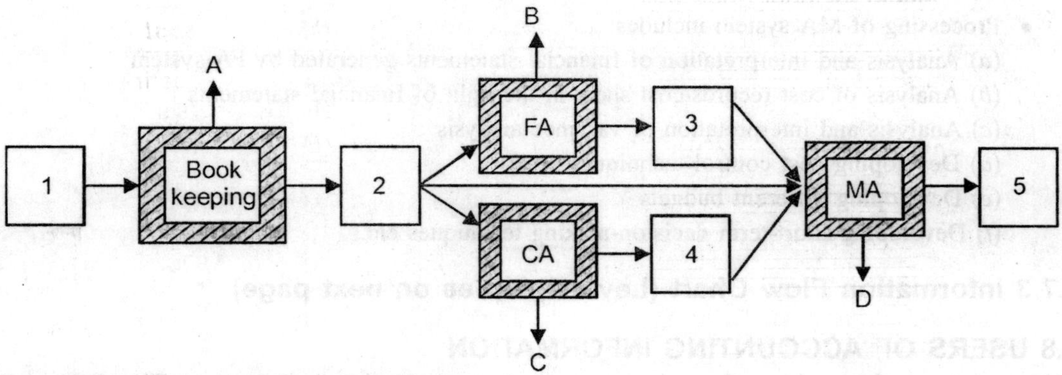

Explanation to above-mentioned symbols

1 – Business transactions/events, which are of financial nature (must be supported by source documents like cash memo, invoice etc), which acts as input data for book-keeping system.

2 – Output generated by book-keeping system which acts as input data for all the main branches of accounting *viz.* FA system, CA system and MA system. This output consists of different ledger books and trial balance.

3 – Statutory financial accounting reports generated by FA system, which acts as input data for MA system. Statutory financial accounting reports consists of financial statements *i.e.* income statement and balance sheet.

4 – Cost accounting reports like various cost sheets showing unit cost at different level of production, which in turn acts as input data for MA system.

5 – Output information generated by MA system fulfilling needs of internal, as well as external users having direct/indirect interest in the organization concerned *e.g.* statement of ratios, fund flow statement/cash flow statement.

A – Accounting theory framework for processing of book-keeping consists of accounting standards, conventions and concepts.

B – Framework of statutory laws and acts like company law, partnership act, SEBI act etc. under which processing of FA system takes place.

C – Framework of predetermined formats, procedures and assumptions under which processing of CA system takes place.

D – Framework of relevant factors (external as well as internal factors) within which processing of management accounting system takes place.

Processing of book-keeping, FA, CA and MA systems are as follows:

- Processing of book-keeping system includes identifying, recording, classifying and summarizing (trial balance only) the business transactions/events, which are of financial nature.
- Processing of FA system includes preparation of financial statements *i.e.* income statement and balance sheet.
- Processing of CA system includes classification, allocation, recording, summarizing and reporting current and prospective costs *i.e.* preparation of various cost sheets showing unit cost at different level of production *i.e.*

(*i*) Cost determination

(*ii*) Cost analysis

(*iii*) Cost control

- Processing of MA system includes:
  (*a*) Analysis and interpretation of financial statements generated by FA system
  (*b*) Analysis of cost records/cost sheet in the light of financial statements
  (*c*) Analysis and interpretation of variance analysis
  (*d*) Developing cost control techniques.
  (*e*) Developing different budgets
  (*f*) Developing short-term decision-making techniques etc.

1.7.3 Information Flow Chart (Level 3) (See on next page)

1.8 USERS OF ACCOUNTING INFORMATION

Different users, for making their decisions require accounting information. These users may be classified as:

Users of Accounting Information

(*i*) Internal users (Management at all levels)

(*ii*) External users

(*a*) Direct users (Interest) (owners/shareholders, investors, creditors, employees, customers, lenders, management and tax authorities)

(*b*) Indirect users (Interest) (regulatory agencies, researchers, banks, government agencies, labour unions, trade associations, public and others)

(*i*) **Internal users:** Top, middle and bottom level of management executives are the internal users of accounting information. They need it for making decisions. These users are interested in the profitability, operational efficiency and financial soundness of the business. The top-level management is concerned with accounting information related to planning, the middle level is interested in planning and controlling and the lower level with operational affairs.

(*ii*) **External users:** External users may have direct interest or indirect interest.

(*a*) **External users having direct interest:** The existing and the prospective creditors and investors have direct interest in the accounting information. The sources of information for external users are financial statements and reports of Directors and Auditors.

Investors assess the financial soundness and net worth of the business so that they may decide about buying, selling or holding investment in the business. Creditors, such as banks, lenders, debenture holders and financial institutions assess the risk involved in granting loans, servicing of the existing loans to the business.

(*b*) **External users having indirect interest:** These users such as department of company affairs, registrar of joint stock companies, sales tax and income tax authorities, labour unions, prospective customers, creditors, stock exchange's trade associations and others who are interested in the affairs of the business. They have to make their own decision on the basis of the financial reports of the business.

1.7·3 Information Flow Chart (Level 3)

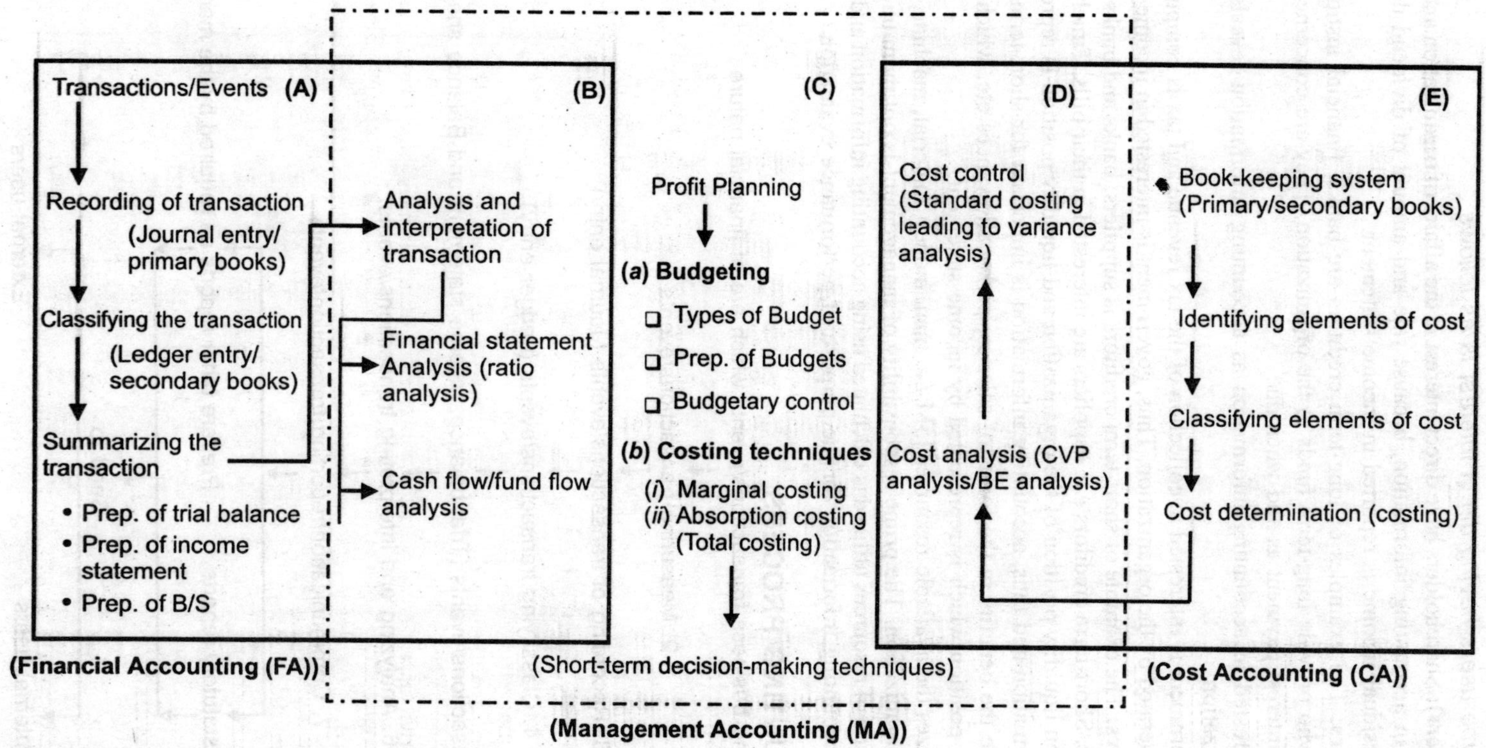

(A): Information flow exclusive to financial accounting
(B): Information flow common to both financial accounting and management accounting
(C): Information flow exclusive to management accounting
(D): Information flow common to both management accounting and cost accounting
(E): Information flow exclusive to cost accounting

A brief description of some users having direct interest is as follows

1. **Shareholders (owners):** Shareholders have direct interest in the affairs of organization and therefore they are interested in accounting information, because rate and amount of dividend depends on residual income. Residual income is reported in income statement.
2. **Long-term creditors:** The examples of long-term creditors are banks, financial institutions and debenture holders who provide long-term funds to the organization. They are concerned with the debt servicing and interest payment as and when due.

   Thus, they are interested in accounting information as accounting information reveals financial health of the organization.
3. **Government:** Government is interested in collection of the tax revenue and tax is computed on the basis of income, generated by the organization. Thus, government is interested in income statement.
4. **Short-term creditors:** The example of short-term creditors is suppliers; banks and banks providing overdraft facility etc. Short-term creditors *e.g.* suppliers are interested in their bills. Timely payment of bills depends upon liquidity position of the organization and liquidity position is represented by the accounting information and thus, accounting information is important for short-term creditors.
5. **Employees:** Receive the benefits in the forms of salaries, perks, allowances etc. which in turn is dependent on profit position which is represented by income statement.
6. **Management:** Utilizes the available resources [5M *i.e.* man, money, material, machine, method + time + I.T.] of the organization. The prime responsibility of management is optimum utilization of resources. The position of resources utilized is calculated using accounting information and therefore, management uses accounting information for the purpose of performance evaluation.

1.9 STEPS IN ACCOUNTING PROCESS

1. Identifying business transactions/events which are of financial nature

↓

2. Measuring transactions/events

↓

3. Recording of transactions/events (Journal entry)

↓

4. Classifying transactions/events (Ledger entry)

↓

5. Summarizing transactions/events (Trial balance, Income statement and Balance sheet)

↓

6. Analyzing and interpreting transactions/events.

↓

7. Communication/reporting transaction/events

↓

Prepare statutory reports | Prepare other reports as required by the management

↓

Send to

↓

Internal users | External users

Note:

- **Accounting Cycle:** Step 1 to step 5 constitutes accounting cycle. Put differently, accounting cycle starts from identifying and recording of transaction and ends with summarizing transactions *i.e.,* preparation of financial statements (Income statement and B/S).

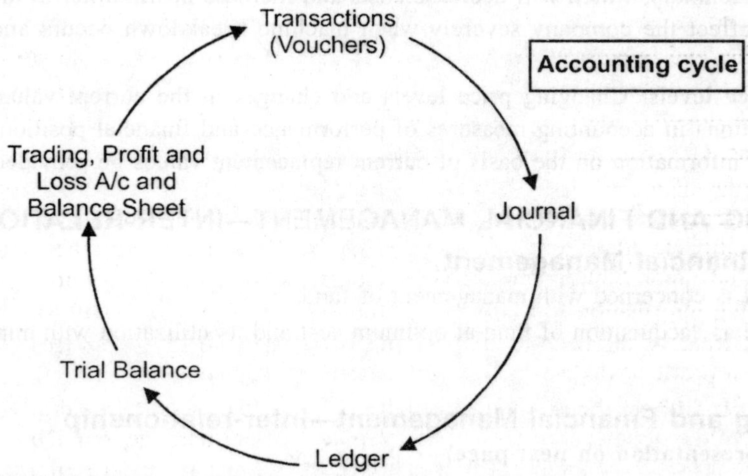

- **Accounting Period:** The time period in completing accounting cycle is known as accounting period and in India it is of one-year duration (1st April to 31st March of next year).

1.10 LIMITATIONS OF ACCOUNTING

Accounting is helpful for business in assessing it's worth *i.e.,* profit or loss, assets and liabilities. It enables the business in deciding its future line of action on the basis of information supplied. Though logical conclusions can be derived from accounting, it can never be taken as granted that the facts supplied by accounting are cent percent true. They may be false, biased and manipulated. Accounting has the following limitations:

1. **Record-keeping:** Accounting records only those transactions/events, which are financial in nature. Transactions/events of non-financial nature do not find place in accounting. Certain very important information such as competency of the management, exit of top-level executive, change in consumers preferences etc. are not recorded in accounting, though they affect the financial soundness of the business.
2. **Accuracy of information generated by accounting system:** Accounting assesses profit or loss and financial position (picture of asset and liability) of the organization concerned on the basis of both the real and assumed estimates. Accountants make the valuation of stock, determine the method of depreciation and maintain various reserves and provisions. Different firms have their own different methods of making provisions, so the results of the business will change with the change in the practice.
3. **Value of assets:** The balance sheet does not show the market value of the assets in the ordinary sense of the word. It usually shows assets, costs adjusted according to the conventional rules of accounting. Again there are certain assets, which do not have real value, but they are shown in our

balance sheet. These assets are like goodwill, patents, preliminary expenses, discount on issue of shares etc. Showing these assets in the book of accounts make the results doubtful.

4. **Window dressing:** Window dressing practices that will improve profitability in the short run may be utilized by the management. Such practices may take the form of postponing the maintenance of plant and machinery, which will decrease costs and increase profitability in the short run, but which would affect the company severely when machine breakdown occurs and production is interrupted.
5. **Changing price levels:** Changing price levels and changes in the current values of assets can produce distortions in accounting measures of performance and financial position. It is desirable that additional information on the basis of current replacement values be provided.

1.11 ACCOUNTING AND FINANCIAL MANAGEMENT—INTER-RELATIONSHIP

1.11.1 Defining Financial Management

Financial management is concerned with management of fund.

It may be defined as "acquisition of fund at optimum cost and its utilization with minimum financial risk."

1.11.2 Accounting and Financial Management—Inter-relationship

(See diagrammatic presentation on next page)

1.11.3 Difference between Accounting System and Financial System

Accounting system	***Financial system***
(*i*) It is information generating system.	(*i*) It is decision-making system.
(*ii*) It is governed by certain laws and Accounting theory framework	(*ii*) It is governed by external factors relevant to organization concerned.
(*iii*) The role of accounting system is: (*a*) Score-keeping (*b*) Attention directing (*c*) Problem solving	(*iii*) The role of financial system is planning and controlling financial decision viz: (*a*) Financing decision (*b*) Investment decision (*c*) Dividend decision.
(*iv*) It takes input data from business transactions/event, which are of financial character.	(*iv*) It takes input data from information generated by different branches of accounting incorporating relevant industrial and economic factors.

Accounting and Financial Management—Inter-relationship

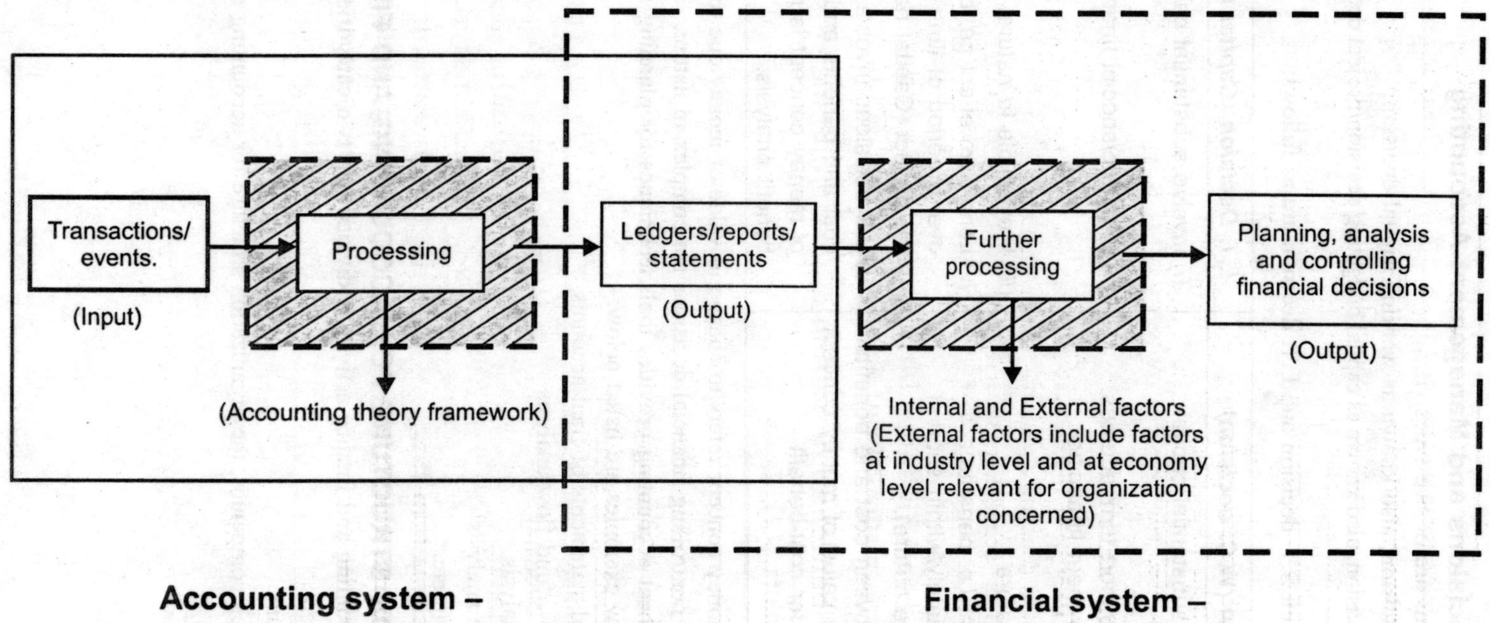

1.11.4 Financial Decisions and Management Accounting

- Financial decisions are of two types *viz.:*

  (*i*) Short-term decision, also known as working capital decision.

  (*ii*) Long-term decision, also known as capital budgeting decision/project decision/capital expenditure decision.

- Difference between S.T. decision and L.T. decision are as follows:

S.T. Decision (W.C. decision)	*L.T. Decision (Capital budgeting decision)*
(*i*) Do not involve substantial capital outlay.	(*i*) Involve substantial capital outlay.
(*ii*) Operating profit/short term-sources are sufficient to meet financing requirement.	(*ii*) Separate/special financing is required.
(*iii*) Reversible in nature	(*iii*) Irreversible in nature.
(*iv*) Short-term effect *i.e.* benefits are realized immediately/within short period (Revenue nature).	(*iv*) Long-term effect *i.e.* benefits are realized over a period of time *i.e.* up to the life of the project (Capital nature).
(*v*) No time lag between cost and benefits and hence time value of money concept is not required for cost-benefit analysis.	(*v*) L.T. decisions involve time lag between cost and benefits and hence time value of money concept is required for cost-benefit analysis.

Note: Time value of money concept refers to change in value of money due to change in time.

- Planning and controlling financial decisions are complex in nature.
- The management accounting provides tools/techniques for planning and controlling financial decisions. Few examples are listed below: -

  (*i*) Projected statements of final accounts

  (*ii*) Cash flow/fund flow analysis

  (*iii*) Ratio analysis

  (*iv*) Variance analysis

  (*v*) Budgeting etc.

1.12 ORGANIZATION STRUCTURE FOR ACCOUNTING AND FINANCE ACTIVITY

In an organization, accounting and finance activity is divided into two categories *viz:*

- Assets management
- Funds management

In case of joint stock companies, the organization structure for accounting and finance activity is as follows:

Director (Finance)

Controller deals with assets management

Controller is responsible for entire accounting activity viz.:

1. Financial accounting, management accounting and cost accounting.
2. Taxation (tax planning)
3. Reporting and auditing.

Treasurer deals with funds management

Treasurer is responsible for cash and near cash resources viz.:

1. Cash management
2. Receivables management (credit policy etc.)
3. Insurance (premium and claims etc.)
4. Loan matters.

Note: In case of medium and small-sized organization, financial controller cum chief accountant is responsible for the entire activities of finance and accounts department.

1.13 UTILITY OF ACCOUNTING AND FINANCIAL MANAGEMENT FOR I.T. PROFESSIONALS

I.T. professionals interact with two things *viz.*

1. **Hardware**–which includes computer and telecommunication media like phone, V-SAT etc.
2. **Software**–which includes customized software developed as per management's requirement and existing software to manage database of the concerned organization using appropriate package. Thus, the problem, from software point of view, before every I.T. professional at business organizations is two fold *viz.*

- Developing application software for different functional areas like production, marketing, purchase, finance, MIS etc. as per requirement of management.
- Managing database of the concerned organization and make them available to right person at right time.

Needless to say for both type of problems stated above, I.T. professionals at work must have at least basic knowledge of accounting and financial management because accounting and financial management are language of business, which makes communication possible. It is important to note that without an understanding of accounting and financial management, one cannot understand the complexities associated with business organization. IT professionals, therefore, equipped with knowledge of accounting and financial management can understand not only the complexities associated with business organization but can recognize the problem which helps in developing Data Flow Diagram (DFD) and Entity Relation Diagram (ER-Diagram) easily, which are essential to software development.

Furthermore, clear understanding of database of the concerned organization leads to efficient management of database, which is possible only when I.T. professionals at work have proper knowledge of accounting and financial management because all the financial database rests with accounts and finance department using definite format and terminology.

Exercises

Q. 1. Explain the term Management Accounting and state what you understand to be its main objectives.

Q. 2. Distinguish between:
- Financial Accounting
- Cost Accounting
- Management Accounting

Q. 3. How does the accounting information assists management in the solution of strategic business problems?

Q. 4. "Accounting as an aid to management in solving tactical business problems". Comment.

Q. 5. Financial accounting has the basic objective of providing financial information to the parties outside the business. Parties inside the business also need information of monetary character and otherwise. Which system of accounting provides this information, and what information is generated for the guidance of the managers to take decisions?

Q. 6. Distinguish between:
- Accounting system and
- Financial system.

Q. 7. Explain the limitations of accounting information.

Q. 8. Describe the users of accounting information.

Q. 9. Describe the utility of Accounting and Financial Management for Information Technology (I.T.) professionals.

Chapter–2

Book-Keeping

LEARNING OBJECTIVES

In this chapter we will study:

- Introduction
- Types of Books of Account
- Book-keeping Process
- Types of Error During Book-keeping Process
- Data Flow Diagram (DFD) for Book-keeping Process
- *Important terms*

2.1 INTRODUCTION

Book-keeping means maintaining books of accounts.

2.2 TYPES OF BOOKS OF ACCOUNT

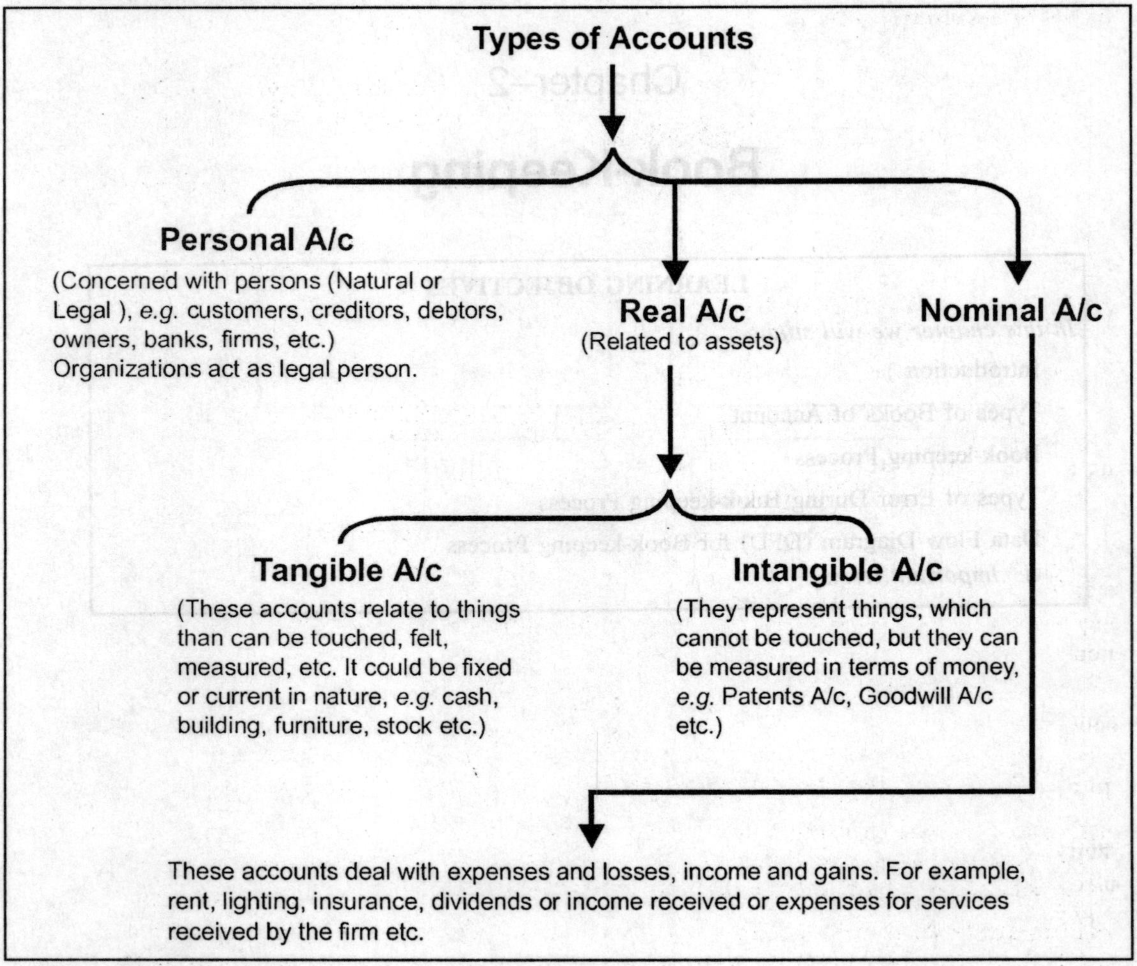

2.2.1 Ground Rule for Entry in Books of Account

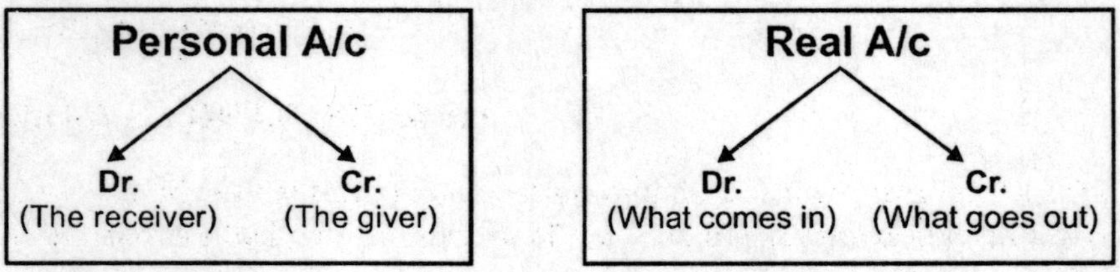

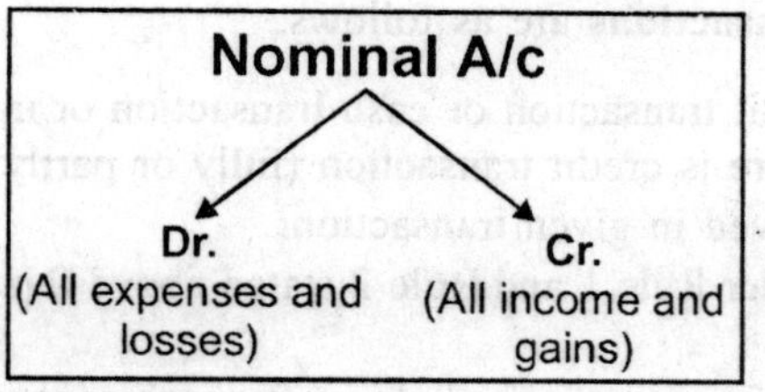

The above ground rule for entry in books of account leads to following another set of rules:

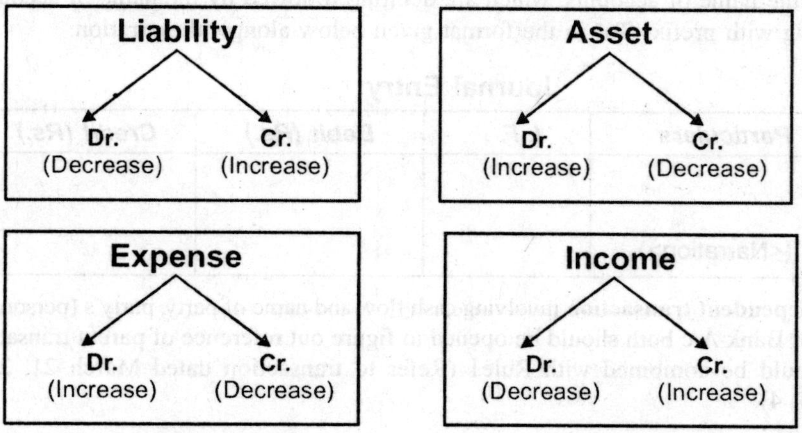

2.3 BOOK-KEEPING PROCESS

The steps involved in book-keeping process are as follows:

Step 1: Identifying financial transactions/events (Vouchers)

↓

Step 2: Recording of transactions/events (Journals)

↓

Step 3: Classifying transactions/events (Ledgers)

↓

Step 4: Summarizing transactions (Trial balance only)

Step 1: Identifying financial transactions/events (Vouchers)

Identifying financial transactions/events means there must be some documentary evidence against transaction to be recorded in books of account *e.g.* cash memo shows cash sale, invoice/bill shows credit sale/purchase, debit note shows goods returned, report of store manager regarding closing stock etc.

These business documents are called source documents and are used in identifying transactions/events to be recorded in books of accounts known as journalisation *i.e.* journal entry.

Step 2: Recording of transactions/events (Journals)

Recording of transaction is done through source documents. Journal is a primary book of accounting. It contains chronological record of transactions. Given below are rules for journal entry followed by some illustrations of journal entries.

Rule for Journal entry

The rules for journal entry in case of **independent transactions** are as follows:

Rule 1: Identify whether the given transaction is credit transaction or cash transaction or mix of these two. Personal A/c will appear only when there is credit transaction (fully or partly).

Rule 2: List all the accounts other than Rule 1 involved in given transaction.

Rule 3: Find out the nature of each account listed under Rule 1 and Rule 2 stated above (Nature means personal A/c, real A/c and nominal A/c).

Rule 4: Apply the **ground rule for entry in books of account** stated above for each account and find out which account is debiting and which account is crediting.

Rule 5: First write the name of accounts, which are debiting followed by the name of accounts, which are crediting with prefix **'To'** in the format given below alongwith narration.

Journal Entry

Date	*Particulars*	*L.F.*	*Debit (Rs.)*	*Credit (Rs.)*
	(<Narration>)			

Rule 6: In case of **dependent transaction** involving cash flow and name of party, party's (personal) A/c and Cash A/c or Bank A/c both should be opened to figure out reference of parent transaction. Thus Rule 6 should be combined with Rule1 (Refer to transaction dated March 21, 2003 under **illustration 4**).

***Note*:**

1. A narration should be written after each journal entry since it narrates the transaction.
2. L.F. stands for Ledger Folio. The transactions entered in journal are later on posted to the ledger. This is given for easy reference.
3. A/c stands for account.
4. Cash transaction includes cash receipt and cash payment arising out of operational activity *e.g.* cash sales, cash purchase, salary paid etc. are cash transactions whereas cash received through owner and bank by way of loan, are credit transactions as owner providing capital and bank providing loans, are creditors and hence according to **Rule 1** stated above personal A/c need to be opened. In case of owner's contribution 'Capital A/c' whereas in case of bank 'Loan A/c' in the name of bank, should be opened.
5. It is evident from journal entry **Rule 5** shown above that book-keeping process follow double entry book-keeping system popularly known as **Mercantile System.**

   "Every transaction involves at least two parties, one for receiving aspect (Dr. entry) and another for giving aspect (Cr. entry), therefore, to record a single transaction simultaneously two books of account are needed (one for Dr. entry and another for Cr. entry). This is known as double entry book-keeping system or mercantile system." **(See Illustrations shown below)**

Illustration 1: Subhra started a business with a capital of Rs. 50,000 on July 1, 2003.

Rule 1: Credit transaction (owner is creditor according to separate entity concept), therefore Subhra's account, *i.e.* capital account will be opened.

Rule 2: Account involved in given transaction other than Capital A/c is Cash A/c. Thus in this case, two accounts are involved:
Subhra's account, *i.e.* Capital account; and Cash account

Rule 3: Capital A/c is a personal A/c and Cash A/c is a real A/c

Rule 4: As per the rules of debit and credit applicable to personal A/c "debit the receiver, credit the giver". As business is a separate entity (entity concept), Subhra is giving money so her account should be credited *i.e.* Capital A/c ....Cr
According to the rules of real A/c "debit what comes in, credit what goes out". In this transaction, cash is coming into the business, so it should be debited.
Cash A/c ....Dr.

Rule 5: Write first the name of account, which is debiting *i.e.* Cash A/c followed by Capital A/c which is crediting with prefix 'To'.

Journal Entry

Date	*Particulars*	*L.F.*	*Debit (Rs.)*	*Credit (Rs.)*
2003 July 1	Cash A/c .... Dr.		50,000	
	To Capital A/c			50,000
	(Being commencement of business)			

(Narration)

Illustration 2. Paid salary Rs. 5,000 to Mr. A by his employer.

Rule 1: Cash transaction, therefore Mr. A's A/c will not be opened.

Rule 2: Thus accounts involved in given transaction are
(*i*) Salary A/c and
(*ii*) Cash Account

Rule 3: Salary A/c is a nominal A/c and Cash A/c is a real A/c

Rule 4: According to the rules of nominal A/c "Debit all expenses and losses, credit all income and gains". For the business it is an expense, so debit it.
Salary A/c........Dr
According to the rules of real A/c "Debit what comes in, Credit what goes out". In this transaction, cash is going out from the business, so it should be credited.
Cash A/c ....Cr

Rule 5: Write first the name of account, which is debiting followed by name of account, which is crediting with prefix 'To'.

Journal entry

Date	*Particulars*	*L.F.*	*Debit (Rs.)*	*Credit (Rs.)*
	Salary A/c .....Dr.		5,000	
	To Cash A/c			5,000
	(Being salary of Rs. 5000 paid to Mr. A)			

Illustration 3. Purchased goods on credit for Rs. 3,000 from Mr. B.

Rule 1: Credit transaction because of credit purchase, therefore Mr. B's A/c will be opened.

Rule 2: Thus accounts involved in given transaction are

(*i*) Mr. B's A/c and

(*iii*) Purchase A/c

Rule 3:

(*iv*) Mr. B's A/c is a personal A/c and Purchase A/c is a nominal A/c

Rule 4: According to the rules stated above

Mr B's A/c... Cr (as it is a personal A/c and Mr. B is the giver of goods)

Purchase A/c...Dr (Expense, so Dr. entry)

Rule 5: Write first the name of account, which is debiting followed by name of account, which is crediting with prefix 'To'.

Journal entry

Date	*Particulars*	*L.F*	*Debit (Rs.)*	*Credit (Rs.)*
	Purchase A/c....Dr.		3000	
	To Mr. B'/s A/c			3000
	(Being purchase of goods on credit)			

Illustration 4: Journalize the transactions given below in the books of Pankaj.

2003

March 1 Pankaj started business with Rs. 50,000. He opens a bank account and deposits Rs. 20,000.

March 2 Bought furniture for Rs. 5,000 and machinery for Rs. 10,000.

March 3 Purchased goods for Rs. 14,000.

March 6 Sold goods for Rs. 8,000.

March 8 Purchased goods from M/s Chowdhry and Co. Rs. 11,000.

March 10 Paid telephone rent for the year by cheque Rs. 500.

March 11 Bought one typewriter for Rs. 2,100 from 'Universal Typewriter Co.' on credit.

March 15 Sold goods to Ram for Rs. 12,000.

March 17 Sold goods to Raj Kumar for Rs. 2,000 in cash.

March 19 Amount withdrawn from bank for personal use Rs. 15,00.

March 21 Received cash from Ram Rs. 11,900 and discount allowed Rs. 100.

March 22 Paid Rs. 5,800 into bank.

March 23 Bought 50 shares in ABC Co. Ltd. at 60 per share, brokerage paid Rs. 20.

March 25 Goods worth Rs. 1,000 found defective were returned to M/s Chowdhry and Co. and balance of the amount due to them settled by issuing a cheque in their favour.

March 28 Sold 20 shares of ABC Co. Ltd. at Rs. 65 per share, brokerage paid, Rs. 20.

March 28 Purchased good worth Rs. 2100 from Bhuwan and supplied them to Raghvendra for Rs. 3000.

March 30 Raghvendra returned goods worth Rs. 100, which in turn were sent to Bhuwan.

March 30 Issued a cheque for Rs. 1,000 in favour of landlord for rent of March.

March 30 Paid salaries of Rs. 1,500 to staff and received Rs. 2,000 from travelling salesman for goods sold by him, after deduction the travelling expenses of Rs. 100.

Journal

Date	Particulars	L.F.	Debit (Rs.)	Credit (Rs.)
2003 March 1	Cash A/c ....Dr. To Capital A/c (being commencement of business)		50,000	50,000
	Bank A/c ....Dr To Cash A/c (being cash deposited in bank)		20,000	20,000
March 2	Machinery and furniture A/c ..Dr. To Cash A/c (being purchase of machinery and furniture for Cash)		15,000	15,000
March 3	Purchase A/c ....Dr. To Cash A/c (being purchase of goods)		14,000	14,000
March 6	Cash A/c To Sales A/c (being goods sold for cash)		8,000	8,000
March 8	Purchase A/c ...Dr. To M/s Chowdhry and Co. (being purchase of goods from M/s Chowdhry and Co. on credit)		11,000	11,000
March 10	Telephone Rent A/c ...Dr. To Bank A/c (being telephone expenses paid by cheque)		500	500
March 11	Typewriter A/c ...Dr. To Universal Typewriter Co. A/c (being purchase of typewriter on credit)		2,100	2,100
March 15	Ram A/c ...Dr. To Sales A/c (being goods sold to Ram on credit)		12,000	12,000

Contd...

Date	Particulars	L.F.	Debit (Rs.)	Credit (Rs.)
March 17	Cash A/c ...Dr. To Sales A/c (being sale of goods for cash)		2,000	2,000
March 19	Drawing A/c ...Dr. To Bank A/c (being withdrawal of cash for personal use by the owner)		1,500	1,500
March 21	Cash A/c ...Dr. Discount allowed A/c ...Dr. To Ram A/c (being cash received from Ram in full settlement and allowed him Rs. 100 as discount)		11,900 100	12,000
March 22	Bank A/c ...Dr. To Cash A/c (being cash deposited in bank)		5,800	5,800
March 23	Investment A/c ...Dr. Brokerage A/c ...Dr. To Cash A/c (being purchase of shares @ Rs. 60 per share from ABC Co. Ltd., payment of Rs. 20 as brokerage)		3,000 20	3,020
March 25	M/s Chowdhry and Co. ...Dr. To Return Outward A/c To Bank A/c (being goods returned to M/s Chowdhry and Co. and final settlement by issuing a cheque)		11,000	1,000 10,000
March 28	Cash A/c ...Dr. To Investment A/c		1,300	1,300
March 28	Investment A/c ...Dr. To Profit & Loss A/c (being 20 shares of XY and Co. Ltd. sold at Rs. 65 per share and profit transferred to Profit & Loss A/c)		100	100

Contd...

Date	Particulars	L.F.	Debit (Rs.)	Credit (Rs.)
March 28	Brokerage A/c ...Dr. To Cash A/c (being brokerage of Rs. 20 written off as an expense)		20	 20
March 28	Purchase A/c ...Dr. To Bhuwan A/c (being purchase made on credit from Bhuwan)		2,100	 2,100
March 28	Raghvendra A/c ...Dr. To Sales A/c (being credit sales made to Raghvendra)		3,000	 3,000
March 29	Return Inward A/c ...Dr. To Raghvendra A/c (being goods returned by Raghvendra)		100	 100
March 29	Bhuwan A/c ...Dr. To Return Outward A/c (being goods purchased from Bhuwan returned)		100	 100
March 30	Rent A/c ...Dr To Bank A/c (being rent paid to landlord for April)		1,000	 1,000
March 30	Salary A/c ...Dr. To Cash A/c (Being salary paid to staff)		1,500	 1,500
March 30	Cash A/c ...Dr. Travelling Expenses A/c. Dr. To Sales A/c (being cash received from travelling salesman after deduction the expenses)		1,900 100	 2,000

***Note*: Return inward and return outward is also termed as sales return and purchase return respectively.**

Working notes:

The above transactions are carried out in the following way:

Note: P⇨Personal A/c, R⇨Real A/c, N⇨Nominal A/c, Dr.⇨Debit, Cr.⇨Credit

1. Transaction on March 1

Rule 1	***Rule 2***	***Rule 3***	***Rule 4***
	A/Cs Involved	*Nature*	*Apply ground Rule for entry in books of account*
Credit transaction	Capital A/c	P	Pankaj is giver, so Cr. his A/c. Capital denotes owner's A/c and is liability.
	Cash A/c	R	Cash comes in, so Dr. it

	A/Cs Involved	*Nature*	*Apply ground Rule for entry in books of account*
Contra transaction	Bank A/c	R	Money received by bank, so Dr. it. (what comes in)
	Cash A/c	R	Cash goes to bank, so Cr. it. (what goes out)

2. Transaction on March 2

Rule 1	***Rule 2***	***Rule 3***	***Rule 4***
	A/Cs Involved	*Nature*	*Apply ground Rule for entry in books of account*
Cash transaction	Machinery and furniture A/c	R	Assets coming in business, so Dr. it
	Cash A/c	R	Cash goes out, so Cr. it

3. Transaction on March 3

Rule 1	***Rule 2***	***Rule 3***	***Rule 4***
	A/Cs Involved	*Nature*	*Apply ground Rule for entry in books of account*
Cash transaction	Purchase A/c Cash A/c	N R	Money spent on buying goods. So Dr. it Cash goes out, so Cr. it

4. Transaction on March 6

Rule 1	***Rule 2***	***Rule 3***	***Rule 4***
	A/Cs Involved	*Nature*	*Apply ground Rule for entry in books of account*
Cash transaction	Cash A/c	R	Cash comes in, so Dr. it.
	Sales A/c	N	Income due to Sales, so Cr. it

5. Transaction on March 8

Rule 1	***Rule 2***	***Rule 3***	***Rule 4***
	A/Cs Involved	*Nature*	*Apply ground Rule for entry in books of account*
Credit transaction	Purchase A/c	N	Money spent on buying goods, so Dr. it.
	Chowdhry and Co. A/c	P	Goods given by Chowdhry and Co. on credit, so Cr. it.

6. Transaction on March 10

Rule 1	Rule 2	Rule 3	Rule 4
	A/Cs Involved	Nature	Apply ground Rule for entry in books of account
Cash transaction	Telephone Rent A/c	N	Expenditure on phone, so Dr. it.
	Bank A/c	R	Cheque payment, so Cr. it.

7. Transaction on March 11

Rule 1	Rule 2	Rule 3	Rule 4
	A/Cs Involved	Nature	Apply ground Rule for entry in books of account
Credit transaction	Typewriter A/c	R	Typewriter comes in, so Dr. it.
	Universal Typewriter Co. A/c	N	Universal Typewriter Co. has given on credit, so Cr. it.

8. Transaction on March 15

Rule 1	Rule 2	Rule 3	Rule 4
	A/Cs Involved	Nature	Apply ground Rule for entry in books of account
Credit transaction	Ram A/c	P	Goods recd. by Ram, so Dr. it.
	Sales A/c	N	Income due to Sales, so Cr. it.

9. Transaction on March 17

Rule 1	Rule 2	Rule 3	Rule 4
	A/Cs Involved	Nature	Apply ground Rule for entry in books of account
Cash transaction	Cash A/c	R	Cash comes in, so Dr. it.
	Sales A/c	N	Income due to sales, so Cr. it.

10. Transaction on March 19

Rule 1	Rule 2	Rule 3	Rule 4
	A/Cs Involved	Nature	Apply ground Rule for entry in books of account
Cash transaction	Drawings A/c	P	Money received by owner, so Dr. it.
	Bank A/c	R	Money from bank goes out, so Cr. it.

11. Transaction on March 21

Rule1-cum-Rule 6	Rule 2	Rule 3	Rule 4
	A/Cs Involved	Nature	Apply ground Rule for entry in books of account
Dependent transaction (Parent trans--action is trans--action dated March 15, 2003)	Cash A/c	R	Cash comes in, so Dr. it.
	Discount Allowed A/c	N	Discount given, so it is an expense, so Dr. it.
	Ram A/c (Personal A/c)	P	Money given by Ram (giver), so Cr. it.

12. Transaction on March 22

Rule 1	*Rule 2*	*Rule 3*	*Rule 4*
	A/Cs Involved	*Nature*	*Apply ground Rule for entry in books of account*
Contra transaction	Bank A/c	R	Money recd. by bank, so Dr. it. (what comes in)
	Cash A/c	R	Cash goes out, so Cr. it. (what goes out)

13. Transaction on March 23

Rule 1	*Rule 2*	*Rule 3*	*Rule 4*
	A/Cs Involved	*Nature*	*Apply ground Rule for entry in books of account*
Cash transaction	Investment A/c	R	Shares purchased *i.e.* comes in, so Dr. it.
	Brokerage A/c	N	Payment to broker, an expense, so Dr. it.
	Cash A/c	R	Cash goes out, so Cr. it.

14. Transaction on March 25

Rule 1	*Rule 2*	*Rule 3*	*Rule 4*
	A/Cs Involved	*Nature*	*Apply ground Rule for entry in books of account*
Cash transaction	Chowdhry and Co. A/c	P	Goods recd. By Chowdhry and Co.(Receiver), so Dr. it.
	Return Outward A/c	N	Reduction of an expenditure (Purchases), so Cr. it.
	Bank	R	Money given by the bank *i.e.* goes out, so Cr. it.

15. Transactions on March 28

Rule 1	*Rule 2*	*Rule 3*	*Rule 4*
	A/Cs Involved	*Nature*	*Apply ground Rule for entry in books of account*
Cash transaction	Cash A/c	R	Cash comes in, so Dr. it.
	Investment A/c	R	Shares sold, so Cr. it.

Rule 1	*Rule 2*	*Rule 3*	*Rule 4*
	A/Cs Involved	*Nature*	*Apply ground Rule for entry in books of account*
Cash transaction	Cash A/c	R	Cash comes in, so Dr. it.
	Sales A/c	N	Income due to Sales, so Cr. it.

Rule 1	*Rule 2*	*Rule 3*	*Rule 4*
	A/Cs Involved	*Nature*	*Apply ground Rule for entry in books of account*
Credit transaction	Investment A/c	R	Profit Rs. 5/- per share [20 × 5 =100] transferred (Asset A/c decreases), so Dr. it.
	Profit & Loss A/c	N	Selling shares is not the core business so whatever profit realized will be entered in Profit & Loss A/c, so Cr. it.

Rule 1	*Rule 2*	*Rule 3*	*Rule 4*
Cash transaction	*A/Cs Involved*	*Nature*	*Apply ground Rule for entry in books of account*
	Brokerage A/c	N	Payment to broker, *i.e.* expense, so Dr. it.
	Cash A/c	R	Cash given to broker, so Cr. it.

Rule 1	*Rule 2*	*Rule 3*	*Rule 4*
Credit transaction	*A/Cs Involved*	*Nature*	*Apply ground Rule for entry in books of account*
	Purchase A/c	N	Expense on buying goods, so Dr. it.
	Bhuwan A/c	P	Sundry creditor (Bhuwan) is giving goods, so Cr. his A/c.

Rule 1	*Rule 2*	*Rule 3*	*Rule 4*
Credit transaction	*A/Cs Involved*	*Nature*	*Apply ground Rule for entry in books of account*
	Raghvendra A/c	P	Sundry debtor (Raghvendra) receives goods, so Dr. it.
	Sales A/c	N	Income due to sales, so Cr. it.

16. Transactions on March 29 and 30

Rule 1	*Rule 2*	*Rule 3*	*Rule 4*
Credit transaction	*A/Cs Involved*	*Nature*	*Apply ground Rule for entry in books of account*
	Return Inward A/c	N	Income decreases due to return, so Dr. it.
	Raghvendra A/c	P	Sundry debtor (Raghvendra) returns goods (giver), so Cr. his A/c.

Rule 1	*Rule 2*	*Rule 3*	*Rule 4*
Credit transaction	*A/Cs Involved*	*Nature*	*Apply ground Rule for entry in books of account*
	Bhuwan A/c	P	Sundry creditor (Bhuwan) receives goods (Receiver), so Dr. it.
	Return-Outward A/c	N	Income enhances due to return outward, so Cr. it.

Rule 1	*Rule 2*	*Rule 3*	*Rule 4*
Cash transaction	*A/Cs Involved*	*Nature*	*Apply ground Rule for entry in books of account*
	Rent A/c	N	Rent paid (Expense), so Dr. it.
	Bank A/c	R	Cheque issued by bank (goes out), so Cr. it.

Rule 1	*Rule 2*	*Rule 3*	*Rule 4*
	A/Cs Involved	*Nature*	*Apply ground Rule for entry in books of account*
Cash transaction	Salary A/c	R	Expenditure on salary, so Dr. entry.
	Cash A/c	R	Cash goes out, so Cr. it.

Rule 1	*Rule 2*	*Rule 3*	*Rule 4*
	A/Cs Involved	*Nature*	*Apply ground Rule for entry in books of account*
Cash transaction	Cash A/c	R	Cash comes in, so Dr. it.
	Travelling Expenses A/c	N	Expense on travelling, so Dr. entry.
	Sales A/c	N	Income due to Sales, so Cr. it.

Some important transactions along with journal (primary) entries, are given below:

1. Invoice received from Shyam Rs. 5000.
2. Goods returned to Shyam or Shyam admitted claim for Rs. 900.
3. Invoice sent to Shyam ——Rs. 2000.
4. Goods returned by Shyam or Shyam's claim admitted Rs. 200.
5. Outstanding salary or salary owing Rs. 2500.
6. Prepaid Insurance or unexpired insurance or insurance paid in advance Rs. 1500.
7. Amount withdrawn by proprietor for personal/domestic/private use Rs. 2000.
8. Goods taken by proprietor for personal/domestic/private use Rs. 1000.
9. Goods given as charity Rs. 800.
10. Shyam paid Rs. 800 in full settlement against Rs. 900 due to him.
11. Shyam becomes bankrupt and paid only Rs 500 against Rs 900 total amount due to him.
12. An amount previously written off as bed debts has now been recovered from Shyam, the old debtor for Rs. 400.
13. Distribution of good as free sample ———Rs. 1000.
14. Loss of goods by fire/theft ———Rs. 500.
15. Distribution of goods to employees ———Rs. 500.
16. Loss of cash by Fire/theft ———Rs. 300.
17. Rs. 5000 as advance received from Mohan against the order for supply of goods worth Rs. 15000.
18. Supplied goods worth Rs. 15000 against previous order from Mohan.
19. Paid income tax amounting Rs. 10000 through cheque.
20. Refund of Income tax ———Rs. 2000.
21. Interest on advance payment of income tax received ——Rs. 1000.
22. Received a VPP (Value Paid Parcel) for goods worth Rs. 1000. Sent an employee with Rs. 1200 for collection of goods. The employee paid Rs. 100 for auto charges and returned the balance.

S.No.	Particulars	L.F.	Debit (Rs.)	Credit (Rs.)
1	Purchase A/c ...Dr. To Shyam A/c (being goods purchased from Shyam)		5,000	5,000
2	Shyam A/c ...Dr. To Purchase Return A/c or Return outward A/c (being goods returned to Shyam)		900	900
3	Shyam A/c ...Dr. To Sales A/c (being goods sold to Shyam)		2,000	2,000
4	Sales Return A/c or Return inward A/c To Shyam A/c (being goods returned by Shyam)		200	200
5	Salary A/c ...Dr. To Outstanding salary A/c (being salaries remaining unpaid)		2,500 2,500	
6	Prepaid Insurance A/c ...Dr. To Insurance A/c (being insurance paid in advance)		1,500	1,500
7	Drawing A/c ...Dr. To Cash A/c (being amount withdrawn by the proprietor)		2,000	2,000
8	Drawing A/c ...Dr. To Purchase A/c (being goods taken by proprietor)		1,000	1,000
9	Charity A/c ...Dr. To Purchase A/c (being goods given as charity)		800	800
10	Cash A/c ...Dr. Discount allowed A/c ...Dr. To Shyam A/c (being cash received from Shyam in full settlement and allowed him Rs. 100 as discount)		800 100	900

Contd...

S.No.	Particulars	L.F.	Debit (Rs.)	Credit (Rs.)
11	Cash A/c ...Dr. Bad debt A/c ....Dr. To Shyam A/c (being Shyam became bankrupt and paid only Rs. 500)		500 400	 900
12	Cash A/c ...Dr. To Bad debt recovered A/c (being recovery of bad debt previously written off)		400 400	
13	Free samples A/c or Advertisement A/c ...Dr. To Purchase A/c (being distribution of goods as free samples)		1,000	 1,000
14	Loss of goods by fire/theft A/c ...Dr. To Purchase A/c (being loss of goods by fire/theft)		500	 500
15	Salary A/c ...Dr. To Purchase A/c (being distribution of goods among employees)		500	 500
16	Loss by fire/theft ...Dr. To Cash A/c (being loss of cash by fire/theft)		300	 300
17	Cash A/c ...Dr. To Advance from Mohan A/c (being goods supplied to Mohan against advance)		5,000	 5,000
18	Mohan A/c ...Dr. Advance from Mohan A/c ...Dr. To Sales A/c (being goods supplied to Mohan against advance)		10,000 5,000	 1,5000
19	Capital A/c ...Dr. To Bank A/c (being payment of income tax through cheque vide receipt no.—— dated ———)		10,000	 10,000

S.No.	Particulars	L.F.	Debit (Rs.)	Credit (Rs.)
20	Cash A/c ...Dr To Capital A/c (being refund of income tax)		2,000	2,000
21	Cash A/c ...Dr To Capital A/c (being Interest on advance payment of income tax received)		1,000	1,000
22	Purchase A/c ...Dr Cartage A/c ...Dr To Cash A/c (being received a VPP (Value Paid Parcel) for goods worth Rs. 1000)		1,000 100	1,100

Practical System of Journalisation of Financial Transactions/Events:

In actual practice, journalisation does not mean recording of transactions in chronological order using only one format of journal entry as shown in **illustration 3** above.

In manual accounting system, the transactions are categorized as per their nature and, for each type of transaction, a separate Journal (primary book) is available where the same has to be recorded. These primary books can be of the following types:

- **(*a*) Purchase Day Book** : It records credit purchase of goods.
- **(*b*) Sales Day Book** : It records credit sale of goods.
- **(*c*) Return Outward Book** : It records good returned to the supplier(s).
- **(*d*) Return Inward Book** : It records good returned by the customer(s).
- **(*e*) Bills Receivable Book** : It records bills accepted by customers.
- **(*f*) Bills Payable Book** : It records bills raised by suppliers.
- **(*g*) Cash Book** : It records cash (and bank) receipts and payments.
- **(*h*) Journal Proper** : It records all residual transactions.

All the above journals are called *daybooks* because transactions are recorded here date-wise.

In computerized accounting system, say, accounting through 'Tally'[1] voucher creation itself act as recording of transactions *i.e.* Journalisation. Depending upon nature of transactions, different types of vouchers are used in tally for Voucher creation/Journalisation.

The important vouchers used by tally for Voucher creation/Journalisation are described below:

- **(*a*) F4: Contra** : To create Contra Voucher—it records transaction between Cash A/c (cash in hand) and Bank A/c (cash at bank).
- **(*b*) F5: Payment** : To create Payment Voucher
- **(*c*) F6: Receipt** : To create Receipt Voucher
- **(*d*) F7: Journal** : To create Journal Voucher
- **(*e*) F8 : Sales** : To create Sales Voucher—it records credit sale of goods.
- **(*f*) F9 : Purchase** : To create Purchase Voucher—it records credit purchase of goods.

1. **'Tally' is the widely accepted Accounting Software (S/w) approved by Chartered Accountant Association of India.**

***Note*:**

1. F4, F5, F6, F7, F8, F9 are functional key's available on keyboard of computer.
2. Subsequent information like different ledgers, trial balance, income statement, balance sheet, fund flow statement and Statement of ratio analysis etc. is automatically generated by tally.
3. For details on Tally see **chapter eleven.**

Specimen of voucher creation in TALLY is shown below:

Specimen for Payment Voucher Creation

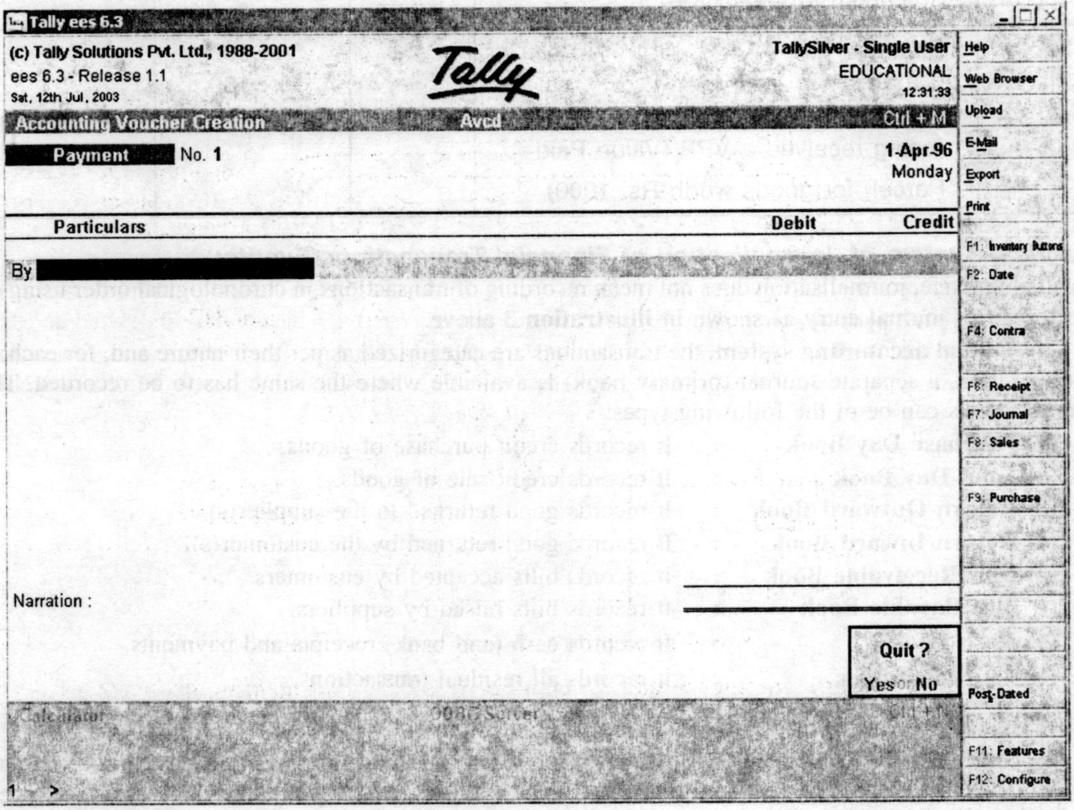

Step 3: Classifying Transactions (ledger entry)

After the Journal entry (*i.e.* recording transactions in primary books), all the amounts are posted to respective ledgers known as *secondary books*. In Journal, each transaction is dealt separately while in the ledger, they appear in a classified form under the particular account. A separate ledger is opened for each type of account. These ledgers are termed as **general ledger**. A ledger has two sides:

(*i*) Debit Side

(*ii*) Credit side

Posting is done in the relevant side of the Ledger based on the Journal entry. By posting, we mean the transfer of debit and credit entries from the Journal to their respective accounts in the Ledger. Reference to the Journal Page number is given in Journal Folio (JF) column of Ledger Accounts. The format for Ledger A/c is as follows:

< Ledger head >

Dr. ***Cr.***

Date	*Particulars*	*JF*	*Amount (Rs.)*	*Date*	*Particulars*	*JF*	*Amount (Rs.)*
	*To balance c/f				*By balance b/d		
	Total		=		Total		=

(***Note:** Only one will appear.)

Rule for ledger entry

Rule 1: While making posting in the ledger, the concerned account, which has been debited or credited in the Journal, should also be debited or credited in the Ledger with same amount in the format shown above. But reference has to be given of the other account, which has been credited or debited in the Journal, as the case may be.

Rule 2: Use prefix 'To' with the accounts, which appear on the debit side and 'By' with the accounts, which appear on the credit side of the ledger A/c.

Remark

In actual practice, however, similar types of ledger accounts are kept in one ledger book e.g., bank having manual system of accounting, maintains different ledger books like ledger book on Saving A/c containing ledger accounts of the entire Saving A/c holders. Similarly ledger accounts of different fixed assets are maintained in fixed asset ledger book.

On the basis of nature of ledger accounts, there are three categories of ledger books viz.

(*i*) Personal books
(*ii*) Real books
(*iii*) Nominal books

Example of personal book is **ledger book on saving account** (mentioned above) as it deals with people *i.e.,* saving account holders. Similarly **fixed asset Ledger book** will be categorized under real books.

Ledgers for Illustration 3: In Illustration 3, twenty-three accounts are created. So 23 ledger accounts will be maintained.

Capital A/c

Dr. **Cr.**

Date	Particulars	JF	Amount (Rs.)	Date	Particulars	JF	Amount (Rs.)
March 30	**To balance c/f**		**50,000**	March 1	By cash		50,000
			50,000				50,000
				March 31	**By balance b/f**		**50,000**

Cash A/c

Dr. **Cr.**

Date	Particulars	JF	Amount (Rs.)	Date	Particulars	JF	Amount (Rs.)
March 1	To Capital A/c		50,000	March 1	By Bank A/c		20,000
March 6	To Sales A/c		8,000	April 2	By Machinery and Furniture A/c		15,000
March 17	To Sales A/c		2,000	March 3	By Purchase A/c		14,000
March 21	To Ram A/c		12,000	March 21	Discount allowed A/c		100
March 28	To Investment A/c		1,300	March 22	By Bank A/c		5,800
					By Investment A/c		3,000
March 28	To Profit & Loss A/c		100	March 23	By Brokerage A/c		20
March 30	To Sales A/c		1,900	March 28	By Brokerage A/c		20
				March 30	By Salary A/c		1,500
				March 30	By Travelling expenses A/c		100
				March 30	**By balance c/f**		**15,760**
			75,300				75,300
March 31	**To balance b/f**		**15,760**				

Bank A/c

Dr. *Cr.*

Date	*Particulars*	*JF*	*Amount (Rs.)*	*Date*	*Particulars*	*JF*	*Amount (Rs.)*
March 1	To Cash A/c		20,000	March 10	By Telephone Rent A/c		500
March 22	To Cash A/c		5,800	March 19	By Drawings A/c		1,500
March 29	To Return Outward A/c		1,000	March 25	By Chowdhry and Co. A/c		11,000
				March 30	By Rent A/c		1,000
				March 30	**By balance c/f**		**12,800**
			26,800				26,800
March 31	**To balance b/f**		**12,800**				

Purchase A/c

Dr. *Cr.*

Date	*Particulars*	*JF*	*Amount (Rs.)*	*Date*	*Particulars*	*JF*	*Amount (Rs.)*
March 3	To Cash A/c		14,000				
March 8	To Chowdhry and Co. A/c		11,000				
March 28	To Bhuwan A/c		2,100	March 30	**By balance c/f**		27,100
			27,100				27,100
March 31	**To balance b/f**		**27,100**				

Sales A/c

Dr. *Cr.*

Date	*Particulars*	*JF*	*Amount (Rs.)*	*Date*	*Particulars*	*JF*	*Amount (Rs.)*
March 30	**To balance b/d**		**27,000**	March 6	By Cash A/c		8,000
				March 15	By Ram A/c		12,000
				March 17	By Cash A/c		2,000
				March 28	By Raghvendra A/c		3,000
				March 30	By Cash A/c		2,000
			27,000				27,000
				March 31	**By balance b/d**		**27,000**

Return Inward A/c

Dr. Cr.

Date	Particulars	JF	Amount (Rs.)	Date	Particulars	JF	Amount (Rs.)
March 29	To Raghvendra A/c		100	March 30	**By balance b/d**		**100**
			100				100
March 31	**To balance b/d**		**100**				

Return Outward A/c

Dr. Cr.

Date	Particulars	JF	Amount (Rs.)	Date	Particulars	JF	Amount (Rs.)
March 30	**To balance b/d**		**1,100**	March 25	By Chowdhry and Co. A/c		1,000
				March 29	By Bhuwan A/c		100
			1,100				1,100
				March 31	**By balance b/d**		**1,100**

Investment A/c

Dr. Cr.

Date	Particulars	JF	Amount (Rs.)	Date	Particulars	JF	Amount (Rs.)
March 23	To Cash A/c		3,000	March 28	By Cash A/c		1,300
March 28	To Profit & Loss A/c		100	March 30	**By balance b/d**		**1,800**
			3,100				3,100
March 31	**To balance b/d**		**1,800**				

Machinery and Furniture A/c

Dr. Cr.

Date	Particulars	JF	Amount (Rs.)	Date	Particulars	JF	Amount (Rs.)
March 2	To Cash A/c		15,000	March 30	**By balance b/d**		**15,000**
			15,000				15,000
March 31	**To balance b/d**		**15,000**				

Raghvendra A/c (Sundry Debtor)

Dr. **Cr.**

Date	Particulars	JF	Amount (Rs.)	Date	Particulars	JF	Amount (Rs.)
March 28	To Sales A/c		3,000	March 29	By Return Inward A/c		100
				March 30	**By balance b/d**		**2,900**
			3,000				3,000
March 31	**To balance b/d**		**2,900**				

Chowdhry and Co. A/c (Sundry Creditor)

Dr. **Cr.**

Date	Particulars	JF	Amount (Rs.)	Date	Particulars	JF	Amount (Rs.)
March 25	To Return Outward A/c		1,000	March 8	By Purchase A/c		11,000
March 25	To Bank A/c		10,000				
			11,000				11,000

Ram A/c (Sundry Debtor)

Dr. **Cr.**

Date	Particulars	JF	Amount (Rs.)	Date	Particulars	JF	Amount (Rs.)
March 15	To Sales A/c		12,000	March 21	By Cash A/c		12,000
			12,000				12,000

Bhuwan A/c (Sundry Creditor)

Dr. **Cr.**

Date	Particulars	JF	Amount (Rs.)	Date	Particulars	JF	Amount (Rs.)
March 29	To Return Outward A/c		100	March 28	By Purchase A/c		2,100
March 30	**To balance c/d**		**2,000**				
			2,100				2,100
				March 31	**By balance b/d**		**2000**

Telephone Rent A/c

Dr. *Cr.*

Date	*Particulars*	*JF*	*Amount (Rs.)*	*Date*	*Particulars*	*JF*	*Amount (Rs.)*
March 10	To Bank A/c		500	March 30	**By balance b/d**		500
			500				500
March 31	**To balance c/d**		**500**				

Typewriter A/c

Dr. *Cr.*

Date	*Particulars*	*JF*	*Amount (Rs.)*	*Date*	*Particulars*	*JF*	*Amount (Rs.)*
March 11	To Universal Typewriter Co. A/c		2,100	March 30	**By balance b/d**		2,100
			2,100				2,100
March 31	**To balance c/d**		**2,100**				

Universal Typewriter Co. A/c

Dr. *Cr.*

Date	*Particulars*	*JF*	*Amount (Rs.)*	*Date*	*Particulars*	*JF*	*Amount (Rs.)*
March 30	**To balance c/d**		**2,100**	March 11	By Typewriter A/c		2,100
			2,100				2,100
				March 31	**By balance b/d**		**2,100**

Drawing A/c

Dr. *Cr.*

Date	*Particulars*	*JF*	*Amount (Rs.)*	*Date*	*Particulars*	*JF*	*Amount (Rs.)*
March 19	To Bank A/c		1,500	March 30	**By balance b/d**		**1,500**
			1,500				1,500
March 31	**To balance c/d**		**1,500**				

Discount Allowed A/c

Dr. Cr.

Date	Particulars	JF	Amount (Rs.)	Date	Particulars	JF	Amount (Rs.)
March 21	To Ram A/c		100	March 30	**By balance b/d**		**100**
			100				100
March 31	**To balance c/d**		**100**				

Salary A/c

Dr. Cr.

Date	Particulars	JF	Amount (Rs.)	Date	Particulars	JF	Amount (Rs.)
March 30	To Cash A/c		1,500	March 30	**By balance b/d**		**1,500**
			1,500				1,500
March 31	**To balance c/d**		**1,500**				

Profit & Loss A/c

Dr. Cr.

Date	Particulars	JF	Amount (Rs.)	Date	Particulars	JF	Amount (Rs.)
March 30	**To balance c/d**		100	March 28	By Investment A/c		100
			100				100
				March 31	**By balance b/d**		**100**

Travelling Expenses A/c

Dr. Cr.

Date	Particulars	JF	Amount (Rs.)	Date	Particulars	JF	Amount (Rs.)
March 30	To Sales A/c		100	March 30	**By balance b/d**		**100**
			100				100
March 31	**To balance c/d**		**100**				

Rent A/c

Dr. Cr.

Date	Particulars	JF	Amount (Rs.)	Date	Particulars	JF	Amount (Rs.)
March 30	To Bank A/c		1,000	March 30	**By balance b/f**		**1,000**
			1,000				1,000
March 31	**To balance c/f**		**1,000**				

Brokerage A/c

Dr. **Cr.**

Date	Particulars	JF	Amount (Rs.)	Date	Particulars	JF	Amount (Rs.)
March 23	To Cash A/c		20	March 30	**By balance b/f**		40
March 28	To Cash A/c		20				
			40				40
March 31	**To balance c/f**		**40**				

Note: The balance is put on the side of the account, which is smaller, and a reference is given that it has been carried forward (c/f) or 'c/d' to the next period.
In the next period, a reference is given that the opening balance has been brought forward (b/f) or 'b/d' from the previous period.

Step 4: Summarizing Transactions/Events (Trial balance only)

TRIAL BALANCE

The trial balance is a statement containing the various ledger balances on a particular date. Trial balance checks the accuracy of ledger balances. The two sides of the trial balance should match. If the two sides do not match then there must be some arithmetical discrepancy in the books of accounts which need to be detected.

Trial balance for illustration 3:

Trial Balance
As on 30th March 2003

Particulars	Debit Amount (Rs.) Dr.	Credit Amount (Rs.) Cr.
Capital A/c		50,000
Cash A/c	15,760	
Bank A/c	12,800	
Purchase A/c	27,100	
Sales A/c		27,000
Machinery and Furniture A/c	15,000	
Investment A/c	1,800	
Brokerage A/c	40	
Typewriter A/c	2,100	
Universal Typewriter and Co. A/c		2,100
Rent A/c	1,000	
Salary A/c	1,500	
Return Inward A/c	100	
Return Outward A/c		1,100
Drawings A/c	1,500	
Raghvendra A/c	2,900	

Contd...

Particulars	*Debit Amount (Rs.) Dr.*	*Credit Amount (Rs.) Cr.*
Travelling Expenses A/c	100	
Profit & Loss A/c		100
Discount Allowed A/c	100	
Telephone Rent A/c	500	
Bhuwan A/c		2,000
Total	**82,300**	**82,300**

Note: A clear scrutiny of trial balance reveals the following rule:

Dr. Column All expenses/losses and assets

Cr. Column All income/gains and liabilities

Suspense Account

If both the sides of the trial balance do not match then a Suspense A/c may be opened to put the difference. This is a temporary account, which has to be written off at the earliest after the error is detected and rectified. If the credit side is less, then the Suspense A/c will be credited. But if the credit side is more, then this account will be debited.

Objective of Trial Balance

The trial balance is prepared with the following objectives:

1. **Helps in detecting arithmetical errors:**
   In case of manual accounting, if there is arithmetical error in calculation of amounts in primary and secondary books, trial balance will not agree and hence need to be detected before preparing final accounts.
2. **Helps in providing ledgers at a glance:**
   Trial balance is Summarizing Transactions/Events as it contains list of all ledger accounts along with their balances. In absence of trial balance it would have been very difficult to assess the position of different ledger accounts from primary and secondary books.
3. **Helps in preparation of final accounts:**
   The ultimate end of maintaining books of account is to ascertain the result of business operation and to provide the picture of assets and liabilities. This is done through preparing income statement and balance sheet, known as final accounts on the basis of information supplied by the trial balance. Thus trial balance acts as a source statement for preparing final accounts.
4. **Helps in identifying items for adjustments in final accounts:**
   While making final accounts certain adjustments regarding closing stock, outstanding and prepaid expenses etc. are to be made. The information furnished by trial balance helps in identifying those items for adjustments in preparing final accounts.

2.4 TYPES OF ERRORS DURING BOOK-KEEPING PROCESS

During book-' eping process starting from Recording of Transaction to Summarizing Transaction (trial balance) number of errors may occur because of lack of knowledge of accountant and because of clerical and arithmetical error. However these errors minimize in case of computerized accounting system (*i.e.* using accounting software for maintaining accounting transactions).

Following is the types of error alongwith its impact over trial balance.

(A) Errors when trial balance agrees: The possible cause of such errors are,

(*a*) Error of accounting principle *e.g.* treating a revenue expense as capital expenditure or vice-versa or treating the sale of a fixed asset as ordinary sale.

(*b*) Clerical errors *e.g.* omitting an entry completely from the primary books, error in voucher entry (primary entry) in terms of amount and in terms of voucher type.

(B) Errors when trial balance does not agree: The possible cause of such errors are clerical errors *e.g.* posting the wrong amount in the ledger, omitting to post the ledger account from the primary books, posting an amount on the wrong side, wrong balancing/totalling of ledger account.

2.5 DATA FLOW DIAGRAM (DFD) FOR BOOK-KEEPING PROCESS

This part is exclusively for I.T. professionals (programmers) as an aid in understanding mechanism involved in book-keeping process regarding data flow.

Context level DFD, I[st] Level DFD and IInd Level DFD for book-keeping process are shown on next page:

1.5 CONTEXT LEVEL DFD

1st LEVEL DFD

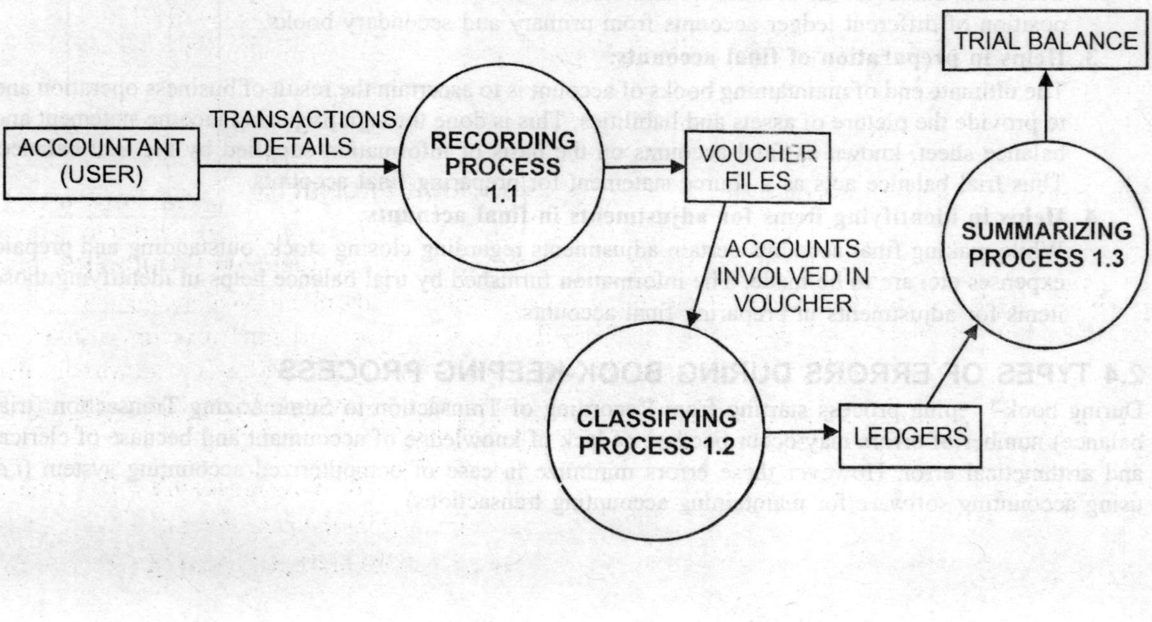

IInd LEVEL DFD

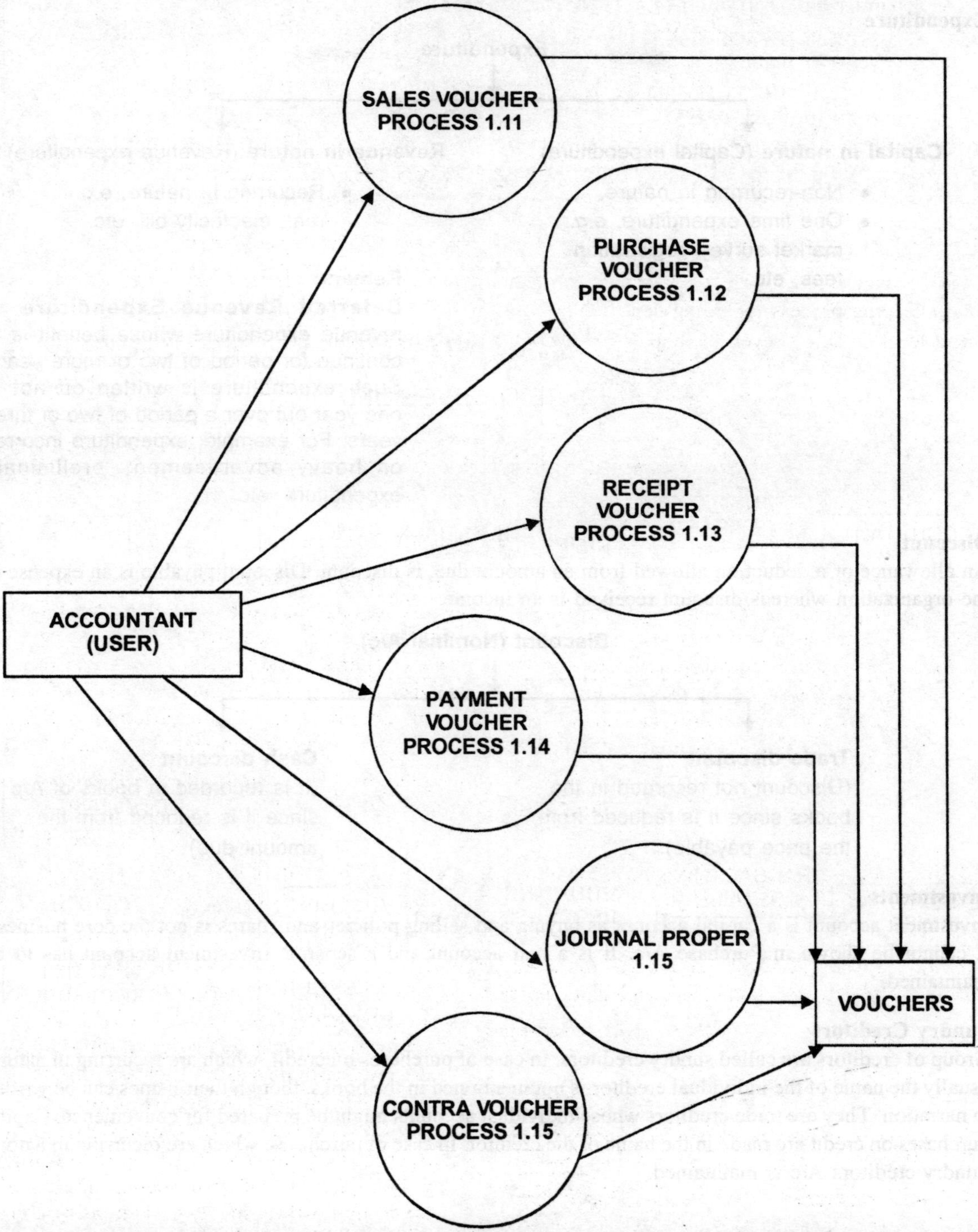

Important Terms

Expenditure

Expenditure

↓

Capital in nature (Capital expenditure)

- Non-recurring in nature.
- One time expenditure, *e.g.* market survey, registration fees, etc.

Revenue in nature (Revenue expenditure)

- Recurring in nature, *e.g.* rent, electricity bill, etc.

Remark:

Deferred Revenue Expenditure: A revenue expenditure whose benefit is to continue for period of two or more years. Such expenditure is written off not in one year but over a period of two or three years. For example, expenditure incurred on heavy advertisement, preliminary expenditure, etc.

Discount

An allowance or a deduction allowed from an amount due, is discount. Discount payable is an expense of the organization whereas discount received is an income.

Discount (Nominal A/c)

↓

Trade discount
(Discount not recorded in the books since it is reduced from the price payable)

Cash discount
(It is recorded in books of A/c since it is reduced from the amount due)

Investments

Investment account is a capital account as buying and selling policies and shares is not the core business. It cannot be shown in Purchase A/c. It is a real account and a separate investment account has to be maintained.

Sundry Creditors

Group of creditors are called sundry creditors. In case of purchases on credit, which are recurring in nature, usually the name of the individual creditor is not mentioned in the books, though their names can be written in narration. They are trade creditors whose individual accounts might be prepared for convenience. Capital purchases on credit are made in the name of the creditor. In case of purchases, which are recurring in nature, Sundry creditors A/c is maintained.

Brokerage

It is a amount paid to broker against trading of securities and hence is an expense.

Drawings

Cash or goods taken by the owner of the business for his personal use. For example, payment of salaries to employees is not a drawing. But, if the owner takes money from the business for the payment of his own expenses, then this is a drawing. Drawings reduce the capital of the owner.

Books of Account

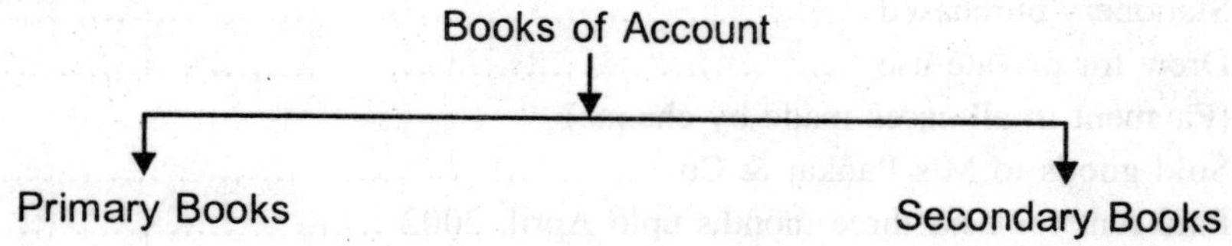

Primary Books

Primary books are books for primary entry and are used for recording business transactions/events, which are of financial nature.

Primary Book (Journals) in Manual Environment	***Primary Book (Journals) in Computerized Environment***
• Subsidiary books like sale, purchase, cash book etc., and Journal proper, are books of primary entry used for recording of business transactions/events, which are of financial nature.	• Different vouchers like receipt, payment, sale, purchase, contra and Journal vouchers are used for recording of transactions/events, which are of financial nature.

Secondary Books

Secondary books are used for ledger entry *i.e.* classifying the transactions/events recorded in primary books.

Secondary Books (Ledgers) in Manual Environment	***Secondary Books (Ledgers) in Computerized Environment.***
• For classifying the recorded transactions/ events, different ledger books are maintained. • Ledger book contains similar type of A/cs. • Cash book acts as primary as well as secondary books.	• Ledger A/cs are automatically generated and are grouped as per requirement.

Exercises

Q. 1. **Describe book-keeping process.**

Q. 2. **Differentiate between primary books and secondary books.**

Q. 3. **Explain the advantages of trial balance, also give the format for trial balance.**

Q. 4. **Describe the possible errors during book-keeping process.**

Q. 5. **Pass the necessary journal entries of the following information, post them into ledgers and prepare trial balance.**

2002		Rs.
Jan. 1	Started business with cash	30,000
Jan. 2	Deposited into bank	10,000
Jan. 5	Purchased machinery for cash	5,000
Jan. 9	Purchased goods from ABC Ltd. at the list price of Rs. 5,000 He allowed 5% trade discount. Payment made by cheque.	
Jan. 11	Paid for electric charges	50
Jan. 11	Paid rent for January, 2002	500
Jan. 11	Stationery purchased	100
Jan. 11	Drew for private use	1000
	(Payment in all cases made by cheque)	
Jan. 20	Sold goods to M/s Pankaj & Co.	4000
Jan. 26	Paid rent for next three months upto April, 2002	1500
Jan. 28	Received a cheque from M/s Pankaj & Co. for Rs. 3,275 in full settlement and sent the cheque to bank	
Jan. 29	Cheque of M/s Pankaj & Co. dishonoured	
Jan. 30	Salaries due to clerk.	200
Jan. 31	Received a new cheque from M/s Pankaj & Co. for Rs. 3,500	
Jan. 31	Interest on capital	50

Q. 6. Pass the necessary journal entries with the following information, post them into ledgers and prepare Trial balance.

2001		Rs.
March 1	Purchased goods for cash	2,000
March 3	Purchased goods from Sunil	7,000
March 5	Sold goods to M/s Black & White for cash	1,500
March 8	Sold goods to Rahul	800
March 9	Paid salaries	500
March 10	Payment received from Rahul in full settlement of his account	750
March 13	Received commission	15
March 16	Deposited into bank	1,400
March 18	Paid general trade expenses	40
March 22	Withdrew from bank for office use	500
March 24	Paid rent	125
March 27	Paid cash to Sunil in full settlement of his account	6,800
March 31	Paid for miscellaneous expenses	200

Q. 7. Journalize the following transactions:

(*a*) Mohan is declared insolvent. I received from his official receiver a first and final dividend of 60 P in a rupee on a debt of Rs. 3000.

(*b*) Received a V.P.P. for Rs. 700. Sent a worker to take delivery of it and he paid Rs.10 for cartage.

(*c*) Received interest on loan from the debtor, Rs. 1,500.

(*d*) Provide interest on Capital (10,000) at 6% for six months.

(*e*) Received Rs. 800 from Narayana in full settlement of a debt to his account for Rs. 850.

Q. 8. Pass the necessary journal entries with the following information, post them into ledgers and prepare trial balance.

2002		Rs.
Feb. 1	Paid salaries	1,500
	Paid rent	900
Feb. 3	Drew for private use	250
Feb. 4	Received commission	100
Feb. 5	Loan taken from A.K. Das	4,000
Feb. 5	Received Rs. 2,000 from Sohan in full settlement of his account for	2,500
Feb. 6	Purchased goods for cash	900
Feb. 17	Cash sales	500
Feb. 18	Bought goods from XYZ & Co. valued at Rs. 5,500 less 10% trade discount	
Feb. 20	Paid wages to workers	200
Feb. 23	Paid office-expenses	50
Feb. 28	Rent received	200

Q. 9. Record the following transactions in the journal and post them into ledgers.

(*i*) Commenced business with cash Rs. 50,000.

(*ii*) Paid rent in advance Rs. 800.

(*iii*) Purchased goods for cash Rs. 18,000 and for credit Rs. 10,000.

(*iv*) Bought scooter for personal use for Rs. 6,000 and the payment made out of business money.

(*v*) Received cash for a bad debt written off last year Rs. 200.

(*vi*) Mr. A, a debtor of the firm became insolvent. A first and final payment @ 75 paise in a rupee was received from his official receivers towards his total dues of Rs. 500.

Q. 10. Describe the objective of trial balance.

Q. 11. Draw context level, 1st level and 2nd level DFD (Data Flow Diagram) for Accounting Information System (AIS).

Chapter–3

Final Accounts

(Financial Statements)

LEARNING OBJECTIVES

In this chapter we will study:

Introduction to Final Accounts

Preparation of Final Accounts—An Introduction

Preparation of Final Accounts for Sole Proprietorship Concern

Difference Between Trial Balance and Balance Sheet

Difference Between Trading Account and Manufacturing Account

Difference Between Trading Account and Profit & Loss Account

Difference Between Income Statement and Balance Sheet

Accounting Theory Framework

- Generally Accepted Accounting Principles (GAAP)
- Accounting Standards (AS)

Final Accounts for Partnership Firm

Final Accounts for Companies

3.1 INTRODUCTION TO FINAL ACCOUNTS

While the Trial Balance checks the accuracy of ledger balances, the final account reveals two facts:

1. Whether the business is in profit or loss during the period covered by the Trial Balance. A Trading and Profit & Loss account also known as income statement is prepared for this purpose.
2. What is the financial position (financial position means picture of assets and liabilities) of the business? This is judged by preparing a balance sheet for the business.

Thus, income statement represents the summary of all the expenses and incomes occurred during the financial year whereas balance sheet represents the financial position of the concerned organization at a particular point of time, usually at the end of financial year *i.e.*, 31st March (in India, financial year starts from 1st April to 31st March).

Final accounts are statutory requirements for all type of registered organizations. They are popularly known as Financial Statements.

3.2 PREPARATION OF FINAL ACCOUNTS—AN INTRODUCTION

Preparation of final accounts is governed by different Acts, Laws, Standards and Principles like Income tax law, Company Act, Partnership Act, Accounting Standards (AS), Generally Accepted Accounting Principles (GAAP) etc., used for valuation of financial transactions/events to standardize accounting information, which in turn depends upon type of organization concerned. In other words, since different types of organizations operates under different legal framework, the methodology/procedure for preparation of final accounts will change accordingly.

Again, there are three main categories of organizations on the basis of incorporation (Registration) *viz.*

1. Sole proprietorship concern
2. Partnership firm
3. Joint stock companies
   (*a*) Private Limited Co.
   (*b*) Public Limited Co.

Thus preparation of final accounts should be dealt separately for all the above category of organizations and are chapterised as under:

Particulars	***Name of Chapter***[1]
1. Accounting for Sole Proprietorship Concern	Final Account
2. Accounting for Partnership Firm	Partnership Account
3. Accounting for Joint Stock Companies	Company Account
4. Accounting for Other Business Activity like Shipping, Leasing etc.	Miscellaneous Account

3.3 PREPARATION OF FINAL ACCOUNTS FOR SOLE PROPRIETORSHIP CONCERN

Preparation of Final Accounts can be studied according to following cases:

Case 1 : Preparation of Final Accounts when Transactions/Events are given.

Case 2 : Preparation of Final Accounts when Ledger balances are given.

Case 3 : Preparation of Final Accounts when Trial balance with additional information is given.

1. Preparation of Final Accounts for partnership firm, joint stock companies and miscellaneous activities are beyond the scope of this book. Only introduction is given here.

Case 1: Preparation of Final Accounts when Transactions/Events are given:

Trading activity:

Steps involved in preparation of Final Accounts when the organization concerned is engaged in trading activity are as follows:

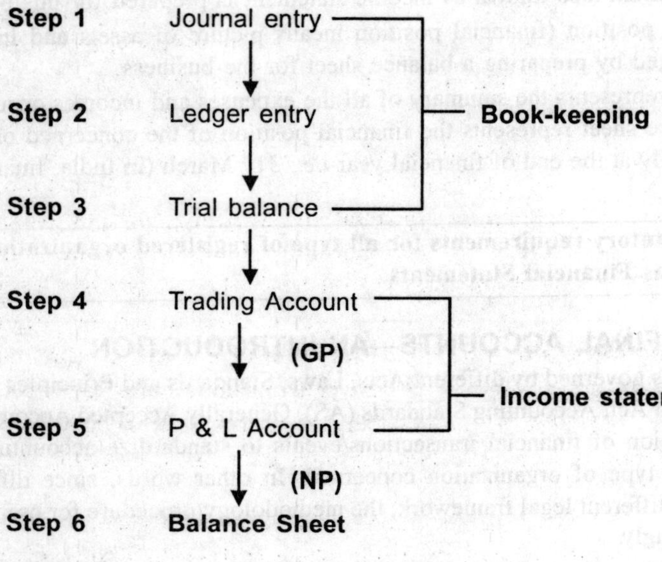

Manufacturing activity:

Steps involved in preparation of final accounts when the organization concerned is engaged in manufacturing activity are as follows:

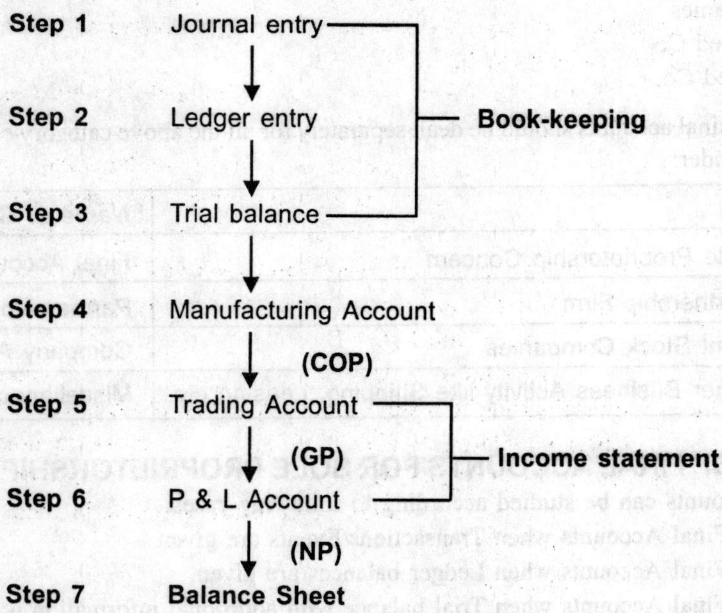

Note:

- **COP** represents cost of production, **GP** represents gross profit and **NP** represents net profit. These are balancing figure of manufacturing account, trading account and Profit & Loss A/c (P & L A/c) respectively.
- In case of trading concern, Income statement is subdivided into trading account and P & L A/c whereas in case of manufacturing concern income statement is subdivided into manufacturing account, trading account and P & L A/c.

The Format for income statement in case of Trading concern is as follows:

Trading and P & L A/c for the year ------

Dr. ***Cr.***

Particulars	***Amount***	***Particulars***	***Amount***
To Opening stock	——	By Sales (less return)	——
To Purchases (less return)	——	****By Gross loss b/d**	——
To Direct wages	——	**(Balancing fig.)**	
To Direct expenses	——		
• Carriage inward			
• Duty and clearing charges			
• Fuel and energy			
• Octroi duty etc.			
To Gross profit (GP) b/d	——		
(Balancing fig.)			
Total	=	**Total**	=
****To Gross loss c/d**	——	**By Gross profit (GP) c/d**	——
To General and administrative expenses	——	**By Other income**	——
• Salaries			
• Rent, rates and taxes		• Rent received	
• Stationary and printing		• Discount received (Cr.)	
• Telephone bill		• Sale of scrap material	
• General expenses		• Commission received	
• Trade expenses		• Interest received	
• Insurance premium		• Dividend received	
• Loss by fire, theft, etc.		• Bad debt recovered	
• Discount allowed			
• Office lighting		****By Net Loss b/d**	——
• Depreciation			

Contd...

Dr. *Cr.*

Particulars	*Amount*	*Particulars*	*Amount*
• Bad debt written off			
• Repairs			
• Audit fee			
• Preliminary expenses written off etc.		** This will happen when total of debit is more than total of credit.	
To Selling and distribution expenses	——		
• Carriage outward			
• Packaging material			
• Salesman commission			
• Conveyance			
• Advertisement			
• Export duty etc.			
To Financial Expenses	——		
• Interest paid			
• Tax paid etc.			
To Net profit (NP) b/d (Balancing fig.)	——		
Total	=	**Total**	=

The format for Income statement in case of manufacturing concern is as follows:

Manufacturing and Trading and P & L A/c for the year -------

Dr. *Cr.*

Particulars	*Amount*	*Particulars*	*Amount*
To Opening stock WIP	——	By Sale of scraps	——
To Opening stock R/M	——	By Closing stock WIP*	——
To Purchases (R/M)	——	**By Cost of production b/d**	——
Less Purchases return		**(balancing fig.)**	
Less Closing stock R/M*		↓	
To Productive wages	——	(or cost of manufacturing)	
To Manufacturing expenses	——		
• Coal, fuel and energy			
• Carriage inward			
• Import duty etc.			

Contd...

Dr. *Cr.*

Particulars	*Amount*	*Particulars*	*Amount*
To Factory Overhead (FOH)	——		
• Factory lighting			
• Factory insurance			
• Repairs to plant and factory building			
• Plant depreciation etc.			
Total	=	**Total**	=
To Cost of production c/d	——	By Sales (less sales return)	——
To Opening stock FG	——	By Closing stock FG	——
To gross profit (GP) b/d (Balancing fig.)	——		
Total	=	**Total**	=
To general and administrative expenses	——	**By gross profit (GP) c/d**	——
• Salaries		By other income	——
• Rent, Rates and Taxes		• Rent received	
• Stationary and printing		• Discount received (Cr.)	
• Telephone bill		• Sale of scrap material	
• General expenses		• Commission received	
• Trade/miscellaneous/ Sundry expenses		• Interest received	
		• Insurance premium	
• Loss by fire, theft etc.		• Dividend received	
• Discount allowed		• Bad debt recovered	
• Office lighting			
• Depreciation other than plant and machinery			
• Bad debt written off			
• Repairs and renewals excluding Factory			
• Audit fee			
• Preliminary expenses written off etc.			
To selling and distribution expenses	——		
• Carriage outward			

Contd...

Dr.			*Cr.*
Particulars	**Amount**	**Particulars**	**Amount**
• Packaging material			
• Salesman commission			
• Conveyance			
• Advertisement			
• Export duty etc.			
To Financial Expenses	——		
• Interest paid			
• Tax paid etc.			
To Net Profit (NP) b/d (Balancing fig.)	——		
Total	=	**Total**	=

Note

1. WIP stands for work in progress *i.e.* semi-finished goods.
2. R/M stands for raw material.
3. FG stands for finished goods.
4. Closing stock of WIP, R/M and FG appear in income statement only when given in additional information.
5. Purchase return is also termed as return outward/return to supplier.
6. Sales return is also termed as return inward/return from customer.
7. Carriage inward is also known as freight inward.
8. Carriage outward is also known as freight outward/cartage outward.
9. For numerical purpose 'wages and salary' goes to Trading A/c whereas 'salary and wages' goes to P & L A/c.

Vertical presentation of Income Statement in case of sole proprietorship concern

Income Statement for the year ------

	Particulars		Amount (Rs.)
	Sales	} Trading A/c	——
Less	Cost of Goods Sold (COGS)		——
	Gross Profit (GP)/(Gross Loss)		——@
Less	Operating Expenses (OE)	} P & L A/c	
	Operating Profit (OP)		——@
Add	Non-operating income/less non-operating losses		——
	Earning Before Interest and Tax (EBIT)		——@
Less	Interest		——
	Earning Before Tax (EBT)		——@
Less	Tax		——
	Earning After Tax/Profit After Tax (PAT)/Net Profit (NP)		——@

↓ Goes to

Balance Sheet (To Capital add Net Profit/less Net Loss, if there is)

Note

- @ Stands for balancing figure.
- OE includes general and administrative expenses plus selling and distribution expenses plus depreciation.
- Interest is tax-deductible item means interest is charged before the tax is levied. Thus, debt capital provides tax shield and hence acts as cheaper source of finance.

The format for balance sheet is as follows:

Balance Sheet as on ————

Liabilities | ***Assets***

Particulars	***Amount***	***Particulars***	***Amount***
Capital	——	Fixed Assets	——
Add Net Profit or Less Net Loss (as per P & L A/c)		• Land and building	
Less drawings		• Plant and machinery	
Long-term loan	——	• Furniture	
		• Fixture and fittings	
		Investments	——
Current liability	——	• Marketable securities	
• Trade creditors/sundry creditors (Crs)		Current assets	——
• Bills Payable (B/P)		• Cash in hand	
• Bank overdraft		• Cash at bank	
• Outstanding expenses e.g. Outstanding Rent/Tax/Wages etc.		• Trade debtors/sundry debtors (Drs)	
		• Bills Receivable (B/R)	
		• Prepaid expenses like Prepaid Rent/ Tax/Wages etc.	
Total	=	**Total**	=

Mechanism involved in preparation of Final Accounts from trial balance

A clear scrutiny of the format for Income statement and balance sheet shown above results into following mechanism: -

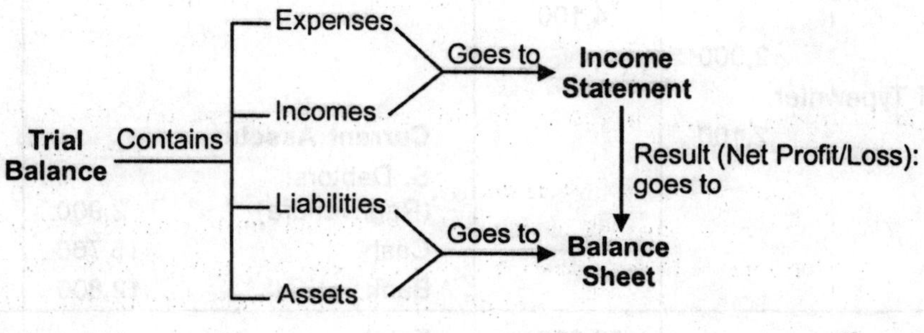

In summarized way:

1. Trial balance contains four items *viz.* Expense, Income, Liability and Assets.
2. Expenses and Incomes go to Income Statement according to format shown above.
3. Liabilities and Assets go to Balance Sheet according to format shown above. Result of Income statement (Profit/Loss) also goes to balance sheet on liability side under reserves or adjusted to Capital A/c in case of sole proprietorship concern.

Final Accounts for Illustration 3

(1) Income Statement for Illustration 3

Dr. *Cr.*

Particulars		*Amount*	*Particulars*		*Amount*
To Purchases	27,100		By Sales	27,000	
Less Return	1,100	26,000	Less Return	100	26,900
To Gross Profit b/d		**900**			
Total		**26900**	**Total**		**26900**
To Brokerage		40	**By Gross Profit c/d**		**900**
To Discount Allowed		100	By P & L A/c		100
To Rent		1,000	**By Net Loss**		**2,240**
To Salary		1,500			
To Telephone Rent		500			
To Travelling Expenses		100			
Total		**3,240**	**Total**		**3,240**

(2) Balance Sheet for Illustration 3

Liabilities		*Amount*	*Assets*		*Amount*
Capital	50,000		**Fixed Assets:**		
Less Drawings	1,500		Machinery and Furniture		1,500
Less Net Loss			Typewriter		2,100
(as per P & L A/c)	2,240	46,260			
			Investment		**1,800**
S. Creditors:		4,100			
Bhuwan	2,000				
Universal Typewriter					
Co.	2,100		**Current Assets:**		
			S. Debtors:		
			(Raghvendra)	2,900	
			Cash	15,760	31,460
			Bank	12,800	
Total		**50,360**	**Total**		**50,360**

Case 2: Steps in preparation of final accounts when ledger balances are given:

Ledger balances

↓

Step 1: Prepare trial balance from given ledger balances as per rule given below.

↓

Step 2: Post the items of trial balance prepared under step 1 to income statement and balance sheet according to format shown above.

Rule for preparation of Trial balance when ledger balances are given is as follows:

Dr. Column	All expenses/losses and assets
Cr. Column	All income/gains and liabilities

Illustration 4: From the following ledger balance prepare final accounts: -

Particulars	*Amount*
Sundry debtors (A)	15,000
Opening stock (E)	50,000
Land and building (A)	10,0000
Capital (L)	25,0000
Rent (Cr.) (I)	6,000
Cash in hand (A)	16,000
Cash at bank (A)	40,000
Wages (E)	30,000
Sundry creditors (L)	70,000
Bills receivable (A)	20,000
Interest given (E)	2,000
Bad debts (E)	5,000
Repairs (E)	3,000
Sales (I)	17,0000
Bills payable (L)	40,000
Furniture and fittings (A)	15,000
Depreciation (E)	10,000
Rates and taxes (E)	8,000
Salaries (E)	20,000
Drawings (A)	20,000
Purchases (E)	10,0000
Office expenses (E)	25,000
Plant and machinery (A)	57,000

Note: 1. Bill receivables (B/R) are those receivables/debtors who has legal evidence (Promissory notes etc.) regarding their transactions.

2. 'A','E','L','I', stands for Asset, Expense, Liability, and Income respectively.

Trial Balance

Particulars	***Debit (A+E)***	***Credit (L+I)***
Sundry debtors	15,000	—
Opening stock	50,000	—
Land and building	10,0000	—
Capital	—	25,0000
Rent received	—	6,000
Cash in hand	16,000	—
Cash at bank	40,000	—
Wages	30,000	—
Sundry creditor	—	70,000
B/R	20,000	—
Interest given	2,000	—
Bad debts	5,000	—
Repairs	3,000	—
Sales	—	17,0000
B/P	—	40,000
Furniture/Fixture	15,000	—
Depreciation	10,000	—
Rent and taxes	8,000	—
Salaries	20,000	—
Drawing	20,000	—
Purchase	10,0000	—
Office expenditure	25,000	—
Plant and machinery	57,000	—
Total	**53,6000**	**53,6000**

Trading and P & L A/c

Particulars	***Amount***	***Particulars***	***Amount***
To Opening stock	50,000	By Sales	17,0000
To Wages	30,000	**By gross loss**	10,000
To Purchase	10,0000		
Total	**18,0000**	**Total**	**18,0000**
To gross loss	10,000	By Other income	
By other exp		• Rent given	6,000
Interest given	2,000	**By net loss**	**77,000**
Bad debts	5,000		
Repairs	3,000		

Contd...

Particulars	Amount	Particulars	Amount
Depreciation	10000		
Rent and tax	8000		
Salaries	20000		
Office Exp.	25000		
Total	**83000**	**Total**	**83000**

Balance Sheet

Liability		Amount	Assets	Amount
Capital	250000		**Fixed Assets:**	
Less drawing	20000		Land and Building	100000
Less net loss	77000		Furniture and Fitting	15000
		153000	Plant and Machinery	57000
Current liability:			**Current assets:**	
Sundry Creditor		70000	Cash in Hand	16000
Bills payable		40000	Cash at Bank	40000
			Sundry Debtor	15000
			Bills Receivable	20000
Total		**263000**	**Total**	**263000**

Case 3: Preparation of final accounts when trial balance with additional information is given: - Adjustment entries (*i.e.,* additional information):

According to going concern concept, an organization never dies, it runs endlessly and therefore it is necessary to evaluate the financial performance and financial position of organization after a fixed interval usually one year, so that the results of one interval can be compared with another. This will help to assess the trend regarding financial performance and position. Financial position means picture of assets and liabilities at given point of time.

Furthermore, to bring the uniformity in process of estimating financial performance and position, it is necessary to match revenues with expenses related to concerned interval only. The revenues and expenses related to other interval must be separated from the interval under consideration. This requires adjustment in both the final accounts. Such items (information), which need to be separated and adjusted accordingly, are known as **'Additional Information'/'Adjustment entries'**. Since the Additional Information comes into the picture after the preparation of Trial Balance, they require double entry—first entry somewhere in income statement and second entry somewhere in Balance Sheet in such a way that Balance Sheet agrees. Similar treatment is given to **'Errors and Omissions'** detected after the preparation of Trial Balance.

Steps in preparation of final accounts when trial balance with additional information is given:

Step1: Post all the items of trial balance to income statement and Balance Sheet according to format shown above.

Step 2: Adjust each additional information one by one in both the final account as they require double entry, keeping in mind that the balance sheet agrees.

Mechanism involved in preparation of final accounts when trial balance with additional information is given:

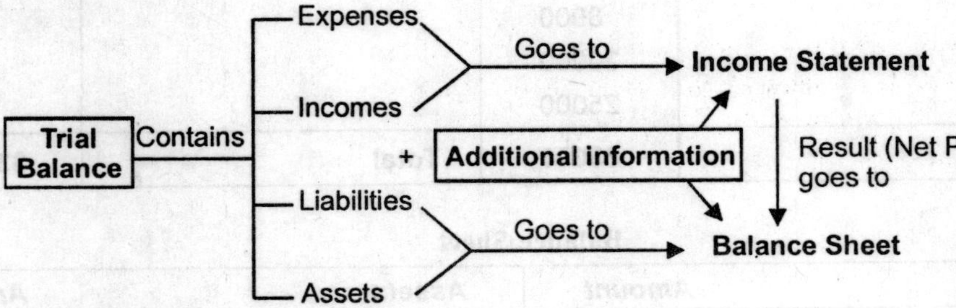

Some important additional information along with adjustment entries in final accounts are given below:

1. Closing Stock → Trading A/c (Cr.); B/S (Current Assets)
2. Outstanding Expenses → P & L A/c (Dr.- Added to concerned expenses); B/S (Current Liabilities)
3. Prepaid Expenses → P & L A/c (Cr. or Expenses, less prepaid expenses); B/S (Current Assets)
4. Outstanding or accrued income (Income due but not received) → P & L A/c (Cr.- Added to concerned income); B/S (Current Assets)
5. Income received in advance or unearned income → P & L A/c (Dr. or deducted from concerned income on credit side); B/S (Current Liabilities)
6. **Depreciation** → **P & L A/c (Dr.)**; **B/S (Fixed Assets, Less Depreciation.)**
7. **Bad Debts** → **P & L A/c (Dr.)**; **B/S (Debtors, Less Bad debts)**
8. **Provision for bad debts** → **P & L A/c (Dr.)**; **B/S (Debtors, Less provision for bad debts)**

9. Provision for discount on debtors	P & L A/c (Dr.)	B/S (Drs., Less provision for discount on debtors)
10. Provision for discount on creditors	P & L A/c (Cr.)	B/S (Crs., Less provision for discount on creditors)
11. Interest on capital	P & L A/c (Dr.)	B/S (Capital, add interest)
12. Interest on drawings	P & L A/c (Cr.)	B/S (Capital, less interest on drawings)
13. Interest on loan (Borrowed)	P & L A/c (Dr.)	B/S: Liability (Loan, add interest on loan)
14. Interest on loan (Advance)	P & L A/c (Cr.)	B/S: Asset (Loan, add interest on loan)
15. Accidental loss of Goods	Trading A/c (Cr. side or deducted from Purchases A/c on Dr. side)	P & L A/c (Dr.) as Loss of stock
16. Goods distributed as free sample	Trading A/c (deducted from Purchases A/c on Dr. side)	P & L A/c (Dr.) as Advertisement A/c
17. Goods given/taken as Charity/Personal use	Trading A/c (deducted from Purchases A/c on Dr. side)	B/S (Capital, less Charity A/c or Drawing A/c)

Remark

The journal entry for above adjustment are given below:

S.No.	Particulars	L.F.	Debit (Rs.)	Credit (Rs.)
1.	Closing stock A/c ...Dr. To Trading A/c			
2.	Expenses A/c ...Dr. To Outstanding expenses A/c			
3.	Prepaid expenses A/c ...Dr. To Expenses A/c			
4.	Accrued income A/c ...Dr. To Income A/c			
5.	Income A/c ...Dr. To Unearned income A/c			
6.	Depreciation A/c ...Dr. To Asset A/c			
7.	Bad Debts A/c ...Dr. To Debtors A/c			
8.	P & L A/c ...Dr. To Provision for bad debts A/c			
9.	P & L A/c ...Dr. To Provision for discount on debtors A/c			
10.	Provision for discount on creditors A/c ...Dr. To P & L A/c			
11.	Interest on capital A/c ...Dr. To Capital A/c			
12.	Drawing A/c ...Dr. To Interest on drawing A/c			
13.	Interest on loans A/c ...Dr. To Loan A/c			
14.	Loans A/c ...Dr. To Interest on loan A/c			
15.	Loss of Stock A/c ...Dr. To Trading A/c or To Purchase A/c			
16.	Advertisement A/c ...Dr. To Purchase A/c			
17.	Charity A/c ...Dr. To Purchase A/c			

Illustration 5: Prepare a trading and P & L A/c for the year ending 31.03.2001 and a balance sheet as on that date from the following trial balance:

Trial Balance

Particulars	*Dr. (Rs.)*	*Cr. (Rs.)*
Opening Stock	16,000	
Capital		45,000
Salaries	13,000	
Drawings	4,000	
Carriage Inwards	500	
Carriage Outwards	1,000	
Sales Return	1,000	
Purchase Return		7,00
Loan to Mr. X	11,000	
Loan from Mr. Y		7,000
Rent	1,300	
Rent Outstanding		200
Purchase	40,000	
Sales		73,100
Debtors	25,000	
Creditors		8,000
Bad Debt	800	
Reserve for Bad Debt		1,200
Discourˌt Allowed/Received	600	
Furniture	11,700	
Wages	500	
Insurance Premium	1,200	
Rent by Sub-letting		800
Cash	700	
Bank	8,000	
Total	**1,36,300**	**1,36,300**

Adjustments

1. Closing Stock Rs. 10,500, but the market value of closing stock was Rs. 9,500.
2. Insurance premium prepaid Rs. 200.
3. Loan to Mr. X, given at 10% interest p.a. and loan taken from Mr. Y carries 9% interest p.a.
4. Depreciation is to be provided at 5% on furniture.
5. Goods worth Rs. 500 have been taken by the proprietor for private use.
6. Bad and doubtful debts are to be provided at 10%.

Solution

Trading Account for the Year ending March 31, 2001

Dr. *Cr.*

Particulars		*Amount*	*Particulars*		*Amount*
To Opening Stock		16,000	By Sales:	73,100	
To Purchase:	40,000		Less Return:	1,000	72,100
Less Return	700	39,000	By Proprietor [I]		500
To Carriage Inward		500	By Closing Stock [II]		9,500
To Wages		500			
To Gross Profit b/d		**25,800**			
Total		**82,100**	**Total**		**82,100**

Profit and Loss Account for the Year ending March 31, 2001

Dr. *Cr.*

Particulars		*Amount*	*Particulars*	*Amount*
To Salary		13,000	By Gross Profit c/d	25,800
To Carriage Outward		1,000	(From Trading A/c)	
To Rent		1,300		
To Reserve for Bad Debts[III]		2,100	By Discount Received	300
To Discount Allowed:		600	By Rent by Sub-letting	800
To Insurance Premium:	1,200		By Interest Receivable [VII]	1,100
Less pre-paid [IV]	200	1,000		
To Interest Payable to Mr. Y[V]		630		
To Depreciation A/c: [VI]		585		
To Net Profit		**7,785**		
Total		**28,000**	**Total**	**28,000**

Working notes

Adjustment (*i*): [II] As per the rule of Conservatism.

Adjustment (*ii*): [IV] Insurance Premium Prepaid.

Adjustment (*iii*): [VII] Loan given to Mr. X is 11,000. Interest on loan is 10% of 11,000 *i.e.* 1,100.
[V] Loan from Mr. Y is Rs. 7,000. Interest payable on loan is 9% *i.e.* Rs. 630.

Adjustment (*iv*): [VI] Furniture is for Rs. 11,700. Depreciation is 5% on furniture *i.e.* Rs. 585.

Adjustment (*v*): [I] Drawing by the proprietor.

Adjustment (*vi*): [III] 10% of Debtor A/c is to be maintained in Reserve for Bad Debt *i.e.* 10% of 25,000 = 2,500. A bad debt of Rs. 800 has been incurred resulting in a balance of Rs. 400 (Rs. 1,200 – Rs. 800 = 400) in Reserve for Bad Debt A/c. In order to maintain Rs. 2,500 in reserve an amount of Rs. 2,100 is required.

***Note*:** Trading Account and Profit & Loss Accounts may be shown together as 'Trading & P/L Account'.

Balance Sheet as on March 31, 2001

Liabilities		*Amount*	*Assets*		*Amount*
Capital	45,000		**Fixed Assets:**		
Less Drawings [I]	4,000		Furniture	11,700	
Less Goods taken			Less Depreciation [VI]	585	
by owner	500				11,115
Add Profit during year	7,785		**Current Assets:**		
		48,285	Loan to Mr. X	11,000	
Loan from Mr. Y [V]	7,000		Add Outstanding		
Add Interest	630		Interest [VII]	1,110	
		7,630			12,100
Rent Outstanding		200	Debtors	25,000	
Creditors		8,000	Less Provision for Bad		
			Debt [III]	2,500	22,500
			Prepaid Insurance [IV]		200
			Cash		700
			Bank		8,000
			Closing Stock [II]		9,500
Total		**64,115**	**Total**		**64,115**

Note:

1. Provision for Doubtful Debts is deducted from Sundry Debtors A/c in the Balance Sheet.
2. Closing Stock (CS) appears in Trading A/c, only when given in Additional Information as well as in B/S (current asset)—Double entry, whereas CS appearing in trial balance, being an asset requires only one entry and hence goes to B/S under current asset. In this case CS do not appear in Trading A/c because it is already adjusted with Purchases A/c.

3.4 DIFFERENCE BETWEEN TRIAL BALANCE AND BALANCE SHEET

Point of difference	*Trial balance*	*Balance sheet*
Objective	The objective of trial balance is to check the accuracy of ledger balances.	The objective of balance sheet is to present financial position at a given point of time.
Requirement	Trial balance is not a statutory requirement.	Balance sheet is a statutory requirement for every registered organization.
Coverage	It includes Expenses, Incomes, Liabilities and Assets.	It includes Liabilities and Assets only.
Time period	It is prepared whenever desired.	Normally it is prepared at the end of accounting period.
Closing stock	Normally Closing stock does not appear in trial balance.	Closing stock appear in balance sheet under Current asset group.

3.5 DIFFERENCE BETWEEN TRADING ACCOUNT AND MANUFACTURING ACCOUNT

Point of difference	***Trading account***	***Manufacturing account***
Objective	The objective is to know the Cost of Goods Sold (COGS).	The objective is to know the Cost of Production (COP)/Cost of Goods manufactured.
Balancing figure	The balancing figure is Gross Profit (GP) or Gross Loss.	The balancing figure is Cost of Production (COP)/Cost of Goods manufactured.
Sale of scrap	The sale of scrap does not appear in trading account.	The sale of scrap appears in manufacturing account on credit side.
Opening Stock (OS) and Closing Stock (CS)	It includes opening and closing stock of finished goods only.	It includes opening and closing stock of semi finished goods *i.e.* WIP and Raw Materials (R/M).

3.6 DIFFERENCE BETWEEN TRADING ACCOUNT AND PROFIT & LOSS ACCOUNT (P & L A/C)

Point of difference	***Trading account***	***Profit and Loss account***
Objective	The objective is to know the Cost of Goods Sold (COGS).	The objective is to know Operating Expenses (OE).
Balancing figure	The balancing figure is Gross Profit (GP) or Gross Loss.	The balancing figure is Net profit (NP) or Net loss.
Treatment of balancing figure	The balancing figure is transferred to P & L A/c.	The balancing figure is transferred to balance sheet on liability side adjusted to Capital A/c in case of Sole proprietorship concern.

Note:

1. Cost of Goods Sold (COGS) = OS + Net purchase + Direct wages + Direct expenses – CS (if given in additional information). Direct expenses are those expenses, which increases COGS.
2. Cost of Production (COP) = OS of WIP + R/M consumed – Sale of scrap – CS of WIP + Productive labour + Manufacturing expenses + Factory overhead.
3. R/M consumed = OS of R/M + Net purchase – CS of R/M.
4. Net purchases = Purchases, less purchases return.
5. Operating Expenses (OE) = General and administrative expenses + Selling and distribution expenses + Depreciation.

3.7 DIFFERENCE BETWEEN INCOME STATEMENT AND BALANCE SHEET

Point of difference	*Income Statement*	*Balance Sheet*
Objective	The objective is to present the summary of expenses and incomes for the accounting period concerned.	The objective of balance sheet is to present financial position at the end of accounting period usually on 31st March.
Balancing figure	The balancing figure tells the result of business operation (Profit/Loss).	It always remains balanced *i.e.* there is no balancing figure.
Coverage	It includes only nominal accounts.	It includes Personal A/c, Real A/c and those Nominal accounts, which are capital in nature and need to be written off over a period of time.
Nature	It is dynamic in nature as it lists the expenses and incomes for the year concerned.	It is static in nature as it lists assets and liabilities at a given point of time usually at the end of year concerned.

Solved Problems

Problem 1. From the following ledger balances, prepare trial balance, income statement and balance sheet:

Particulars	*Amount*
Mr. X's capital	5,00,000
Drawing	20,000
Purchase	2,00,000
Loan	1,00,000
Machinery	50,000
Return to suppliers	50,000
Sales	4,00,000
Return inward	6,00,000
Carriage outward	20,000
Bad debts	5,000
Sundry Drs.	1,00,000
B/R	20,000
Sundry Crs.	50,000
Carriage inward	10,000
Salary and wages	5,000
Depreciation	20,000
Cash in hand	1,00,000
Sale of scrap	5,000
Closing stock	50,000
Prepaid tax	10,000
Outstanding wages	5,000

Open Suspense A/c to balance trial balance if needed.

Solution

Trial Balance

Particulars	*Debit*	*Credit*
Mr. X's Capital	—	5,00,000
Drawing	20,000	—
Purchase	2,00,000	—
Loan	—	1,00,000
Machinery	50,000	—
Return to supplies	—	50,000
Sales	—	4,00,000
Return inward	60,000	—
Carriage outward	20,000	—
Bad debts	5,000	—
Sundry Debtors	1,00,000	—
Bills receivable	20,000	—
Sundry creditors	—	50,000
Carriage inward	10,000	—
Salary and wages	5,000	—
Depreciation	2,000	—
Cash in hand	1,00,000	—
Sale of scrap	—	5,000
Closing stock	50,000	—
Prepaid tax	10,000	—
Outstanding wages	—	5,000
Suspense A/c	4,40,000	—
Total	**11,10,000**	**11,10,000**

Trading and P & L A/c

Dr. *Cr.*

Particulars		*Amount*	*Particulars*		*Amount*
To Purchase	2,00,000		By Sales	4,00,000	
Less: Returns	50,000	1,50,000	Less: Returns	60,000	3,40,000
To Direct Expense:					
Carriage inward	10,000				
To Gross profit		**1,80,000**			
Total		**3,40,000**	**Total**		**3,40,000**

Contd...

Dr. Particulars	Amount	Particulars	*Cr.* Amount
To Salaries and wages	5,000	**By Gross profit**	**1,80,000**
To Depreciation	20,000	By Sale of scrap	5,000
To Carriage outward	20,000		
To Bad debts	5,000		
To Net profit	**1,35,000**		
Total	**1,85,000**	**Total**	**1,85,000**

Balance Sheet

Liabilities		*Amount*	*Assets*	*Amount*
Capital	5,00,000		Fixed Assets:	
Less: Drawing	20,000		Machinery	50,000
	4,80,000			
Add: Net Profit	1,35,000		**Current Assets:**	
		6,15,000	B/R	20,000
			Sundry Debtors	1,00,000
Loan		1,00,000	Cash in hand	1,00,000
Current liability			Closing stock	50,000
Sundry Creditor		50,000	Prepaid tax	10,000
Outstanding wages		5,000	Suspense A/c	4,40,000
Total		**7,70,000**	**Total**	**7,70,000**

Problem 2. A book-keeper has submitted you the following trial balance. You are required to prepare income statement and balance sheet as on 31st March 2002.

Trial Balance as on 31st March 2002

Particulars	*Debit*	*Credit*
Cash in hand	30	
Purchases	8990	
Cash at bank	885	
Fixtures and fitting	225	
Freehold premises	1500	
Lighting and heating	65	
B/R	825	
Returns inward	30	
Salaries	1075	
Debtors	5700	

Contd...

Particulars	Debit	Credit
Opening stock	3000	
Printing	225	
Rates and taxes insurance	190	
Discount allowed	200	
Capital		7610
Sales		11060
Creditors		1950
B/P		1875
Discount received		445
Total	**22940**	**22940**

Solution

Trading and Profit & Loss Account
(for the year ending March 31, 2002)

Dr. *Cr.*

Particulars	*Amount*	*Particulars*		*Amount*
To Opening stock	3000	By Sales	11060	
To Purchase	8990	Less: Return	30	11030
		By Gross loss		960
	11990			**11990**
To Gross loss	960	By Discount received		445
To Salaries	1075	By Net loss		2270
To Rent and tax	190			
To Printing	225			
To Lighting and heating	65			
To Discount allowed	200			
	2715			**2715**

Balance Sheet
(as on 31st March 2002)

Liabilities		*Amount*	*Assets*	*Amount*
Current Liability:			*Current assets:*	
Creditor		1950	Cash in hand	30
Bills payable		1875	Cash at bank	885
Proprietorship:			Debtor	5700
Capital	7610		Bills receivable	825
Loss	2270	5340	*Fixed assets:*	
			Fixture and fitting	225
			Freehold premise	1500
Total		**9165**	**Total**	**9165**

Problem 3. Prepare final accounts from the trial balance given below:

Trial Balance as on 31st March 2002

Particulars	*Debit*	*Credit*
Cash in hand	30	
Purchases	8990	
Cash at bank	885	
Fixtures and fitting	225	
Freehold premises	1500	
Lighting and heating	65	
B/R	825	
Returns inward	30	
Salaries	1075	
Debtors	5700	
Opening stock	3000	
Printing	225	
Rents and taxes insurance	190	
Discount allowed	200	
Capital		7610
Sales		11060
Creditors		1950
B/P		1875
Discount received		445
Total	**22940**	**22940**

Additional Information

- Closing stock at the end of year amount Rs. 5000.
- Outstanding wages was Rs. 1000.
- Dep. charges at the rate of 10% on furniture and fixture.

Solution

Trading and P & L A/c

Particulars	*Amount*	*Particulars*	*Amount*
To Opening stock	3000	Sales (less return)	11030
To Purchase	8990		
To Out. wages	1000	Closing stock	5000
To Gross profit	3040		
	16030		16030
To Salary	1075	By Gross profit	3040

Contd...

Particulars	*Amount*	*Particulars*	*Amount*
To Printing	225	By Discount received	445
To Rents and tax insurance	190		
To Discount allowed	200		
To Lighting and heating	65		
To Depreciation	23		
To Net profit	1708		
	3485		**3485**

Balance Sheet

Liabilities	*Amount*	*Assets*	*Amount*
Capital	7610	Furniture and fitting	202
Net profit	9318	Freehold Premises	1500
Creditors	1950	*Current assets:*	
Bills payable	1875	Cash in hand	30
Out. wages	1000	Cash at bank	885
		B/R	825
		Drs.	5700
		Current liabilities	5000
Total	**14142**	**Total**	**14142**

Problem 4. Following is the trial balance as on 30th June 2001.

Trial Balance

Particulars	*Debit*	*Credit*
Land and building	20000	
Machinery	50000	
Furniture and fixtures	4000	
Opening stock	16300	
Purchases	80000	
Salaries	6000	
Carriage on sales	1500	
Freight on purchases	2000	
Custom duty on purchases	8000	
Advertising	5400	
Wages	15000	
Rent	3000	
Postage and stationary	1500	
General expenses	3200	

Contd...

Particulars	Debit	Credit
Repairs to Machinery	2000	
Loan to Kumar @ 9%	5000	
Prepaid insurance	200	
Sundry debtors	20000	
Cash in hand	250	
Cash at bank	3100	
Capital		80000
Sundry creditors		8000
Discount received		400
Outstanding expenses		1550
Sales		150500
Repairs and rewards (provision)		6000
Total	**246450**	**246450**

The additional information is as follows:

1. Closing stock was worth Rs. 14900.
2. Dep. is to be written of @ 3% on land and building, 10% on machinery and 5% on furniture and fixture.
3. Provision for repairs and renewals are credited with Rs. 1500 every year.
4. Provision for bad debts is 5% on Sundry debtors.

Prepare income statement and balance sheet.

Solution

Trading and P & L A/c
(for the year ending 30th June 2001)

Particulars	Amount	Particulars	Amount
To Opening stock	16300	By Sales	150500
To Purchase	80000	By Closing stock	14900
To Freight on purchase	2000		
To Custom duty	8000		
To Wages	15000		
To Gross profit	44100		
	165400		165400
To Provision for R and R	1500	By Gross profit	44100
To Depreciation	5800	By Discount received	400
To Carriage on sales	1500		
To Pro. for bad debts	1000		
To Advertisement	5400		
To Salaries	6000		

Contd...

Particulars	Amount	Particulars	Amount
To Rent	3000		
To Postage and stationary	1500		
To General expenses	3200		
To Repair of machinery	2000		
To Net profit	13600		
Total	**44500**	**Total**	**44500**

Balance Sheet
(as on 30th June 2001)

Liabilities		Amount	Assets	Amount
Capital	8000		Land & Building (less–dep)	19400
Add N.P.	13600	93600	Machinery (less–dep)	45000
Creditors		8000	For Furniture (less–dep)	3800
Outstanding expenses		1550	Prepaid insurance	200
Prov. for Repairs & Rewards		6000	Sundry debtors	
Add: Provision every year		1500	Less: Prov. for bad debts	19000
			Cash in hand	250
			Cash at bank	3100
			Loan to Kumar	5000
			Closing stock	14900
Total		**110650**	**Total**	**110650**

3.8 ACCOUNTING THEORY FRAMEWORK

To bring uniformity in accounting information, accountants all over the world follow certain common practices known as concepts, conventions and postulates while recording financial transactions. These practices come under preview of accounting theory framework.

Accounting theory framework can be studied in two parts:

3.8.1 Part I: Generally Accepted Accounting Principles (GAAP) *i.e.* concepts, conventions and postulates etc.

3.8.2 Part II: Accounting Standards (AS)

Part I
[Accounting principles]
(Accounting principles are first practicalized then theorized)

3.8.1.1 Concepts

A concept is a general notion or thought.

Accounting is based on a few basic concepts, they are:

1. Money Measurement Concept

According to this concept, in the books of account, only those business transactions are recorded which can be expressed in terms of money. The advantages of expressing facts in monetary terms is that money provides a common denominator by means of which heterogeneous facts about a business can be expressed in terms of numbers that can be added and subtracted.

This concept can better be illustrated by taking the following example.

Example: **A business owns the following assets:**

Land	5 acres
Building Space	2500 sq. metres
Machines	5
Stock of Raw Material	1,500 kgs.
Trucks	5
Motor Cars	2
Trade Debtors	Rs. 1,20,000
Bank Balance	Rs. 5,000

These different units of measurement cannot be added together to produce meaningful information. If these assets can be expressed in terms of money they will reveal the total property and assets of the business.

Land	Rs. 2,00,000
Buildings	15,00,000
Machines	50,00,000
Stock of Material	60,000
Trucks	1,50,000
Motor Cars	50,000
Trade Debtors	1,20,000
Bank Balance as on 31st March 2001	5,000
Total	Rs. 70,85,000

Remark

Money provides a common denominator for measuring value and implies a basic similarity between one rupee and another, but it may not be a fact particularly in a period of inflation. In the assets shown above, the bank balance is expressed in the rupee value of 2001, but the amounts for land, buildings, machines etc. are in terms of rupee value of ten years back when they were purchased. The rupee of ten years back was worth more than a rupee of today, because the purchasing power of the present rupee has gone down due to high degree of inflation in the economy.

2. Business Entity Concept

According to this concept, for accounting purposes, an organization is taken as a separate legal entity and it is distinct from owner itself. In other words, irrespective of the form of organization a business has got its own individuality as distinguished from those persons who own, control or otherwise are associated with the business.

If the business transactions and personal transactions of the owner of the business are mixed up then the twin financial statements *i.e.* the balance sheet and profit and loss account will not correctly disclose the true financial position and profitability of the business. Management is entrusted with the funds of a

business and it is expected of them to make the best use of these resources. Through the medium of financial accounting and reporting of the business transactions the owners will judge how well this responsibility has been discharged. For these reasons the business must have its own personality.

3. Going Concern Concept

According to this concept, accounting assumes that the business is a going concern and not a gone concern. In other words, an organization never dies. It will continue to operate in the future. Its success is judged by the surplus, which it generates from the sale of goods and services over the cost of the resources used.

Production resources such as plant and machinery, land and building which have been acquired and whose period of usefulness has not expired *i.e.* which could not be consumed in creating output are shown in books of account at their book-value and not at their current market value. They are acquired to remain in the business; so long it is a going concern, for earning revenues and are not meant for resale. But when it is a gone concern and is about to be liquidated or sold, accounting would attempt to measure what the business is currently worth. Under this arrangement the current resale value of the assets becomes relevant.

4. Cost Concept

This fundamental concept of accounting is closely related to the going concern concept. According to this concept, an asset is ordinarily recorded in the books of account at its acquisition cost. This cost then becomes the basis for all subsequent accounting for the asset. The market value of an asset may change with the passage of time, but for accounting purpose it continues to be shown in the books at its book-value *i.e.* the cost at which it was acquired minus the provision for depreciation.

There is therefore a wide difference between the accounting concept of cost and the economic concept of value, which means what the asset is currently worth.

Example: A business purchased a piece of land for Rs. 100,000/-. It was recorded in the books of account for Rs. 100,000/-. In course of time its economic value has shot up, with the result that its current market value is Rs. 500,000/-. No change would ordinarily be made in accounting record to reflect this fact.

5. Dual-Aspect Concept

According to this concept, at least two parties are involved in every transaction, one for receiving aspect and another for giving aspect and therefore to record a single transaction simultaneously two books of account are required. In other words, every transaction has dual aspect (a) the yielding of a benefit, and (b) the receiving of that benefit. It is impossible to think of one without the other; a giver necessarily implies a receiver and a receiver necessarily implies a giver.

Example: Suppose Gopal starts a business with a capital of Rs. 50,000/-. Then the business now has an asset cash of Rs. 50,000/- and Gopal, the proprietor has a claim against this asset also of Rs. 50,000.

Balance sheet

Gopal's Capital	Rs. 50,000	Cash	Rs. 50,000

If the business later on purchased furniture on credit from Krishna Kumar for Rs. 5,000/-, the Furniture Account receives the benefit and Krishna Kumar gives the benefit. The accounting record would now show the following position.

Balance sheet

Gopal's Capital	Rs. 50,000	Cash	Rs. 50,000
Krishna Kumar	5,000	Furniture	5,000
	55,000		**55,000**

It follows that in order to have a complete record of each transaction, there must be a double entry.

Thus to record a single transaction at least two book of accounts are needed simultaneously, one for receiving aspect (*i.e.* debit entry) and another for giving aspect (*i.e.* credit entry). This is also known as **"double entry book-keeping system"**.

6. Accrual Concept

According to this concept, income/profit arises from the operations of a business when the sales revenue exceeds the cost of sale. Cost of sale includes manufacturing cost plus non-cash charges like depreciation. The income so accrued will increase the owners equity.

Remark: (Difference between income *i.e.* profit and cash)

It is important to remember that income and cash are not synonyms. They are not interchangeable, because their nature is different. If a business has made a profit of Rs. 50,000/-, it does not mean that it has the same amount of cash. Income is added to the capital of the business and is shown on the liabilities side. The income shown on the liability side increases owner's equity and is absorbed in the assets shown on the assets side of the balance sheet. It is not necessary that it may be in the form of cash. It is important to recognize that income is associated with changes in owner's equity and has no necessary relation to changes in cash. Income connotes prosperity of the business. The higher the income the better off is the business and therefore the owners. An increase in cash does not necessarily mean that the business is doing well and the owners are better off. The increase in cash may have been due to the sale of machine or decrease in some other asset or an increase in liability, with no effect on owner's equity at all.

Example: Suppose in the manufacture of 5000 units of X product the following expenses are incurred and revenues earned.

(a) Cash expenses—	
Process material @ Rs. 5/- per unit	Rs. 25,000
Process wages @ Rs. 3/- per unit	15,000
Overheads, paid in cash	10,000
Total	50,000
(b) Non-cash expenses—	
Depreciation etc.	5,000
Cost of 5000 units of finished stock [(a)+(b)]	**55,000**
Selling Price @ Rs. 15/- per unit	75,000
Income	Rs. **20,000**

In understanding how this income came about we will have to consider the two aspects of this event separately. The sum of Rs. 75,000/- received from sales revenue and the decrease in finished stock of goods of Rs. 55,000/-. Rs. 75,000/- will result in the increase in owner's equity and a corresponding increase in the asset of the business. Rs. 55,000/- will cause a decrease in assets *i.e.* of the finished stock of goods and corresponding decrease in owner's equity. These two aspects show the only two ways in which the business operations can affect owner's equity. They can increase or decrease it.

Conclusions

- Any increase in the owner's capital resulting from the operations of the business is called revenue.
- Any decrease in the owner's capital resulting from the operations of the business is called an expense.

- Income is thus the excess of revenues over expenses.
- Income is tied to owner's equity and has no direct link to changes in cash.

7. Realization Concept

According to this concept, revenue is considered as being earned on the date when the goods are delivered to the customer whereas profit is not recognized to have been earned till it is realized in cash or a third party has legally become liable to pay the amount. In fact cash is received from the customer when the customary period of credit allowed, has expired.

Example: JK company manufacturers sewing machines at Lucknow. During the month of December 2001 it manufactured 12 dozen machines and booked 5 dozen by rail to its customer at Agra. The invoice for Rs. 25,000/- was sent on 1st January 2002. The period of credit allowed by the company was 2 months after delivery. The revenue from this transaction was realized not in the month of December 2001, the month of manufacture, not in March 2002 in which cash was received but in January, the month in which they were delivered *i.e.* when the exchange took place. The accounting practice is to show the date of realizing revenue, the date the product was booked, shipped or the date shown as the invoice to the customer, whichever is later.

8. Matching Concept (Match Expenses against Revenue)

At the end of the financial year, all costs (expenses) of the organization are to be matched against the revenue of the organization. Income made by the business during a period can be measured only when the revenue earned during a period is compared with the expenditure incurred for earning that revenue.

Surplus ⇒ Profit or excess of revenue over expenses.

Deficit ⇒ Loss or excess of expenditure over revenue or income.

3.8.1.2 Accounting Conventions

Accounting convention means established usage.

The three essential elements of convention are:

(1) Consistency

(2) Conservatism

(3) Materiality

1. Consistency

The element of consistency requires that once a business has decided to adopt a particular method, it will consistently follow the same in years to come. For example, a company has adopted the straight-line method of charging depreciation on its plant and machinery, then it will continue charging depreciation on this asset under the same method. If the company later on switches over to diminishing balance method of charging depreciation, then comparison of its accounting figure from one year to another would become difficult. Another example is the valuation of inventory. There are different methods of valuing the assets *viz.*

- Actual cost based on LIFO and FIFO methods.
- Average cost.
- Standard cost.
- Market price.

If the company has adopted actual cost based on LIFO method, it should adhere to it. Suppose it changes over to market price subsequently for valuation of inventory, it will distort the figure of profit and comparison of profit form one year to another will be misleading. The essence of the element of consistency in accounting is very well made out in this case.

2. Conservatism

The element of conservatism in relation to accounting conventions may be stated as follows. "Anticipate no profit, and provide for all possible (conceivable) losses." On the basis of conservatism the value of closing stock for preparing final accounts is shown at cost or market price whichever is lower.

Example: The following example will show how conservatism pays in the long run. A company has taken a contract of Rs. 10,00,000/- for the construction of a building in one year. The work commenced on 1st April 2001 and is to be completed by 31st March 2002. The company closes its books of account on 31st December every year. There is a penalty clause for late completion of the work @ Rs. 5,000/- per month. On 31st December 2001 only half of the work could be completed and was certified by the architect. Due to labour trouble and difficulty in procuring cement, bricks and iron, it was estimated that the work would take six months more for completion and will not be finished by 31st March 2002 as provided in the contract.

According to the agreement the company will have to pay a penalty of Rs. 15,000/- @ Rs. 5,000/- per month for the late completion of the work. Conservatism demands that the company should make provision for the conceivable loss of Rs. 15,000/-. A worker has also sued the company for claiming compensation of Rs. 5,000/- under the Workmen's Compensation Act. The case has not been so far decided by the court, but the company must also make provision for this liability. In case if the work is completed earlier and the claim of the worker has not been so far decided by the court, the company must also make provision for this liability. In case if the work is completed earlier and the claim of the worker is not upheld by the court, which will naturally reduce the estimated loss to the company, it will not lose anything by providing for all liabilities, which have not occurred, to that extent.

The cost of half of the work completed as on 31st December 2001 as revealed by the books came to Rs. 4,50,000/- and the amount received for half of the work certified was Rs. 5,00,000/-. Thus the estimated earnings of the company would be Rs. 50,000/-.

Conservatism demands that the company should not show this amount as profit on this contract for the year ending 31st December 2001. This profit may not result due to the following reasons:

(1) Increase in wages due to the frequent labour trouble which disrupts the work,

(2) Increase in the cost of other inputs,

(3) Provision for penalty arising out of late completion of the work, and lastly

(4) Compensation claimed by a worker.

If for the above reasons the estimated profit of Rs. 50,000/- is not taken into consideration in preparing final accounts of 2001, and if these contingencies do not take place or their impact is lesser, the company will not lose anything, but will surely gain by way of its improved financial position.

3. Materiality

According to this convention it is expected that accounting information should disclose all the material information. By the term material information, we mean that information which would have changed the result of business operation, in case it would have been disclosed. This does not mean that accounting should be over-burdened with information. This can better be explained by taking an example. A new lead pencil is an asset to the business. Every time the pencil is used its value decreases. In theory the business can ascertain everyday the number of partly-used pencils. But the labour and time involved for this insignificant matter will be huge and no sensible accountant would think of doing this exercise.

There is no line of demarcation between significant and insignificant events. Much will depend on the common sense of the accountant and the policy, which is followed by the business concern.

Under materiality convention, accountants furnish certain information in footnotes. Most common information given in footnotes are:

(1) Information regarding contingent liabilities.

(2) Information regarding market price of investments.

The accountant should always keep in mind that materiality does not mean leaking business secrets. It stresses not to reveal vital information, which are of strategic importance.

3.8.1.3 Postulates

Accountants make various assumptions that implement the principles/conventions they have adopted. Such assumptions are:

(1) The enterprise for which the accounting is performed will remain in business. The rupee amounts shown in the balance sheet are, therefore, going concern values.

(2) The value of money, that is, its purchasing power is constant.

(3) The entire income from sales is earned at the moment the sales take place even though a considerable amount of time may have been required to produce the item sold.

Thus, the rupee amount of assets in the balance sheet and the amount of net profit or loss in the profit and loss account is produced by certain conventional method, implemented by various postulates, which have been developed in course of time. These stated rupee amounts do not provide precise measurement of the financial statement items and do not necessarily bear any relation to the market value of the assets of the business or the price at which they could be replaced.

Role of Personal Judgement of Accountant in Book-keeping System

Although the procedure for stating how much of a particular expenditure is to be assigned to revenue and how much is to be carried forward as an asset is governed by conventions and postulates. The application of these conventions and postulates depends on the personal judgement of the accountant. Even though the intentions of accountants are of the best, the human quality of judgement plays an unconscious part. Perfectly honest and capable individuals on the basis of physical facts frequently reach very different conclusions. Let us see how judgement enters into the estimation of three items—the valuation of inventory, the determination of a reserve for doubtful debts and the determination of the rate of depreciation to be charged on the various classes of the fixed assets.

Valuation of Inventory

The inventory could be carried at cost or market, whichever is lower and still have widely different valuations depending upon the method of computations: first in first out, last in first out, average cost, standard cost, and so on. In every case someone must decide which method of valuation will be used. That particular method will affect the valuation of the inventory in the balance sheet, the cost of goods sold, and hence the net profit in the profit and loss account.

Reserve for Doubtful Debts

The amount of reserve to be set aside for doubtful debts is likewise an exercise of judgement alone, based perhaps on past experience.

Depreciation

When it comes to depreciation, judgement enters into two necessary decisions. First, the rates of depreciation to be used for various types of fixed assets, and second, the method of depreciation to be adopted. The rate of depreciation, which is based upon the useful life expectancy of an asset, is engineering rather than an accounting problem. Useful life expectancy in itself is a generality. The method of depreciation selected will give different values to assets over the years and different charges to profit and loss account affecting net profit, even though the same life expectancy is used.

Remark

"One might question the usefulness of accounting statements whose fairness rests so heavily upon judgement rather than upon demonstrated facts. But as against such doubts it should be borne in mind that the judgement employed is an informed one. It is concerned with actualities and is not mere imagination. The accounting statements reflect the summary of all relevant information relating to the transactions involved."

3.8.1.4 Accounting systems

The two systems of accounting are as follows:

1. Cash System of Accounting

Accounting entries are made only when cash is received or paid, *i.e.* when actual cash exchange takes place.

No entry is made when a payment or receipt is merely due, *e.g.* government system of accounting and small business enterprise.

2. Mercantile or Accrual System of Accounting

Accounting entries are made on the basis of amounts having become due for payment or receipt. In this system, the sale is recognized soon after delivery, *e.g.* corporate accounting *i.e.* accounting for corporate.

Part II
[Accounting Standards (AS)]

3.8.2.1 Meaning of Accounting Standard

The uniform, definite and universally accepted accounting rules developed by International Accounting Standards Committee (IASC) are known as accounting standard.

3.8.2.2 Need for Accounting Standard

It was felt that there were different accounting concepts, conventions, customs, traditions and rules prevailing in different nations leading to misunderstanding, uncertainty and often resulting in scandal. Confusion prevailed at the national level also. This created need to develop universally accepted and internationally standardized accounting terminology, commonly known as accounting standard.

3.8.2.3 Development of International Accounting Standard

In 1973, an International Accounting Standards Committee was formed with 16 accounting bodies from 9 nations as founder members. The committee agreed to formulate and publish in public interest standards to be observed in the presentation of audited financial statements and to promote their worldwide acceptance and observance.

3.8.2.4 International Accounting Standard (IAS) issued by IASC

IAS –1: Disclosure of Accounting Policies

IAS –2: Valuation and Presentation of Inventories

IAS –3: Consolidated Financial Statements

IAS –4: Depreciation accounting

IAS –5: Information to be disclosed in financial statements

IAS –6: Accounting responses to changing prices.

IAS –7: Statement of changes in financial position and so on …

3.8.2.5 Development of Accounting Standard in India

In India, Institute of Chartered Accountants of India works as the counterpart of International Accounting Standards Committee. The institute has formulated and issued accounting standards of recommendatory nature. These standards are known as Accounting Standards (AS).

3.8.2.6 Accounting Standards (AS) issued by Institute of Chartered Accountants of India (ICAI) on February 8, 2002

AS – 1: Disclosure of accounting policies. (Effective from 1-4-1991)
AS – 2: Valuation of inventories. (Effective from 1-4-1999)
AS – 3: Cash flow statement. (1-4-1997)
AS – 4: Contingencies and events occurring after balance sheet date. (1-4-1995)
AS – 5: Prior period and extraordinary items and changes in accounting policies. (1-4-1996)
AS – 6: Depreciation accounting. (1-4-1995)
AS – 7: Accounting for construction contracts. (1-4-1999)
AS – 8: Accounting for research and development. (1-4-1991)
AS – 9: Revenue recognition. (1-4-1991)
AS – 10: Accounting for fixed assets. (1-4-1991)
AS – 11: Accounting for the effects of changes in foreign exchange rates. (1-4-1995)
AS – 12: Accounting for government grants. (1-4-1994)
AS – 13: Accounting for investments. (1-4-1995)
AS – 14: Accounting for amalgamations. (1-4-1995)
AS – 15: Accounting for retirement benefits in the final statements of employers. (1-4-1995)
AS – 16: Borrowings cost. (1-4-2000)
AS – 17: Segment reporting. (1-4-2001)
AS – 18: Related party disclosure. (1-4-2001)
AS – 19: Leases (1-4-2001)
AS – 20: Earning per share. (1-4-2000)
AS – 21: Consolidated financial statements. (1-4-2001)
AS – 22: Accounting for taxes on income (1-4-2001)
AS – 23: Accounting for investments associates in consolidated financial statements. (1-4-2002)
AS – 24: Discontinued operations. (8-02-2002)

3.8.2.7 Objectives of the Accounting Standards (AS)

(*i*) To bring out uniformity in financial reporting and to ensure consistency and comparability in the data published by the organization.

(*ii*) Standard must provide a generally understood and accepted measure of the phenomena of concern.

(*iii*) Standard should significantly reduce the amount of manipulation of the reported numbers that is likely to occur in the absence of the standards.

3.8.2.8 Is Accounting Theory Framework Good or Bad?

Though accounting theory framework imposes constraints during book-keeping process, it has positive aspects too. Following are the benefits of accounting theory framework.

1. Accounting theory framework discussed above brings uniformity in accounting information from one year to another and from one company to another company, making comparison/inter-firm comparison possible.
2. Strict implementation of accounting theory framework reduces the chances of window dressing and standardizes the accounting information.
3. Accounting information produced under accounting theory framework soon after incorporating relevant factors, becomes valuable information for decision-making purposes.

Note

By relevant factors we mean:

"All those micro factors (industry level) and macro factors (economy level), which affects the organization concerned, constitute relevant factors."

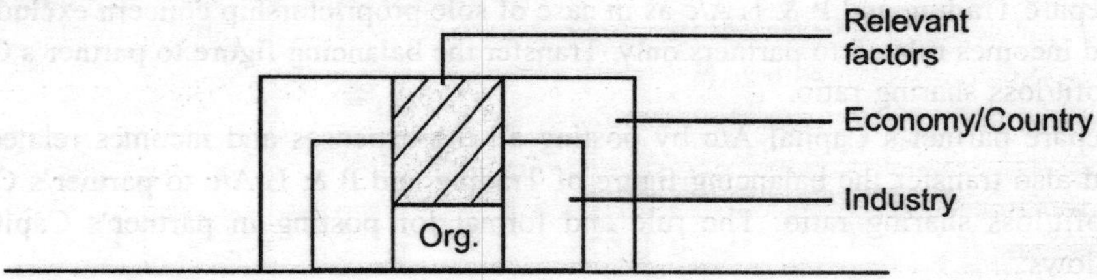

3.9 FINAL ACCOUNTS FOR PARTNERSHIP FIRM

3.9.1 Introduction

Any organization registered under Partnership Act 1932 is defined as partnership firm. Partnership Act defines partnership as follows:

"Partnership is the relation between persons who have agreed to share the profits of a business carried on by all or any of them acting for all."

Partners carry business according to partnership deed.

3.9.2 Partnership Deed

Partnership deed is the written/oral agreement between partners for the conduct of the business. It includes –

- Share of profit/loss
- Interest on capital drawing
- Salary, rent, commission etc.
- Nature of business
- Provisions regarding admission, retirement of partners, etc.

However, in those situations where partnership deed remains silent, the general provisions of Partnership Act will apply e.g.

1. No interest is to be allowed on Capital in case such provision is not given in partnership deed.
2. No interest is to be charged on Drawings made by the partners.

3. If any partner apart from his share capital, advances loan to the firm, he is entitled to receive interest at 6% per annum.
4. In the absence of partnership deed, profits and losses are to be shared equally by partners irrespective of their capitals contributed to the firm.

3.9.3 Final Accounts of Partnership

(*a*) The method of preparing final accounts of a partnership firm is not different from the one followed for the preparation of final accounts for a sole proprietorship concern.

(*b*) There will be a separate capital account for each partner. The amount of profit or loss, drawings etc. will be all credited or debited to that accounts.

(*c*) Steps involved in preparation of final accounts from trial balance are given below.

3.9.4 Preparation of Final Accounts from Trial Balance

Steps involved in preparation of final accounts from trial balance in case of partnership business is as follows:

Step 1: Prepare Trading and P & L A/c as in case of sole proprietorship concern excluding expenses and incomes related to partners only. Transfer the balancing figure to partner's Capital A/c in profit/loss sharing ratio.

Step 2: Prepare partner's Capital A/c by posting all the expenses and incomes related to partners and also transfer the balancing figure of Trading and P & L A/c to partner's Capital A/c in profit/loss sharing ratio. The rule and format for posting in partner's Capital A/c is as follows:

Rule:

Partner's Capital A/c → Dr. (Decrease)
Partner's Capital A/c → Cr. (Increase)

Format:

Let 'A' and 'B' be two partners.

Dr. ***Cr.***

Date	Particulars	A	B	Date	Particulars	A	B
	To Balance b/d:						
	A's Capital A/c	-------					
	B's Capital A/c		--------				
	Total	=	=		**Total**	=	=

Step 3: Prepare a Balance Sheet as in case of sole proprietorship concern by posting balancing figure of partner's Capital A/c (under step 2) on liability side under head partner's Capital A/c *e.g.* A's Capital A/c and B's Capital A/c in above case.

3.9.5 Mechanism Involved in Preparation of Final Accounts for Partnership Firm

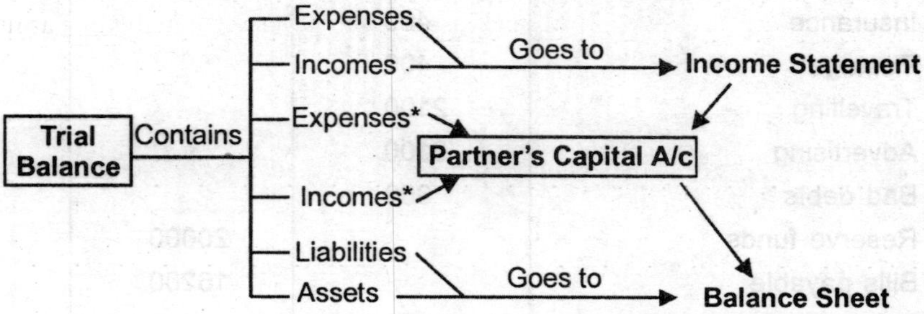

*** denotes expenses and incomes related to partners only e.g. interest on capital, interest on drawings, salaries to partners are some incomes/expenses related to partners.**

Illustration 6

Following is the trial balance of a partnership firm as on 31st March 2001 where 'A' and 'B' are partners. Interest on capitals and drawings are allowed @ 6% per annum. 'B' is also entitled to salary of Rs. 6000 per annum. The profit sharing ratio is 3:1.

Additional Information

- Closing stock amounting to Rs. 5000 — R/M (Raw Material)
  Rs. 10000 — FG (Finished Goods)
- Goods taken by 'B' for personal use amounting to Rs. 2000.
- Provide additional provision of Bad Debts @ 3% per annum.
- Material not recorded amount to Rs. 2000.
- Provision for depreciation:
  Land and Building (L & B) — @ 3% per annum
  Plant and Machinery and Furniture (P & M & F) — @ 10% per annum

Prepare Final Accounts

Trial Balance

Particulars	*Dr.*	*Cr.*
A's Capital A/c		50000
B's Capital A/c		20000
Opening stock—R/M	4000	
Opening stock—FG	9000	
Purchases	74000	
Sales		174080
Purchases return		200
Sales return	400	
Wages	42400	
Salaries	12000	

Contd...

Particulars	Dr.	Cr.
Insurance	400	
Postage	400	
Travelling	2100	
Advertising	6100	
Bad debts	300	
Reserve funds		20000
Bills payable		16200
Discount allowed	580	
Discount received		340
Land and building	16000	
Plant and machinery	59000	
Furniture	600	
Debtors	42000	
Creditors		15820
Cash	1600	
Bank	6000	
Power	3000	
Lighting	500	
Provision for bad debts		500
Carriage	760	
Office expenses	4000	
A's Drawing	9000	
B's Drawing	3000	
Total	**297140**	**297140**

Solution

Income Statement

Manufacturing A/c and Trading and P & L and P & L (Appr.) A/c

Particulars		Amount	Particulars	Amount
To Opening Stock—R/M		4000	By Cost of production	116960
To Purchases	74000			
Less Return	200			
Less Closing stock	5000			
Less Material not recorded	2000	66800		
To Power		3000		
To Carriage		760		
Total		**116960**	**Total**	**116960**

Contd...

Particulars		*Amount*	*Particulars*		*Amount*
To cost of production		**116960**	By Sales	174080	
To Finished goods	9000		Less Return	400	173680
Less Goods taken by B	2000	7000			
			By Closing stock - FG		10000
To Gross Profit (GP)		**59720**			
Total		**183680**	**Total**		**183680**
To Salary		12000	**By GP**		**59720**
To Insurance		400	By Discount received		340
To Postage		400			
To Travelling expenses		2100			
To Discount allowed		580			
To Advertising		6100			
To Lighting		500			
To Office expenses		4000			
To Bad debts		300			
To Depreciation					
— P and M and F		5960			
— Building		480			
To Provision for bad debts		1260			
To Net Profit (NP)		**25980**			
Total		**60060**	**Total**		**60060**
To Interest on capital:		8400	By NP		25980
A :	6300				
B :	2100		By Interest on drawings:		720
To Salary to B		6000	A's Capital A/c	540	
To Balance b/d:		12300	B's Capital A/c	180	
A's Capital A/c	9225				
B's Capital A/c	3075				
Total		**26700**	**Total**		**26700**

Partner's Capital Account

Dr. (decrease) *Cr. (increase)*

Particulars	*A*	*B*	*Particulars*	*A*	*B*
To Drawings	9000	3000	By Balance	50000	20000
To Interest on drawings	540	180	By Interest on capital	6300	2100
To Goods taken by B		2000	By P & L (App.) A/c	9225	3075
To Balance b/d	55985	25995	By Salary to B		6000
Total	**65525**	**31175**	**Total**	**65525**	**31175**

Balance Sheet

Liabilities	***Amount***	***Assets***		***Amount***
A's Capital A/c	25995	Land and building	16000	
B's Capital A/c	55985	Less Depreciation	480	15520
Reserve fund	20000	P and M and F	59600	
Bill payable	16200	Less dep.	5960	53640
Creditors	15820	Debtors	42000	
		Less Provision for bad debt	1760	40240
		Cash		1600
		Bank		6000
		Closing stock—R/M	5000	
		Add Material not recorded	2000	7000
		Closing stock—FG		10000
Total	**134000**	**Total**		**134000**

3.10 FINAL ACCOUNTS FOR COMPANIES

- The monetary transactions of a limited company are recorded in the same manner as those of a sole trading concern or partnership firm. The special transactions related to formation of company are governed by provisions of Companies Act 1956 amended up to date. The general principles applicable to preparation of trading and profit and loss account as well as balance sheet of sole proprietorship concern also hold good in respect of final accounts of a limited company. However, the preparation and presentation of final accounts of company are governed strictly by the provisions of Companies Act 1956 amended up to date.
- There is a range of provisions contained in Companies Act 1956 which regulate the accounting for, and the record of, business transactions of a company but only certain salient points profoundly affect the preparation of final accounts. They are,
  1. The balance sheet and profit and loss account of a company are to be drawn up in strict conformity with the provisions of section 211 and schedule VI of Companies Act 1956.
  2. Annual accounts of a company which are statutorily required to be filed with the registrar of companies, comprises of balance sheet, profit & loss account, and every other documents annexed or attached to balance sheet and profit & loss account. The auditor's report on annual accounts is attached to balance sheet of the company. This annual accounts of a company must give a 'true and fair view, of the state of affairs of a company at the end of financial year including the profit or loss position under Section 211 of the Company Act. Truly speaking, the provisions of Companies Act regulates every aspect of not only the preparation of final accounts but also the accounting for business transactions.

Balance Sheet of Companies

- **Distinction between a Company's Balance Sheet and Firm's Balance Sheet**

A Company's Balance Sheet is different from a Firm's Balance Sheet in the following respects:

1. A company's Balance Sheet is prepared in the order of permanence whereas a partnership firm's Balance Sheet is usually prepared in the order of liquidity.

2. For a company's Balance Sheet, there are two standard forms prescribed under the Companies Act 1956 whereas, there is no standard form prescribed under the Indian Partnership Act 1932 for a partnership firm's Balance Sheet.
3. In case of a company's Balance Sheet, previous year's figures are required to be given whereas, it is not so in the case of a partnership firm's Balance Sheet.

- **Form of Balance Sheet:**

Balance Sheet
(Main Headings only)
(As per Section 211, Schedule VI, Part I)

LIABILITIES	*Previous Yr.*	*Current Yr.*	*ASSETS*	*Previous Yr.*	*Current Yr.*
Share Capital			**Fixed Assets**		
Authorized: ———Shares of Rs.—— each			(1) Goodwill (2) Land (3) Buildings		
Issued: ———Shares of Rs. —— each			(4) Leaseholds (5) Railway sidings (6) Plant and machinery		
Subscribed: ———Shares of Rs.—— each			(7) Furniture and fittings (8) Development of property		
Paid-up capital: Rs. —— per share called up			(9) Patent, trade marks and designs		
Less: Unpaid calls			(10) Livestock and		
Add: Forfeited shares (Amount originally paid-up)			(11) Vehicles, etc.		
Reserves and Surplus			**Investments**		
(1) Capital reserves			(1) Investment in government or trust or trust securities		
(2) Capital redemption reserve					
(3) Share premium account					
(4) Other reserves, specifying the nature of each reserve			(2) Investment in shares, debentures or bonds		
(5) Profit & Loss account or surplus *i.e.* balancing figure carried over as per Profit & Loss (appropriation) account			(3) Immovable properties (4) Capital of partnership firms		
(6) Proposed additions to reserves			**Current Assets, Loans and Advances** **A. Current Assets:**		
(7) Sinking funds			(1) Interest accrued on investment		

Contd...

LIABILITIES	*Previous Yr.*	*Current Yr.*	*ASSETS*	*Previous Yr.*	*Current Yr.*
Secured loans					
(1) Debentures			(2) Stores and spare parts		
(2) Loans and advances from banks			(3) Loose tools		
(3) Loans and advances from subsidiaries			(4) Stock-in-trade		
			(5) Work-in-progress		
(4) Other loans and advances			(6) Sundry debtors		
			(7) Cash balance in hand		
Unsecured loans					
(1) Fixed deposits			(8) Bank balance		
(2) Loans and advances from subsidiaries			**B. Loans and Advances:**		
(3) Short-term loans and advances			(9) Loans and advances to subsidiaries		
(4) Other loans and advances			(10) Loans and advances to partnership firm in which company or any of its subsidiaries is a partner		
Current Liabilities and Provisions					
A. Current Liabilities					
(1) Acceptances					
(2) Sundry creditors					
(3) Subsidiary companies					
(4) Advance payment and unexpired discounts			(11) Bill of exchange		
(5) Unclaimed dividends			(12) Advances recoverable in cash or kind or value to be received, e.g. rates, taxes, insurances, etc.		
(6) Other liabilities					
(7) Interest accrued but not due on loans					
B. Provisions			(13) Balances with custom, port trust, etc.		
(8) Provision for taxation					
(9) Proposed dividends					
(10) Provision for contingencies			**Miscellaneous Expenditure** (to the extent not written off or adjusted)		
(11) Provision for provident fund schemes					
(12) Provision for insurance, pension and similar staff benefit schemes			(1) Preliminary expenses		
(13) Other provisions			(2) Expenses including		

Contd...

LIABILITIES	*Previous Yr.*	*Current Yr.*	*ASSETS*	*Previous Yr.*	*Current Yr.*
			commission or brokerage or underwriting of subscription of shares or debentures (3) Interest paid out of capital during construction (4) Development expenditure not adjusted (5) Other sums, specifying nature		
Total			**Total**		
Footnote may be added as the following: (1) Claims against the company not acknowledged as debts (2) Uncalled liability on shares partly paid-up (3) Arrears of fixed cumulative dividends (4) Estimated amount of contracts remaining to be executed on capital account and not provided for (5) Other sums for which the company is contingently liable					

Note: Amounts shown above dotted line (———) are excluded from total of Balance Sheet.

Profit & Loss Account of Companies

No standard form has been prescribed by law for the profit & loss account of a company as has been done for the balance sheet. This is due to the reason that there are many different types of companies and industries, with their own peculiar characteristics, for which one set form cannot be suitable. However, the part II of schedule VI of the Companies Act has specified presentation and disclosure requirements in respect of items of income and expenditure.

Vertical presentation of Final Accounts for Joint Stock Companies (condensed form)

Income Statement for the year ———

	Particulars		Amount (Rs.)
	Sales	Trading A/c	——
Less	Cost of Goods Sold (COGS)		——
	Gross Profit (GP)/(Gross Loss)		——@
Less	Operating Expenses (OE)	P & L A/c	——
	Operating Profit (OP)		——@
Add	Non operating income/Less non operating losses		——
	Earning Before Interest and Tax (EBIT)		——@
Less	Interest		——
	Earning Before Tax (EBT)		——@
Less	Tax		——
	Profit After Tax (PAT)/Net Profit (NP)		——@
Less	Provision for dividend	P & L (appropr.) A/c	——
Less	Transfer to general reserve		——
Less	Transfer to other reserves		——
	Profit & Loss A/c		——@

↓ Goes to

Balance Sheet liability side (under the head Reserves and Surplus as Profit & Loss A/c or Retained Earnings (RE)

***Note*:**

- @ Stands for balancing figure.
- OE includes general and administrative expenses plus selling and distribution expenses plus depreciation.
- Interest is tax-deductible item means interest is charged before the tax is levied. Whereas dividend is not tax-deductible item means dividend is paid after tax is paid. This is the reason why debt is cheaper source of finance as compared to equity.

Balance Sheet as on ———

Particulars		Amount (Rs.)
Fixed Assets (FA)		—
Investment		—
Current Asset (CA)	—	
Less Current Liability (CL)	—	
Net Working Capital (NWC)		—
Total		==

Contd...

Particulars	Amount (Rs.)
Financed by:	
Equity capital	—
Reserves and surplus (R and S)	—
Long-term debt:	
Debentures/bonds	—
Term loans	—
Total	==

Remark

In case of sole proprietorship concern Net Profit (NP)/Net Loss goes to balance sheet and is adjusted with capital account as follows:

Capital Account
Add Net Profit/Less Net Loss

Illustration

From the following information prepare financial statements of ABC Ltd. for the year ending 31, March 2005.

Trial Balance
(As on 31st March 2005)

Particulars	Dr. (Rs.)	Cr. (Rs.)
Stock	6,80,000	
Furniture and fixture	5,00,000	
Discount allowed	40,000	
Loan to directors	80,000	
Bad debts	35,000	
Advertisement	20,000	
Purchases	23,19,000	
Commission	1,20,000	
Plant and machinery	8,60,000	
Rent	25,000	
Current account with bank	45,000	
Cash in hand	8,000	
Interest on bank loan	1,16,000	
Preliminary expenses	10,000	
Wages	9,00,000	
Consumables	84,000	
Freehold land	15,46,000	

Particulars	*Dr. (Rs.)*	*Cr. (Rs.)*
Tools and equipment	2,45,000	
Goodwill	2,65,000	
Debtors	2,87,000	
Bills receivable	1,53,000	
Dealer aids	21,000	
Insurance premium (Marine)	30,000	
Trade expenses	72,000	
Distribution freight	54,000	
Debenture interest	20,000	
Equity Capital (Shares of Rs. 10 each)		25,00,000
11% Debentures		5,00,000
Bank loan		6,45,000
Bills payable		1,25,000
Creditors		1,56,000
Sales		42,68,000
Rent received		46,000
Transfer fees		10,000
Profit & loss account		1,39,000
Accumulated depreciation—machinery		1,46,000
Total	**85,35,000**	**85,35,000**

The Closing Stock valued as on 31, March 2005 is Rs. 8,23,000.

Solution

ABC Limited

Profit & Loss Account for the Year ending March 31, 2005

Dr. *Cr.*

Particulars	*Amount*	*Particulars*	*Amount*
To Stock	6,80,000	By Sales	42,68,000
To Purchases	23,19,000	By Rent received	46,000
To Consumables	84,000	By Transfer fees	10,000
To Wages	9,00,000	By Closing stock	8,23,000
To Bad debt written off	35,000		
To Discount allowed	40,000		
To Rent paid	25,000		
To Commission paid	1,20,000		
To Interest on bank loan	1,16,000		
To Advertisement	20,000		

Contd...

Dr. Particulars	Amount	Particulars	Cr. Amount
To Dealer aids	21,000		
To Insurance (Marine)	30,000		
To Trade expenses	72,000		
To Distribution freight	54,000		
To Debenture interest	20,000		
To Net profit	6,11,000		
Total	**51,47,000**	**Total**	**51,47,000**

ABC Limited
Balance Sheet as at March 31, 2005

Liabilities		*Amount*	*Assets*	*Amount*
Equity Share Capital (2,50,000 shares of Rs. 10 each)		25,00,000	**Fixed Assets**	
			Goodwill	2,65,000
			Freehold land	15,46,000
			Furniture and fixture	5,00,000
Reserves and Surplus			Plant and machinery	7,14,000
Profit & Loss Account	1,39,000	7,50,000	Tools and equipment	2,45,000
Add: Current year's net profit	6,11,000		**Investments**	
			Current Assets, Loans and Advances	
Secured Loan				
11% Debentures		5,00,000	**Current Assets:**	
Bank loan		6,45,000	Stock	8,23,000
			Debtors	2,87,000
Unsecured Loans			Current account	45,000
			Cash in hand	8,000
Current Liabilities and Provisions			**Loans and Advances:**	
			Loans to Director	80,000
Bills payable		1,25,000	Bills payable	1,53,000
Sundry creditors		1,56,000		
			Miscellaneous Expenses	
			Preliminary expenses	10,000
Total		**46,76,000**	**Total**	**46,76,000**

Exercises

Q. 1. What are Final Accounts? What purpose do they serve?

Q. 2. Distinguish between Profit & Loss Account and Balance Sheet, also give their format.

Q. 3. Differentiate between Trading Account and Profit & Loss Account. What is the purpose of preparing trading and profit & loss account?

Q. 4. Distinguish between Trial Balance and Balance Sheet.

Q. 5. Explain the format of trading account. Illustrate your answer with suitable example.

Q. 6. What adjustments are necessary at the time of preparing Final Accounts? Give two examples.

Q. 7. What do you understand by Manufacturing Account? What items are found in a Manufacturing Account?

Q. 8. Distinguish between:

(*i*) Current Assets and Fixed Assets.

(*ii*) Current Liabilities and Long-term Liabilities.

Q. 9. What do you understand by financial statements? Discuss the significance of financial statements to various parties interested in business concern.

Q. 10. Define Profit & Loss account or Income Statement. Explain the format of profit & loss account.

Q. 11. Briefly describe the following:

(*i*) Gross Profit

(*ii*) Net Profit

(*iii*) Operating Profit

Q. 12. What do you understand by

(*a*) Cost of Goods sold

(*b*) Direct expenses

(*c*) Indirect expenses

Q. 13. Briefly describe the steps involved in preparation of final accounts in case of (*a*) Manufacturing business (*b*) Trading business of sole proprietorship concern.

Q. 14. Write short note on

(*a*) Final Accounts for Partnership firm

(*b*) Final accounts for Companies

Q. 15. Briefly describe meaning, need and objective of Accounting standards in India and explain in what context they differ from International Accounting Standard (IAS).

Q. 16. Describe Generally Accepted Accounting Principles (GAAP) with the help of suitable examples.

Q. 17. From the following balances draw up a Trading and Profit & Loss Account and Balance Sheet.

Particulars	***Amount (Rs.)***
Prakash's Capital	20,000
Bank Overdraft	5,000
Machinery	13,400
Cash in hand	1,000
Fixtures & Fittings	5,500
Opening Stock	45,000
Bills Payable	7,000

Contd...

Particulars	*Amount (Rs.)*
Creditors	40,000
Debtors	63,000
Bills Receivable	5,000
Purchases	50,000
Sales	1,29,000
Return from customers	1,000
Return to creditors	1,100
Salaries	9,000
Manufacturing wages	4,000
Commission and T.A.	5,500
Trade Expenses	1,500
Discount (Cr.)	4,000
Rent	2,200

The closing stock amounted to Rs. 52,000.

Q. 18. From the understated Trial balance of M/s Rashu Brothers prepare (*a*) Manufacturing Account (*b*) Trading and Profit & Loss Account and (*c*) Balance Sheet.

Trial Balance as on 31st December 2004

Debit balances	*Amount (Rs.)*	*Credit balances*	*Amount (Rs.)*
Wages	20,000	Sales	1,74,000
Stock (Raw Materials) 1.1.2004	5,710	Profit and Loss Balance	12,000
Purchases	88,274	1.1.2004	
Carriage Inward	3,686	Capital	1,30,000
Repairs	6,000		
Salaries (factory)	2,100		
Salaries General	1,000		
Rates and Taxes	2,240		
Travelling Expenses	3,550		
Insurance (Factory)	700		
Insurance General	80		
Bad debts	410		
General Expenses	2,942		
Carriage Outward	9,424		
Various Assets	1,13,884		
Stock (Finished goods) 1.1.2004	56,000		
Total	**3,16,000**	**Total**	**3,16,000**

The Closing Stocks are as follows:

Raw materials	Rs. 40,000
Work-in-progress	12,000
Finished goods	6,000

Part – II

Management & Cost Accounting

Chapter–4

Ratio Analysis

LEARNING OBJECTIVES

In this chapter we will study:

- Introduction
- Concept of Ratio
- Types of Ratios
- Measurement and Interpretation of Ratios
- Application of Ratios
- Methodology for Ratio Analysis
- Du-pont Chart for Ratio Analysis
- Advantages of Ratio Analysis
- Limitations of Ratio Analysis

4.1 INTRODUCTION

Ratio analysis is a technique used to evaluate the financial health of the concerned organisation from interested groups' point of view using different ratios as a tool. It comprises of two terms *viz.* ratio and analysis and therefore both the terms should be dealt separately while studying ratio analysis.

Ratio Analysis

Ratio + **Analysis**[1]

Ratio	Analysis[1]
• Concept of Ratio	• Trend Analysis
• Types of Ratios	• Inter-firm Comparison
• Measurement of Ratios	• Comparison with Industrial Average
• Interpretation of Ratios	• Horizontal/Vertical Analysis

4.2 CONCEPT OF RATIOS

Absolute financial data of an organization does not provide useful information but whenever it is compared with another financial data of the same organization it provides useful information and constitutes a ratio.

Illustration

Suppose following is the data related to Company A.

Profit — Rs.10,000

Sales — Rs.1,00,000 ——— Data dealt separately is not useful.

[(Profit/Sales)*100/Sales = 10%] is useful information as it represents profit margin ratio.

4.3 TYPES OF RATIOS

There are various groups, which are interested in financial health of the organization. These groups are Owners/Shareholders, Short-term creditors (suppliers, suppliers of short-term loans), Long-term creditors (Debenture holders, Banks and Financial Institutions providing term loans), Management and government.

Furthermore, the risk and return perceived by abovesaid groups are varying in nature and since risk–return trade off is the objective of any group, this leads to basis for classification of financial health. Thus financial health of the organization can viewed as follows:

1. Financial health from owner's point of view.
2. Financial health from short-term creditor's point of view.
3. Financial health from long-term creditor's point of view.
4. Financial health from management's point of view.
5. Financial health from government's point of view.

Here **Financial health** means **ability to serve** the concerned group.

The classification of ratios is done on the basis of the purpose of different groups mentioned above having direct interest in the organization concerned.

---

1. Analysis refers to application of ratios in different ways (mentioned above) for the purpose of planning financial decisions and in solving decision-making problems. This portion is beyond the scope of this book.

There are five broad categories of ratios on the basis of its nature:

1. Liquidity ratios
2. Profitability ratios
3. Solvency ratios
4. Turnover ratios
5. Market ratios

- Liquidity ratios measure liquidity position of the organization. Liquidity means ability to meet short-term obligations. Short-term obligation includes bills payables, outstanding expenses, bank overdraft etc.
- Profitability ratios measure profitability position *i.e.* ability to earn profit. Higher the ratio better it is.
- Solvency ratios measure solvency position of the organization. Solvency means ability to meet long-term obligations. Long-term obligation includes loan repayments, debt servicing *i.e.* interest payments etc.
- Turnover ratios measure position of resources utilization. A higher turnover ratio indicates better utilization of resources. Resources include fixed assets, current assets, working capital etc.
- Market ratios reflect performance of the organization within industry concerned/economy. Market ratios are useful to secondary market (stock market) investors.

Table 1 and **Table 2** stated below, describe the summary of ratios with groups having direct interest.

Table 1

Groups having direct interest	***Relevant ratios***
Owners/shareholders	- Profitability ratios - Market ratios
Short-term creditors	- Liquidity ratios -Turnover ratios
Long-term creditors	- Solvency ratios
Management	- Turnover ratios - Market ratios
Government.	- Profitability ratios - Market ratios

Table 2 (Summary of ratios)

Type of ratios	***Name of the ratios***
Liquidity ratios	1. Current Ratio (CR) 2. Quick Ratio (QR) 3. Cash Ratio
Profitability ratios	1. Gross Profit Margin (GPM) 2. Operating Profit Margin (OPM) 3. Net Profit Margin (NPM)

Contd...

Type of ratios	*Name of the ratios*
	4. Return on Investment (ROI):- • Return on Net worth (RO Net worth) • Return on Capital Employed (ROCE) • Return on Total Asset (ROTA)
Solvency ratios	1. Debt-equity ratio 2. Fixed charge coverage ratio
Turnover ratios	1. Fixed Asset Turnover Ratio (FATOR) 2. Current Asset Turnover Ratio (CATOR) 3. Total Asset Turnover Ratio (TATOR) 4. Debtors Turnover Ratio (Drs TOR)/Average Collection Period (ACP). 5. Creditors Turnover Ratio (Crs TOR)/Average Payable Period (APP) 6. Working Capital Turnover Ratio (WCTOR) 7. Stock Turnover Ratio (*a*) Raw material turnover ratio (*b*) Work in progress turnover ratio (*c*) Finished goods turnover ratio
Market ratios	1. Dividend Payout Ratio (D/P ratio) 2. Price-Earning Ratio (P/E Ratio) 3. Dividend Yield 4. Earnings Yield

4.4 MEASUREMENT AND INTERPRETATION OF RATIOS

Liquidity Ratio

Liquidity ratio measures liquidity position of the organization. Liquidity means ability to meet short-term obligations *i.e.* current liabilities (bank overdraft, bills payable, outstanding expenses etc.).

Remark

Liquidity of asset is different from liquidity of organization stated above. Liquidity of asset means ease of convertibility of that asset into cash.

The extent of liquidity depends upon the level of current assets. (Current assets are those, which convert into cash within one year *e.g.* cash, debtors, stock, marketable securities, prepaid expenses, loans and advances (given) etc.).

Types of Liquidity Ratios

The different types of liquidity ratios are as follows:

1. Current ratio
2. Quick ratio or acid test ratio

3. Cash ratio or super quick ratio.
   - Higher the liquidity ratios, higher will be the liquidity position.
   - Higher the liquidity ratios, higher will be the amount of Working Capital (WC).
   - Working capital means excess of Current Assets (CA) over Current Liabilities (CL).

$$\textbf{Current Ratio (CR)} = \frac{\textbf{Current Assets (CA)}}{\textbf{Current Liability (CL)}}$$

- A very high Current Ratio indicates inadequate employment of funds.
- A very low Current Ratio indicates that business is trading beyond its resources and is signal of danger for management.
- CR is a measure of margin of safety to short-term creditors *i.e.* higher the CR, greater the safety of funds of short-term creditors.

$$\textbf{Quick Ratio} = \frac{\textbf{Current Assets – Inventory (Stock)}}{\textbf{Current Liability}}$$

- Quick ratio is used to measure the liquidity position, when stock (inventory) is doubtful.

$$\textbf{Cash Ratio} = \frac{\textbf{(Cash + Marketable Securities)}}{\textbf{Current Liability}}$$

- Cash ratio is the most penetrating test regarding the liquidity position and is used when debtors are also doubtful.
- A very high cash ratio is not desirable because it indicates the organization has an idle cash balance leading to decrease in profitability.

Note: The ideal current ratio is 2:1
The ideal quick ratio is 1:1
The ideal cash ratio is 0.5:1

Profitability Ratios

Profitability Ratios measures the profitability position of the organization. Profitability means ability to earn more profit.

Following are the different types of profitability ratios:

1. Gross Profit Margin (GPM)
2. Operating Project Margin (OPM) and Operating Ratio (OR)
3. Net Profit Margin (NPM)
4. Return on investment
   (*i*) Return on Net Worth
   (*ii*) Return on Capital Employed (ROCE)
   (*iii*) Return on Total Assets (ROTA)

$$\textbf{Gross Profit Margin} = \frac{\textbf{Gross Profit}}{\textbf{Sales}} \times \textbf{100}$$

$$\textbf{Operating Profit Margin} = \frac{\textbf{Operating Profit}}{\textbf{Sales}} \times \textbf{100}$$

$$\textbf{Operating Ratio} = \frac{\textbf{Operating Expenses}}{\textbf{Sales}} \times 100$$

$$\textbf{Net Profit Ratio} = \frac{\textbf{Net Profit}}{\textbf{Sales}} \times 100$$

- **Higher the profitability ratios (GPM, OPM, NPM), higher will be the profitability position of the concerned organization.**
- **Lower the operating ratio (OR = OE/Sales), the better it is.**
- **In case gross profit margin is satisfactory but the operating profit margin is not satisfactory then it indicates that the organization is incurring huge operating expenses. Again if operating profit margin is satisfactory but net profit margin is not satisfactory then it indicates that the organization has heavy debt burden. In this situation, to improve the net profit margin, the organization should try to reduce debt burden in order to reduce the interest payment obligation leading to improvement of net profit and hence net profit margin.**

Note

Income Statement for the Year ——

	Particulars		***Amount (Rs.)***
	Sales	Trading A/c	——
Less	Cost of Goods Sold (COGS)		——
	Gross Profit (GP)/(Gross Loss)		——@
Less	Operating Expenses (OE)	P & L A/c	——
	Operating Profit (OP)		——@
Add	Non operating income/less non operating losses		——
	Earning Before Interest and Tax (EBIT)		——@
Less	Interest		——
	Earning Before Tax (EBT)		——@
Less	Tax		——
	Profit After Tax (PAT)/Net profit (NP)		——@
Less	Provision for dividend	P & L (appropr.) A/c	——
Less	Provision for tax		——
Less	Transfer to general reserves		——
	Profit & loss A/c		——@

↓ Goes to

Balance sheet liability side (under the head 'Reserves and surplus' as Profit & Loss A/c or Retained Earnings (RE))

- @ Stands for balancing figure.
- OE includes general and administrative expenses plus selling and distribution expenses plus depreciation.
- Gross Profit (G.P.) = Sales – Cost of Goods Sold (COGS)

- Operating Profit (OP) = G.P. – Operating Expenses (O.E.)
- Earning Before Interest and Tax (EBIT) = OP + Non-Operating Profit (NOP)/Less Non-Operating Expenses (NOE)
- Net Profit (N.P.) = EBIT – (Interest + tax).
- Interest is tax-deductible item which means interest is charged before the tax is levied. Whereas dividend is not tax-deductible item which means dividend is paid after tax is paid. This is the reason why debt is cheaper source of finance as compared to equity.

Return on Investment—There are three approaches regarding definition of investment.:

Investment → Total Asset (TA)
Investment → Net worth or equity
Investment → Capital Employed (CE)

$$\textbf{ROTA} = \frac{\textbf{Net Profit}}{\textbf{Total Asset}} \times \textbf{100}$$

- ROTA measures overall profitability of the organization because TA includes total resources of the organization.
- ROTA is the most popular measure of Return On Investment (ROI).

$$\textbf{Return on net worth or equity} = \frac{\textbf{NP}}{\textbf{Net worth of equity}}$$

$$= \frac{\textbf{Net Profit}}{\textbf{(Equity Capital + Reserve \& Surplus)}}$$

- Return on equity measures the productivity of the owner's capital (*i.e.* risk capital) employed in the firm.

$$\textbf{ROCE} = \frac{\textbf{Net Profit}}{\textbf{Capital Employed (CE)}}$$

CE = Total long-term fund = Total asset – Current liability

- **Higher the return on investment (ROTA, RO net worth, ROCE) higher will be the profitability.**

Solvency Ratios

Solvency ratios measure solvency position of the concerned organization. Solvency means ability to meet long-term obligations. There are two categories of liabilities arising out of long-term obligations *i.e.* long-term creditors *viz.* fixed charge/interest payment obligation and principal repayment. Thus there are two ratios to measure the solvency position.

1. Fixed Charge/Interest Coverage Ratio (for fixed charge obligation):

$$\textbf{Fixed Charge/Interest Coverage Ratio} = \frac{\textbf{EBIT}}{\textbf{Fixed Charges}} \quad \textbf{(Unit – Times)}$$

- **Higher the ratio, better it is.**
- **This ratio indicates the extent of EBIT towards fixed charge/interest payment obligation.**

2. Debt Equity (D/E) ratio (for principal repayment obligation):

$$\text{D/E ratio} = \frac{\text{Long-term Debt}}{\text{(Equity Capital + Reserve \& Surplus)}}$$

- Lower the ratio, better it is.
- D/E ratio measures the margin of safety of principal amount invested by long-term creditors. More the equity, more safe will be principal of long-term creditors.
- Equity capital acts as cushion to long-term creditors.
- Leverage means making use of low cost debt capital in order to boost the earnings on equity *i.e.* return on equity. Low cost debt means, Rate of earnings > Interest rate of debt capital.
- Trading on equity is possible when leverage exits.

Illustration (Trading on equity):

(In Rs.)

Particulars	*Company A*	*Company B*
Equity	1,00,000	40,000
Long-term debt at 10% rate of interest	-	60,000
Total capital employed	1,00,000	1,00,000
EBIT (Earnings Before Interest and Tax)–15% (say)	15,000	15,000
Less: Interest	-	6,000
EBT (Earning Before Tax)	15,000	9,000
Less: Tax @ 40% (say)	7,500	3,600
EAT (Earnings After Tax)/PAT/NP	7,500	6,400
Return on equity = (NP/Equity) x 100	7.5%	10.6%

From above table it is clear that Company B is in better position as it gives more return to its shareholders in comparison to Company A. This is known as trading on equity. Thus trading on equity means maximizing shareholder's wealth (measured in terms of return on equity) through use of low cost debt capital in total capital employed.

Here we can trace out that trading on equity is possible because leverage exists. Company B has used low cost debt capital means Rate of earning (Rate of EBIT—15%) > Interest rate of debt capital—10%). This excess earning (15% – 10% = 5%) goes to equity as equity shareholders have residual claim on income.

Turnover Ratios

- It measures the position of resources utilization. Resources include 5M (men, machine, material, money, method) + IT.
- Higher the turnover ratio, better it is. The unit of turnover ratio is 'Times'. The different turnover ratios are as follows:

$$\text{'X' Turnover Ratio ('X' T.O.R.)} = \frac{\text{Cost of Goods Sold (COGS)}}{\text{Average 'X'}}$$

$$\text{Average 'X'} = \frac{\text{Opening Balance (X)} + \text{Closing Balance (X)}}{2}$$

↓

TA, FA, CA etc.

- Total Asset Turnover Ratio (T.A.T.O.R.) $= \dfrac{\text{Cost of Goods Sold (COGS)}}{\text{Average total asset}}$
- Fixed Asset Turnover Ratio (F.A.T.O.R.) $= \dfrac{\text{Cost of Goods Sold (COGS)}}{\text{Average fixed asset}}$
- Current Asset Turnover Ratio (C.A.T.O.R.) $= \dfrac{\text{Cost of Goods Sold (COGS)}}{\text{Average current asset}}$
- Working Capital Turnover Ratio (W.C.T.O.R.) $= \dfrac{\text{Cost of Goods Sold (COGS)}}{\text{Average current asset}}$

Note:

- If previous year's Balance Sheet (B/S) is not given, then replace average figure with closing balance figure.
- If COGS is not available, replace it with sales figures.

Stock or Inventory Turnover Ratio

- Stock Turnover Ratio $= \dfrac{\text{(COGS)}}{\text{Average Stock}}$ (unit in times)

  Average Stock $= \dfrac{\text{Opening stock + Closing stock}}{2}$

  If COGS is not available, replace it with sales.

- Stock velocity or stock holding period $= \dfrac{\text{360 or 365}}{\text{Stock turnover ratio}}$ days

  or, Stock velocity or stock holding period $= \dfrac{360 \times \text{Average stock}}{\text{COGS}}$

- **Stock turnover ratio shows how fast (in times) the average stock is sold during the year. Higher the stock turnover ratio, better it is.**
- **Stock velocity shows the average time (in days) the stocks remain lying in warehouse before being sold.**
- **Lower inventory turnover ratio shows that the stock is blocked and not immediately sold means stock is piling up in warehouse.**
- **In case of manufacturing organization, there are three categories of stocks *viz.* raw material stock, semi finished goods or work in progress and finished goods stock.**
- **The formula shown above is meant for finished goods stock. The formula for other category of stocks are as follows:**
  - **Raw Material Stock Turnover Ratio** $= \dfrac{\text{Raw material consumed during the year}}{\text{Average raw material stock}}$

- Work-in-Progress (WIP) Turnover Ratio $= \dfrac{\text{Cost of manufacturing during the year}}{\text{Average work - in - progress stock}}$

- The raw material stock turnover ratio measures how many times the average raw material stock is being send for production during the year.

Note: A high inventory turnover ratio may be caused by maintaining a low level of inventory as inventory turnover ratio is inversely proportional to average inventory (see formula). This may result into frequent stock outs leading to possible loss of sales and customer goodwill.

This favourable high turnover ratio may be used for window dressing *i.e.* a firm may prepare its balance sheet at a point when its level of inventory is very low. As a result, it may appear that the firm has a very comfortable liquidity position alongwith adequate inventory turnover, which is not correct.

Debtors Turnover Ratio

- Debtors Turnover Ratio $= \dfrac{\text{Credit sales}}{\text{Average debtors}}$ (unit is times)

If credit sales are not available, replace it with sales.

- Average Collection Period (ACP) $= \dfrac{360 \text{ or } 365}{\text{Debtors turnover ratio}}$ days

$$\text{ACP} = \frac{360 \times \text{Average debtors}}{\text{Credit sales}}$$

Or, Average Collection Period (ACP) $= \dfrac{12 \text{ Months}}{\text{Debtors turnover ratio}}$ months

- Debtors' turnover ratio shows how promptly debtors are making payments.
- Higher the ratio shows debtors are paying frequently.
- ACP shows the average time (in days) taken by the debtors in making the payment.
- Lower the ACP (or higher the debtors turnover ratio), better it is because it reduces the chances of bad debts.

Creditors Turnover Ratio

- Creditors Turnover Ratio $= \dfrac{\text{Credit purchases}}{\text{Average creditors}}$ (unit is times)

If Credit Purchases are not available, replace it with purchases.

- Average Payable Period (APP) $= \dfrac{360 \text{ or } 365}{\text{Creditors turnover ratio}}$ Days

$$\text{APP} = \frac{360 \times \text{Average creditors}}{\text{Credit purchase}}$$

Or, Average Payable Period (APP) $= \dfrac{12 \text{ Months}}{\text{Creditors turnover ratio}}$ Months

- **Creditors turnover ratio shows how frequently trade creditors (suppliers) are paid. This ratio reflects the credit worthiness of the organization.**

- Higher the ratio shows organization is paying frequently.
- APP shows the average time (in days) taken by the organization in clearing suppliers' bill (Bills payable).
- Lower the APP (or higher the creditors turnover ratio), better it is, because it improves credit worthiness of the concerned organization. Again a very high creditors turnover ratio is not desirable as it shows that the organization is not fully utilizing the credit period extended by suppliers.
- Creditors turnover ratio acts as spontaneous source of finance as in case of favourable credit worthiness fund can be made available through postponement of payment of suppliers' bill.

Market Ratios

- Market ratios reflect the performance of concerned organization in secondary market.
- Market ratios are useful for investors of stock market as it helps in fundamental analysis of concerned organization.
- Following are different types of market ratios:

1. Dividend per Share (DPS) $= \dfrac{\text{Total distributable profit}}{\text{Number of outstanding shares}}$

2. Earnings per Share (EPS) $= \dfrac{\text{Earnings available to equity shareholder}}{\text{Number of outstanding shares}}$

   OR Earnings per Share (EPS) $= \dfrac{\text{PAT less preference dividend}}{\text{Number of outstanding shares}}$

   Where PAT = Profit after Tax

3. Dividend payout ratio (D/P Ratio) $= \dfrac{\text{DPS}}{\text{EPS}} \times 100$

   - 40% Dividend payout ratio means organization has paid Rs. 40 as dividend against earnings of Rs. 100.

4. Price-Earning Ratio (P/E Ratio) $= \dfrac{\text{MP}}{\text{EPS}} \times 100$

   - P/E Ratio is a multiplier used for evaluating market value of share as:
     Market Price per share = (P/E) × EPS

5. Earnings yield $= \dfrac{\text{EPS}}{\text{MP}} \times 100$

6. Dividend yield $= \dfrac{\text{DPS}}{\text{MP}} \times 100$

Where MP is market price per share.

Note1:

1. Stock velocity ≡ Stock (Inventory) holding period
2. A/R velocity ≡ Average Collection Period (ACP)
3. A/P velocity ≡ Average Payable Period (APP)

4. Cost of sales ≡ COGS (Cost of Goods Sold in case Closing stock is zero)
5. If Gross Profit (GP) = x% of sales, where x = GPM (Gross Profit Margin) is given, then GP can be written in terms of COGS as given below,

$$GP = \left(\frac{x\%\text{ of sales} \times 100}{(100 - x\%\text{ of sales})}\right)\%\text{ of COGS}$$

e.g.

If GPM = 20%

Then GP = 20% of sales as GPM = (GP/sales) × 100

Or,

$$GP = \left(\frac{20 \times 100}{(100 - 20)}\right)\%\text{ of COGS}$$

Or,

GP = 25% of COGS

Note 2:

The three turnover ratios *viz.* inventory turnover ratio, debtors turnover ratio, and creditors turnover ratio have bearing on the liquidity of the concerned firm.

The combined effect of the three turnover ratios is summarized below:

Inventory holding period	= 2 Months	(Say)
Add: Debtors collection period	= +1.5 Months	
Less: Creditors payment period	= – 3 Months	
Total	= 0.5 Months	

As a rule, the shorter the period, the better is the liquidity position and vice-versa.

Note 3:

Relationship between working Capital (WC) and Liquidity

- Working capital represents capital employed in current asset components *viz.* cash, stock and debtors.
- Though WC is not a ratio but it is frequently used as a measure of firm's liquidity position.
- An enterprise should have sufficient WC in order to be able to meet the claims of creditors and meeting day to day needs of business. The greater the amount of WC, the greater the liquidity of the firm. In other words,

  Liquidity ∝ WC

  Thus, inadequate working capital is the 1st sign of financial problems for concerned firm.

4.5 APPLICATION OF RATIOS

Following are different ways for application of ratios, which help in planning financial decisions and in solving decision-making problems.

- Trend analysis
- Inter-firm comparison
- Comparison with industrial average *i.e.,* digging out strength and weakness.

4.6 METHODOLOGY FOR RATIO ANALYSIS

Methodology for ratio analysis is as follows:

Step 1: Selection of relevant data from the financial statements depending upon the objective of the analysis.

↓

Step 2: Calculation of appropriate ratios from the above data.

↓

Step 3: Comparison of the calculated ratio with the ratios of the same firm in the past, or the ratios developed from projected financial statements or the ratios of competitor firms or comparison with the average ratios of the industry to which the firm belongs.

↓

Step 4: Interpretation of ratios.

Note: The source of financial data for ratio analysis may be the audited financial statements published in annual report of the organization concerned.

4.7 DU-PONT CHART FOR RATIO ANALYSIS

- Du-Pont chart is designed by Du-Pont Company of America.
- This chart shows how change in any resource/monetary activity of organization affects overall profitability measured in terms of return on total asset.
- This chart helps the management to exercise control, as it incorporates all the resources/monetary activities of the organization.

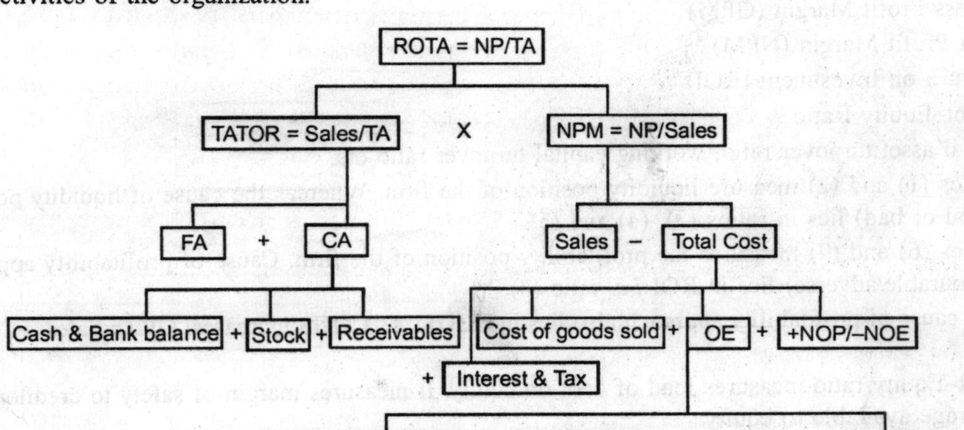

Where,

TATOR : Total Asset Turnover Ratio
NP : Net Profit
NPM : Net Profit Margin
TA : Total Asset
FA : Fixed Asset
CA : Current Asset
OE : Operating Expenses
NOP : Non Operating Profit
NOE : Non Operating Expenses

- According to this chart:

Return on Investment = Asset Turnover × Profit Margin

Illustration

Return on Investment = Asset Turnover × Profit Margin

12 % = 6 % × 2 % ——— case 1

OR 12 % = 2 % × 6 % ——— case 2

This means ROI can be achieved by increasing asset turnover (= Sales/TA) in case profit margin is low (case 1) or by increasing profit margin in case asset turnover is low (case 2).

Dealers and footpath traders work on this principle as with low profit margin they achieve ROI through higher asset turnover (case 1). Whereas showroom traders with low asset turnover achieve ROI through higher profit margin.

To assess the financial position of the firm or for inter-firm comparison, the following steps should be followed-

Evaluate the following ratios and make assessment as suggested below:

1. Current Ratio (CR)
2. Quick Ratio (QR)
3. Inventory Turnover Ratio
4. Debtors Turnover Ratio or ACP
5. Creditors Turnover Ratio or APP
6. Gross Profit Margin (GPM)
7. Net Profit Margin (NPM)
8. Return on Investment (ROI)
9. Debt–Equity Ratio
10. Total asset turnover ratio, working capital turnover ratio etc.

- Ratios (1) and (2) measure liquidity position of the firm. Whereas the cause of liquidity position (good or bad) lies in ratios (3), (4) and (5).
- Ratios (6) and (7) measures the profitability position of the firm. Cause of profitability approach (favourable/adverse) lies in ROI *i.e.* ratio (8).

Again, cause of profitability approach also lies in COGS. As COGS increases, GP (= Sales – COGS) decreases.

- Debt–Equity ratio measures load of debt on equity. It measures margin of safety to creditors and leverage available to equity.

- Ratio (10), (3) and (4) measures the efficiency of management. Lower the T.A.T.O. ratio means under utilization of assets (resources). In this situation, the level of activity can be enhanced without making capital investment.

Illustration: (Application of ratios as tool in decision-making problem)
From the following information taken from the records of two companies (A and B) of the same industry, answer the questions given at the end using ratios as tool.

Particulars	*Company A*	*Company B*
Cash	2,10,000	3,20,000
Debtors	3,30,000	6,30,000
Stock	12,30,000	9,50,000
Plant and equipment	16,95,000	24,00,000
Total Assets	**34,65,000**	**43,00,000**
Sundry creditors	9,00,000	10,50,000
8% Debentures	5,00,000	10,00,000
Equity share capital	11,00,000	17,50,000
Retained earnings	9,65,000	5,00,000
Total Liabilities	**34,65,000**	**43,00,000**
Sales	56,00,000	82,00,000
Cost of Goods Sold (COGS)	40,00,000	64,80,000
Other Operating Expenses (OE)	8,00,000	8,60,000
Interest expenses	40,000	80,000
Income taxes	38,00,000	3,90,000
Dividends	10,000	1,80,000

Questions

1. Which company is using the shareholder's money more profitably?
2. Which company is better able to meet its current debts?
3. If you were to purchase the debentures of one company, which company's debenture would you buy?
4. Which company collects its receivables faster, assuming all sales to be credit sales?
5. Which company has extended credit for a greater period by the creditors, assuming all purchases (equivalent to COGS) to be credit purchases?
6. How long does it take each company to convert an investment in stock to cash?

Solution
Following are the relevant ratios used for answering the above questions:

S.No.	Relevant ratios	Company A	Company B
1	Return on equity	18.40 %	17.33 %
2	**Liquidity Ratios:**		
2.1	Current ratio	1.88	1.81
2.2	Quick ratio	0.6	0.9
2.3	Cash ratio	0.23	0.30
3	**Solvency Ratios:**		
3.1	Debt service coverage ratio	20 times	10.7 times
3.2	Debt–equity ratio	0.24	0.44
4	Average collection period	21 days	27 days
5	Average payable period	81 days	58 days
6	Stock holding period	110 days	53 days

Answer to Question No. 1:
From the above table it is evident that return on equity in case of Company A is comparatively more than Company B, therefore it can be concluded that Company A is using shareholders' money more profitably as compared to Company B, as return on equity represents yield on shareholders' fund.

Answer to Question No. 2:
From the above table it is evident that CR in case of Company A is slightly higher than Company B but QR and cash ratio in case of Company B is higher than Company A and since QR and cash ratio are more rigorous test for assessing liquidity position as compared to CR it can be concluded that liquidity *i.e.* ability to meet current debts in case of Company B is more than Company A.

Answer to Question No. 3:
From the above table it is evident that solvency position of Company A is better than Company B which represents ability to meet long-term obligations in terms of interest payment obligation as well as principal repayment obligation. It can, therefore, be concluded that one should purchase debentures of Company A instead of Company B.

Answer to Question No. 4:
Since ACP of Company A is comparatively less than Company B which means average collection time for Company A is less than Company B, it can be concluded that Company A collects its receivables faster than Company B.

Answer to Question No. 5:
Since APP of Company B is comparatively less than Company A which means average payment time for Company B is less than Company A, it can be concluded that Company A has extended credit for a greater period by the creditors than Company B.

Answer to Question No. 6:
Since Stock holding period of Company B is comparatively less than Company A which means stock holding time for Company B is less than Company A, it can be concluded that Company A is holding its stock before being sold for a greater period than Company B.

Working notes

Given,

Sales	56,00,000	82,00,000
Less: COGS	40,00,000	64,80,000
GP	16,00,000	17,20,000
Less: OE	8,00,000	8,60,000
OP/EBIT	8,00,000	8,60,000
Less: Interest expenses	40,000	80,000
EBT	7,60,000	7,80,000
Income tax	3,80,000	3,90,000
PAT/NP	3,80,000	3,90,000

1. Return on net worth or equity $= \dfrac{\textbf{NP}}{\textbf{Net worth or equity}}$

$$= \frac{\textbf{Net Profit}}{\textbf{(Equity capital + Reserve \& surplus)}}$$

For Company A:

$$\text{Return on equity} = \frac{3{,}80{,}000}{(11{,}00{,}000 + 9{,}65{,}000)}$$

$$\text{Return on equity} = \frac{3{,}80{,}000}{20{,}65{,}000} \times 100$$

$$\text{Return on equity} = 18.40\ \%$$

For Company B:

$$\text{Return on equity} = \frac{3{,}90{,}000}{(17{,}50{,}000 + 5{,}00{,}000)}$$

$$\text{Return on equity} = \frac{3{,}90{,}000}{22{,}50{,}000} \times 100$$

$$\text{Return on equity} = 17.33\ \%$$

2.1 Current Ratio (CR) $= \dfrac{\textbf{Current Asset (CA)}}{\textbf{Current Liability (CL)}}$

For Company A:

$$CR = \frac{(2{,}10{,}000 + 3{,}30{,}000 + 12{,}30{,}000)}{9{,}00{,}000}$$

$$CR = \frac{17{,}00{,}000}{9{,}00{,}000}$$

$$CR = 1.88$$

For Company B:

$$CR = \frac{(3{,}20{,}000 + 6{,}30{,}000 + 9{,}50{,}000)}{10{,}50{,}000}$$

$$CR = \frac{19,00,000}{10,50,000}$$

$$CR = 1.81$$

2.2 Quick Ratio (QR) $= \dfrac{\textbf{(Current asset – Stock)}}{\textbf{Current Liability (CL)}}$

For Company A:

$$QR = \frac{[(2,10,000 + 3,30,000 + 12,30,000) - 12,30,000]}{9,00,000}$$

$$QR = \frac{5,40,000}{9,00,000}$$

$$QR = 0.6$$

For Company B:

$$QR = \frac{[(3,20,000 + 6,30,000 + 9,50,000) - 9,50,000]}{10,50,000}$$

$$QR = \frac{9,50,000}{10,50,000}$$

$$QR = 0.9$$

2.3 Cash Ratio $= \dfrac{\textbf{(Cash + Marketable securities)}}{\textbf{Current Liability (CL)}}$

For Company A:

$$\text{Cash ratio} = \frac{2,10,000}{9,00,000}$$

$$\text{Cash ratio} = 0.23$$

For Company B:

$$\text{Cash ratio} = \frac{3,20,000}{10,50,000}$$

$$\text{Cash ratio} = 0.30$$

3.1 Debt service coverage ratio (for fixed charge obligation):

Debt service coverage ratio $= \dfrac{\textbf{EBIT}}{\textbf{Interest expenses}}$ **(Unit – times)**

For Company A:

$$\text{Debt service coverage ratio} = \frac{8,00,000}{40,000}$$

$$\text{Debt service coverage ratio} = 20 \text{ times}$$

For Company B:

$$\text{Debt service coverage ratio} = \frac{8,60,000}{80,000}$$

$$\text{Debt service coverage ratio} = 10.7 \text{ times}$$

3.2 Debt–Equity (D/E) ratio (for principal repayment obligation):

D/E ratio $= \dfrac{\textbf{Long-term debt}}{\textbf{(Equity capital + Reserve \& surplus)}}$

For Company A:

$$\text{D/E ratio} = \frac{5,00,000}{20,65,000}$$

$$\text{D/E ratio} = 0.24$$

For Company B:

$$\text{D/E ratio} = \frac{10,00,000}{22,50,000}$$

$$\text{D/E ratio} = 0.44$$

4. Average Collection Period (ACP):

$$\text{ACP} = \frac{360 \times \text{Average debtors}}{\text{Credit sales}}$$

For Company A:

$$\text{ACP} = \frac{360 \times 3,30,000}{56,00,000}$$

$$\text{ACP} = \frac{1188}{56}$$

$$\text{ACP} = 21 \text{ days}$$

For Company B:

$$\text{ACP} = \frac{360 \times 6,30,000}{82,00,000}$$

$$\text{ACP} = \frac{2268}{82}$$

$$\text{ACP} = 27 \text{ days}$$

5. Average Payable Period (APP):

$$\text{APP} = \frac{360 \times \text{Average creditors}}{\text{Credit purchases}}$$

For Company A:

$$\text{APP} = \frac{360 \times 9,00,000}{40,00,000}$$

$$\text{ACP} = \frac{36 \times 9}{4}$$

$$\text{APP} = 81 \text{ days}$$

For Company B:

$$\text{APP} = \frac{360 \times 10,50,000}{64,80,000}$$

$$\text{APP} = \frac{37800}{648}$$

$$\text{APP} = 58 \text{ days}$$

6. Stock holding period:

$$\text{Stock holding period} = \frac{360 \times \text{Average stock}}{\text{COGS}}$$

For Company A:

$$\text{Stock holding period} = \frac{360 \times 12{,}30{,}000}{40{,}00{,}000}$$

$$\text{Stock holding period} = \frac{36 \times 123}{40}$$

Stock holding period = 110 days

For Company B:

$$\text{Stock holding period} = \frac{360 \times 9{,}50{,}000}{64{,}80{,}000}$$

$$\text{Stock holding period} = \frac{34200}{648}$$

Stock holding period = 53 days

4.8 ADVANTAGES OF RATIO ANALYSIS

- **Financial Health:** Ratio analysis helps in analyzing financial health of the concerned organization from different interested groups' (Suppliers, Lenders, Employees, Management, Government and Investors) point of view.
- **Planning and Forecasting:** Ratio analysis over a period of time for concerned organization helps the management in planning and forecasting future activities.
- **Corrective Measures:** Ratio analysis helps in identifying strength and weaknesses of the concerned organization. It also helps in identifying causes for weakness and thus helps in taking corrective action in time.
- **Decision Making:** Ratio analysis helps in improving operational efficiency of the concerned organization.
- **Usefulness:** Ratio analysis is the simplest tool for fundamental analysis, which is of great help to Investors. Furthermore, information expressed in financial statements and presented through ratio analysis is easily understandable and hence more useful for all those having interest in the organization.

4.9 LIMITATIONS OF RATIO ANALYSIS

- **Reliability:** The accuracy of ratio analysis depends upon the accuracy of data used for ratio analysis. Since for the purpose of ratio analysis, data is taken from financial statements *viz.* income statement and balance sheet, and most of the time financial statements get manipulated, careful interpretation of ratio analysis after thorough investigation is required.
- **Comparative measure:** Ratio analysis depicts only comparative picture of financial health of the concerned organization. It does not give absolute measure of financial health.
- **Distorted result:** Inter-firm comparison on the basis of ratio analysis may be misleading because of different practices followed by different firms in respect of inventory valuation, cost of investments etc.
- **External factor:** Price level changes make ratio analysis difficult.

Exercises

Q. 1. State whether the following statements are 'true' or 'false':

(*a*) A ratio is a quotient.

(*b*) Liquidity ratios indicate financial soundness of a company.

(*c*) Gross profit margin covers administrative and selling expenses.

(*d*) Debt ratios have no implications in overall capital structure of the company.

(*e*) Earning per share shows turnover ratio.

Q. 2. State whether following transactions will result in decline, improvement or have no effect on current ratios.

(*a*) Payment of a current liability.

(*b*) Purchase of fixed assets in cash.

(*c*) Cash collected form debtors.

(*d*) Issue of new shares.

(*e*) Sell 15% debenture.

Q. 3. Give the formula for calculating the following ratios:

(*a*) Current ratio

(*b*) Acid test ratio

(*c*) Debt equity ratio

(*d*) Inventory turnover ratio

(*e*) Gross profit margin

(*f*) Earning per share

(*g*) Return on investment.

Q. 4. Describe three liquidity ratios.

Q. 5. Discuss the important turnover ratios.

Q. 6. Which ratios are used to evaluate financial structure of the company? Discuss.

Q. 7. A firm's current assets and current liabilities are Rs. 600 and 1,500 respectively. How much can the firm borrow from the bank without reducing the current ratio below 1:5?

Q. 8. A company's net profit margin is 5%, total assets turnover ratio is 1.5 times, debt to total assets ratio is 0.7. What is the return for the company?

Q. 9. Which of the following ratios are more likely to be of interest to the short-term creditors and why?

(*a*) Inventory turnover.

(*b*) Debt to equity ratio.

Q. 10. Explain the following financial ratios

(*a*) Acid test ratio

(*b*) Debt equity ratio

(*c*) Stock turnover ratio

Q. 11. Which financial ratios are most likely to be consulted by you if you identify ourself with the following position and why?

(*a*) Equity investor

(*b*) Long term lender

(*c*) Trade creditors

Q. 12. 'The higher the rate of return on investment, the better the corporate management'. Is this statement true for all companies? Explain.

Q. 13. (*a*) A firm's sales are Rs. 4,50,000, cost of goods sold is Rs. 2,40,000 and inventory is Rs. 90,000. What is Stock turnover? Also calculate the gross margins.

(*b*) The only current assets possessed by a firm are cash Rs. 1,05,000, inventories Rs. 5,60,000 and debtors Rs. 4,20,000. If the current ratio for the firm is 2 to 1, determine its current liabilities. Also, calculate the firm's quick ratio.

Q. 14. What ratio would you use to measure profitability of a company?

Q. 15. Discuss the significance and limitations of ratios as tools for decision-making?

Q. 16. Write a short note on the merit and demerit of ratio analysis.

Q. 17. What is the difference between current and acid test ratios?

Q. 18. If a company has sales of Rs. 2,00,000 and average accounts receivable of Rs. 40,000, what are its accounts receivable turnover ratio and average collection period?

Q. 19. A company has sales of Rs. 7,50,000, cost of goods sold of Rs. 4,00,000 and inventory of Rs. 1,50,000. What is its inventory turnover ratio ?

Q. 20. A company's request for a line of credit at a bank was turned down. The bank said company's 2:1 current ratio was not adequate. Give reasons why a 2:1 current ratio was found inadequate.

Q. 21. A company has a gross profit margin of 10% and asset turnover of 3. What is its ROI?

Q. 22. A company has current liabilities of Rs. 2,00,000, mortgage of Rs. 3,00,000 and bonds of Rs. 5,00,000. Its total equity is Rs. 1,50,000. What is its debt equity ratio?

Q. 23. A company has net income after tax of Rs. 4,00,000 and pays cash dividend of Rs. 2,40,000 on its Rs. 2,00,000 shares when the stock is selling for Rs. 20. What is the dividend yield and dividend payout ratio of the company.

Q. 24. The total sales of a firm are Rs. 4,00,000 and it has a gross profit margin of 20 percent. If the company has an average inventory of Rs. 50,000, determine the inventory turnover.

Q. 25. A company has an inventory of Rs. 18,00,000, debtors of Rs. 1,15000 and an inventory turnover of 6. The gross profit margin of the company is 10 percent and its credit sales are 20 percent of total sales. Calculate the average collection period (assume a 360 day year).

Q. 26. A company has shareholders equity of Rs. 2,00,000. Total assets are 160 percent of the shareholders equity while the assets turnover is 4. If the company has an inventory turnover of 5, determine the amount of inventory.

Q. 27. A firm has cost of Rs. 2,00,000, sales of Rs. 2,50,000 and asset turnover of 4. What is the rate of return on asset?

Q. 28. A firm has profit before interest and taxes of Rs. 30,000, total assets of Rs. 5,00,000 and total liabilities Rs. 3,00,000. What is its (1) return of equity (2) interest coverage?

Q. 29. Determine the P/E ratio of a firm that has a net profit after taxes of Rs. 1,50,000 and 30,000 outstanding shares selling at a market price of Rs. 10 per share. What rate of return do share holders expect?

Q. 30. A company has a net profit after taxes of Rs. 1,20,000 and pays a cash dividend of Rs. 48,000 on it and 36,000 outstanding shares when the share is selling for Rs. 12. What is the yield and dividend payout?

Q. 31. The XYZ company financial statement contain the following information.

	Previous Year (Rs)	Current Year (Rs)
Cash	2,00,000	1,60,000
Sundry Debtors	3,20,000	4,00,000
Temporary Investment	2,00,000	3,20,000
Stock	18,40,000	21,60,000
Prepaid Expenses	28,000	12,000
Total Current Asset	25,88,000	30,25,000
Total Asset	56,00,000	64,00,000
Current Liabilities	6,40,000	8,00,000
10% Debentures	16,00,000	16,00,000
Equity Share Capital	20,00,000	20,00,000
Retained Capital	4,68,000	8,12,000

Statement of profit for the year ended June 30, current year

		Rs.
Sales		40,00,000
Less cost of goods sold	–28,00,000	
Less interest	–1,60,000	
Net profit for current year		10,40,000
Less taxes @ 50%	–5,20,000	
Earning after taxes		5,20,000
Dividends declared on Equity shares		2,20,000

From the above appraise the financial position of the company from the point of view

1. Liquidity
2. Solvency
3. Profitability
4. Activity

Q. 32. You have been supplied data for the Royal Plastic Company Ltd. Indicate the company's strengths and weakness in terms of liquidity, solvency and profitability as revealed by your analysis.

Balance Sheet Dec. 31 Current year

Liabilities	*Rs.*	*Assets*	*Rs.*
Equity share capital	1,00,000	Plant and equipment	1,51,000
10% preferences share capital	40,000	Cash	12,300
Retained earnings	27,400	Debtors	36,000

Contd...

Liabilities	*Rs.*	*Assets*	*Rs.*
Long term debts	34,000	Stock	60,800
Sundry creditors	31,500		
Outstanding expenses	1,200		
Other current liabilities	26,000		
	2,60,100		**2,60,100**

Statement of Profit for the year ending December 31

	Rs.	*Rs.*	
Sales net		2,25,000	
Less cost of goods sold	52,500		
Selling expensed	29,500		
Administrative expensed	14,800		
Research & development	65,00		
Interest	2,900	2,06,200	
Earnings before tax			18,800
Less income taxes			9,400
Net income			9,400
Dividends paid to equity holders			5000

Q. 33. From the following information of a textile company complete the proforma balance sheet if its sales are Rs. 32,00,000

Sales to net worth	2.3 times
Current debt to net worth	42%
Total debt to net worth	75%
Current ratio	2.9 times
Net sales to inventory	4.7 times
Average collection period	64 days
Fixed asset to net worth	53%

Proforma Balance Sheet

Net worth	?	Fixed asset	?
Long term debt	?	Cash	?
Current debt	?	Stock	?
		Sundry debtors	?

Q. 34. The following is the summary of the financial ratios of a company relating to its liquidity position.

	Year 1	*Year 2*	*Year 3*
Current ratio	2.00	2.13	2.28
Acid test ratio	1.20	1.10	0.90
Debtors turnover	10.00	8.00	7.00
Stock turnover	6.00	5.00	4.00

The current ratio is increasing while is acid test ratio is decreasing. Explain the contributing factors for this apparently divergent trend.

Chapter–5

Fund Flow Statement (FFS)

LEARNING OBJECTIVES

In this chapter we will study:

Introduction

Preparation of Fund Flow Statement (FFS)

- Preparation of FFS on the basis of total resource
- Preparation of FFS on the basis of Net Working Capital (NWC)
- Preparation of FFS on the basis of Cash (CFS)

Difference between FFS and CFS (Cash Flow Statement)

Difference between FFS and Income Statement

Difference between FFS and Balance Sheet

5.1 INTRODUCTION

- When we move from one balance sheet to another balance sheet, the picture of assets and liabilities get changed. There may be several reasons to explain, as income statement, which deals only with incomes and expenses, is silent about change in assets and liabilities. This change can be explained correctly with the help of FFS, because FFS depicts the change in assets and liabilities during the financial year *i.e.* between two successive balance sheets. That is why FFS is also referred as **statement of change in financial position (or statement of change in assets and liabilities).** Financial position means position of assets and liabilities.

  Thus FFS is a supplementary statement in addition to statutorily required financial statements *viz.* Balance Sheet and Income Statement.
- FFS represents flow of fund (fund inflow *i.e.,* sources of fund and fund outflow *i.e.* application of fund) through business organization during financial year *i.e.* between two successive balance sheets.

  Thus FFS bridges the gap between two successive balance sheets and is dynamic in nature whereas balance sheet is static in nature as it represents position of assets and liabilities at a given point of time.
- Almost all the big companies prepare their FFS to bring transparency in their accounting information as FFS provides useful information like, why the concerned organization has not paid the dividend in case it has earned a huge profit. FFS also helps in fundamental analysis as well as in working capital management. Working capital is the capital required for day-to-day working of the concerned organization.

5.2 PREPARATION OF FUND FLOW STATEMENT (FFS)

- For the purpose of FFS, there are three approaches regarding definition of fund *viz.*
  1. Fund means total resource.
  2. Fund means Net Working Capital (NWC). NWC means current assets minus current liabilities.
  3. Fund means cash. Cash means cash in hand and cash at bank *i.e.* bank balance.
- Thus there are three approaches for the preparation of FFS *viz.*
  1. Preparation of FFS on the basis of total resource.
  2. Preparation of FFS on the basis of net working capital.
  3. Preparation of FFS on the basis of cash.
- FFS prepared on the basis of cash is popularly known as Cash Flow Statement (CFS).
- For the preparation of fund flow statement, two successive balance sheets are must.

5.2.1 Preparation of Fund Flow Statement (FFS) on the Basis of Total Resources

In this method, the successive balance sheets are compared and changes in each item of balance sheets are noted and classified as a source of fund or application of fund as mentioned below:

Sources: (Sources of fund)

1. Increase in liability side item
2. Decrease in asset side item

Application: (application of fund)

1. Increase in asset side item
2. Decrease in liability side item

Illustration 1:

From the following balance sheets, prepare FFS on total resource basis.

Balance Sheets

(In Rs.)

Liabilities	*As on March 31,2004*	*As on March 31,2005*
Capital	31,250	31,250
Reserve and surplus	50,000	70,000
Debentures	20,000	20,000
Long-term loans	42,500	30,000
Sundry creditors	6,250	25,000
Bank loan		25,000
Provision for dividend	—	5,000
Total	**1,50,000**	**2,06,250**

Assets	*As on March 31,2004*		*As on March 31,2005*	
Fixed asset	1,25,000		2,00,000	
Less Depreciation	62,500		68,750	
Net fixed asset		62,500		1,31,250
Stock		37,500		50,000
Debtors		25,000		12,500
Cash		25,000		12,500
Total		**1,50,000**		**2,06,250**

Solution:

Fund Flow Statement

Sources of Fund	*Amount*	*Application of Fund*	*Amount*
Decrease in debtors	12,500	Increase in net fixed asset	68,750
Decrease in cash	12,500	Increase in stock	12,500
Increase in reserve and surplus	20,000	Decrease in long-term loan	12,500
Increase in sundry creditors	18,750		
Increase in bank loan	25,000		
Increase in provision for dividend	5,000		
Total	**93,750**	**Total**	**93,750**

5.2.2 Preparation of Fund Flow Statement (FFS) on the Basis of Net Working Capital (NWC)

The format for the preparation of FFS on the basis of NWC is as follows:

Sources of Fund	*Amount*	*Application of Fund*	*Amount*
1. Fund Provided by Operation (FPO)	–	1. Payment of dividend	–
2. Issue of shares	–	2. Payment of tax	–
3. Issue of debentures/ borrowings	–	3. Redemption of debenture/ Repayment of borrowings	–
4. Sale of non-current assets	–	4. Purchase of non-current assets	–
5. Non-operational receipts	–	5. Increase in net working capital*	–
6. Decrease in networking capital*	–		
Total	=	**Total**	=

Note:

1. *In case of change in net working capital, either there will be increase in NWC or there will be decrease in NWC. Decrease in NWC as shown above will act as source of fund whereas increase in NWC will act as application of fund.
2. Non-current assets means fixed assets, intangible assets and investments like fixed deposits etc.
3. It is a practice to deal with dividend and tax separately for the purpose of FFS to make FFS more informative. That is why payment of dividend and payment of tax are shown separately on application of fund side.
4. The mechanism involved in calculation of different items of FFS is given below.

Schedule for change in NWC

- Technically, **provision for dividend/provision for tax** both are current liabilities but for the purpose of calculation of change in NWC, they are excluded from the list of current liability. The reason behind treating them as items of non-current liability is the practice of dealing with them and hence showing them separately in FFS.
- Following methods can be used to calculate change in NWC:

Method I:

$$\textbf{Change in NWC} = (NWC)_{\text{current year}} - (NWC)_{\text{previous year}}$$

If $(NWC)_{\text{current year}} > (NWC)_{\text{previous year}}$

there will be increase in NWC,

$$\textbf{Increase in NWC} = (NWC)_{\text{current year}} - (NWC)_{\text{previous year}}$$

If $(NWC)_{\text{current year}} < (NWC)_{\text{previous year}}$

there will be decrease in NWC,

$$\textbf{Decrease in NWC} = (NWC)_{\text{previous year}} - (NWC)_{\text{current year}}$$

where, Net Working Capital (NWC) = Current Asset (CA) – Current Liability (CL)

Method II:

Particulars	*Increase*	*Decrease*
Increase in current assets components	–	
Decrease in current assets components		–
Increase in current liabilities components		–
Decrease in current liabilities components	–	
Total	**A (say)**	**B (say)**

If A > B,
there will be increase in NWC,

Increase in NWC = A – B

If A < B,
there will be decrease in NWC,

Decrease in NWC = B – A

Thus according to this method, increase in CL components are transferred to decrease column, whereas decrease in CL components are transferred to increase column.

Illustration 2:
From the following balance sheets of ABC Ltd., calculate change in NWC:

(In Rs.)

Particulars	*2002*	*2003*
Assets:		
Goodwill	20,000	10,000
Cash	50,000	1,40,000
Debtors	1,96,000	1,80,000
Closing stock	1,74,000	2,40,000
Short-term investment	30,000	20,000
Land	30,000	54,000
Preliminary expenses	10,000	6,000
Total	**5,10,000**	**6,50,000**
Liabilities:		
Trade creditors	1,00,000	90,000
Bills payable	40,000	70,000
Debentures	–	40,000
Share capital	2,50,000	3,00,000
Profit & Loss A/c	1,20,000	1,50,000
Total	**5,10,000**	**6,50,000**

Solution:

Method I :

Change in NWC = $(NWC)_{\text{current year}} - (NWC)_{\text{previous year}}$

Or Change in NWC = $(NWC)_{2003} - (NWC)_{2002}$

Or Change in NWC = $(CA - CL)_{2003} - (CA - CL)_{2002}$

Or Change in NWC = $(5{,}80{,}000 - 1{,}60{,}000)_{2003} - (4{,}50{,}000 - 1{,}40{,}000)_{2002}$

Or Change in NWC = $(4{,}20{,}000)_{2003} - (3{,}10{,}000)_{2002}$

Since $(NWC)_{2003} > (NWC)_{2002}$

Therefore,

Increase in NWC = 4,20,000 – 3,10,000

Increase in NWC = Rs. 1,10,000

Method II:

Particulars	*Increase*	*Decrease*
Increase in current assets components:		
Cash	90,000	
Closing stock	66,000	
Decrease in current assets components:		
Debtors		16,000
Short-term investment		10,000
Increase in current liabilities components:		
Bills payable		30,000
Decrease in current liabilities components:		
Trade creditors	10,000	
Total	**1,66,000**	**56,000**

Thus,

Increase in NWC = 1,66,000 – 56,000

Increase in NWC = Rs. 1,10,000

Thus both the methods give same change in NWC.

Illustration 3:

From the following balance sheets of XYZ Ltd., calculate change in NWC:

(In Rs.)

Particulars	*2003*	*2004*
Liabilities:		
Equity share capital	4,80,000	7,20,000
Preference share capital (redeemable)	2,40,000	1,20,000
General reserve	48,000	72,000

Contd...

Particulars	*2003*	*2004*
P & L A/c	43,000	64,800
Proposed dividend	67,200	93,600
Sundry creditors	70,000	1,00,000
Bills payable	14,000	27,200
Outstanding salary	19,200	14,400
Provision for taxation	67,200	76,800
Total	**10,48,800**	**12,88,800**

Assets:		
Discount on issue of shares	1,20,000	96,000
Factory	2,40,000	1,20,000
Machinery	2,16,000	4,58,400
Fixed deposit with Syndicate bank	24,000	84,000
Sundry debtors	1,80,000	2,59,200
Stock	2,04,000	1,87,200
Bank	30,600	50,000
Cash	10,200	17,200
Preliminary expenses	24,000	16,800
Total	**10,48,800**	**12,88,800**

Solution:

Schedule for change in NWC:

Particular	*Increase*	*Decrease*
Increase in current assets components:		
Sundry debtors	79,200	
Bank	19,400	
Cash	7,000	
Decrease in current assets components:		
Stock		16,800
Increase in current liabilities components:		
Sundry creditors		30,000
Bills payable		13,200
Decrease in current liabilities components:		
Outstanding salary	4,800	
Total	**1,10,400**	**60,000**

Increase in NWC = 1,10,400 – 60,000

= Rs. 50,400

Illustration 4:

From the following balance sheets of Reshma and Co., calculate change in NWC:

(In Rs.)

Particulars	*2004*		*2005*	
Liabilities:				
Equity share capital	60,000		80,000	
General reserve	34,000		42,000	
P & L A/c	12,000		15,000	
Debentures	40,000		30,000	
Sundry creditors	18,000		21,800	
Bank overdraft	6,000		5,000	
Provision for taxation	18,000		17,000	
Proposed dividend	6,000		7,200	
Total	**1,94,000**		**2,18,000**	
Assets:				
Fixed assets	1,60,000		1,90,000	
Less depreciation	46,000		58,000	
Net fixed asset		1,14,000		1,32,000
Long-term investment		20,000		16,000
Current assets		51,000		63,500
Preliminary expenses		5,000		4,000
Discount on issue of debentures		4,000		2,500
Total		**1,94,000**		**2,18,000**

Solution:

Schedule for change in NWC:

Particulars	*Increase*	*Decrease*
Increase in current assets components:		
Current assets	12,500	
Decrease in current assets components:		-
Increase in current liabilities components:		
Sundry creditors		3,800
Decrease in current liabilities components:		
Bank overdraft	1,000	
Total	**13,500**	**3,800**

Increase in NWC = 13,500 – 3,800

= Rs. 9,700

Calculation of Fund Provided by Operation (FPO)

- Fund provided by operation is major source of fund to FFS.
- The objective of FPO is to calculate fund provided by operation and therefore while calculating FPO those items should be adjusted which do not affect flow of fund like depreciation, expenses written off etc. and non-operational incomes like sale of scrap material, rent received etc.
- The format for calculation of FPO is given below:

Calculation of FPO

Particulars	*Amount*
Net Profit as per P & L A/c or **change in Profit & Loss A/c as per P & L (Appropriation) A/c***	– –
Add:	
Items which do not decrease operating fund:	
• Depreciation charged during the year.	
• Expenses/losses written off like goodwill written off, bad debt written off, preliminary expenses written off, discount on issue written off etc.	
• Loss on sale of non-current assets like fixed assets, long-term investments etc.	
• Transfer to general reserve*	
• Transfer to provision for dividend*	
• Transfer to other provisions like tax*	
Less:	–
Items which do not increase operating fund:	
• Profit on sale of non-current assets like fixed assets, long-term investments etc.	
• Non-operating receipts** like sale of scrap material, dividend receipt, interest receipt etc.	
** Non-operating receipts are shown separately as source of fund in FFS that is why they are excluded from calculation of FPO. *Items marked with (*) *i.e.* transfer to general reserve, provision for div. etc. are required to be adjusted for calculation of FPO when **change in Profit & Loss A/c as per P & L (appropriation) A/c** is given. Items marked with (*) need not be adjusted in case **Net Profit as per P & L A/c** is given as these items come after Net Profit (see income statement shown below)	
Fund Provided by Operation (FPO)	–

Remark:

Income Statement for the year ———

	Particulars		*Amount (Rs.)*	
	Sales	Trading A/c	—	
Less	Cost of Goods Sold (COGS)		—	
	Gross Profit (GP)/(Gross Loss)		—@	
Less	Operating Expenses (OE)		—	P & L A/c
	Operating Profit (OP)		—@	
Add	Non-operating income/Less non-operating losses		—	
	Earning Before Interest and Tax (EBIT)		—@	
Less	Interest		—	
	Earning Before Tax (EBT)		—@	
Less	Tax		—	
	Profit After Tax (PAT)/Net Profit (NP)		—@	
Less	Provision for dividend	P & L (appropr.) A/c		
Less	Provision for tax			
Less	Transfer to/provision for general reserve			
	Profit & Loss A/c		—@	

Goes to ↓

Balance sheet liability side (under the head reserves and surplus as Profit & Loss A/c or Retained Earnings (RE))

Note:

- @ Stands for balancing figure.
- OE includes general and administrative expenses plus selling and distribution expenses plus depreciation.
- Interest is tax-deductible item means interest is charged before the tax is levied. Whereas dividend is not tax-deductible item means dividend is paid after tax is paid. This is the reason why debt is cheaper source of finance as compared to equity.

Illustration 5:

Calculate FPO from the following details:

P & L A/c

Particulars	*Amount*	*Particulars*	*Amount*
To Salary	30,000	By Gross profit	80,000
To Sundry expenses	10,000	By Profit on sale of machinery	10,000
To Loss on sale of furniture	5,500	By Rent received	5,000
To Discount allowed	1,500		
To Goodwill written off	8,000		

Particulars	*Amount*	*Particulars*	*Amount*
To Pre. expenses written off	2,000		
To Depreciation	13,000		
To Net profit	25,000		
Total	**95,000**	**Total**	**95,000**

Solution:

Calculation of FPO:

(In Rs.)

Particulars	*Amount*
Net profit as per P & L A/c	25,000
Add:	
Items which do not decrease operating fund:	
• Depreciation charged during the year (non-cash items)	13,000
• Goodwill written off (non-cash items)	8,000
• Preliminary expenses written off (non-cash items)	2,000
• Loss on sale of furniture (non-cash items)	5,500
Less:	
Items which do not increase operating fund:	
• Profit on sale of machinery*	10,000
• Rent received**	5,000
***** **This is non-cash profit and therefore need to be adjusted.**	
****** **This is non-operating receipt and is shown separately in FFS on sources of fund side.**	
FPO	**38,500**

Illustration 6:
Calculate FPO from the following Income Statement:

Income Statement

Particulars	*Amount*	*Particulars*	*Amount*
To Salary	36,000	By Gross income	1,91,000
To Insurance	4,500	By Refund of tax	7,000
To Rent, rates and taxes	10,000	By Dividend received	2,000
To Commission paid	6,000	By Discount received from creditors	7,500
To Dep.			
—— Plant	15,000	By Commission received	15,000
—— Furniture	4,000		
To Provision for doubtful debts	3,000		
To Discount allowed to customer	15,000		

Contd...

Particulars	Amount	Particulars	Amount
To Discount on issue of shares written off	10,000		
To Underwriting commission on shares written off	8,000		
To Provision for taxation	32,000		
To Provision for general reserve	25,000		
To Proposed dividend	20,000		
To Net income	34,000		
Total	**2,22,500**	**Total**	**2,22,500**

Solution:

Calculation of FPO:

(In Rs.)

Particulars	Amount
Net income as per income statement	34,000
Add:	
Items which do not decrease operating fund:	
• Depreciation (non-cash items)	
□ Plant	15,000
□ Furniture	4,000
• Discount on issue of shares written off	10,000
• Underwriting commission on shares written off	8,000
• Proposed dividend (See note)	20,000
• Provision for tax	32,000
• Provision for general reserve	25,000
	1,48,000
Less:	
Items which do not increase operating fund:	
• Refund of tax*	7,000
• Dividend received*	2,000
• Discount received from creditors**	7,500
* These are non-operating receipts and are shown separately in FFS on sources of fund side.	
** This is non-cash profit and therefore required to be adjusted.	
FPO	**1,31,500**

Note: Provision means kept aside. Provisions do not require cash outflow and hence need to be adjusted.

Exercise: Calculate FPO and prepare FFS for illustration 2 given above.

Calculation of FPO:

(In Rs.)

Particulars		**Amount**
Change in P & L A/c		30,000
Add:		
Items which do not decrease operating fund:	(non-cash items)	
• Goodwill written off		10,000
• Preliminary expenses written off		4,000
FPO		**44,000**

Fund Flow Statement

Sources of Fund	***Amount***	***Application of Fund***	***Amount***
FPO	44,000	Purchase of land	24,000
Issue of share capital	50,000	Increase in NWC	1,10,000
Issue of debenture	40,000		
Total	**1,34,000**	**Total**	**1,34,000**

Problems on preparation of FFS

There are two categories of problems on FFS *viz.*

Case 1: Preparation of FFS when two successive balance sheets without additional information, are given.

Case 2: Preparation of FFS when two successive balance sheets with additional information, are given.

The combined rules for both the cases alongwith exercises based on rules are given below:

S. No.	***Items***	***Position***	***Rule***
1	Proposed dividend (See note)	Only in balance sheet (B/S)	OB (Previous year's fig.) ------ Shown as application of fund in FFS CB (Current year's fig.) ------ Added to change in P & L A/c* while calculating FPO *(In case Net profit (NP) is given, then do not add CB while calculating FPO)
2	Proposed dividend (See note)	Only in additional information	Same amount is shown as application of fund as well as added to change in P & L A/c while calculating FPO.
3	Proposed dividend is given in both *i.e.* B/S as well as additional information. ***Note:*** Proposed dividend/provision for dividend given in balance sheets under current liabilities should be treated as non-current liability and thus excluded from calculation of change in working capital.		Calculate provision for dividend and amount of div. paid during the year using following equation:[1] OB (Previous year's fig.) + Provision – Amount paid = CB (Current year's fig.) Provision → Added to change in P & L A/c while calculating FPO Amount paid → Shown as application of fund in FFS (given in additional information) ***Note:*** It is practice to deal proposed dividend/provision for dividend separately for the purpose of FFS *i.e.* why it is excluded from the list of current liability and shown separately on application of fund side in FFS.
Note:	1. In case of provision for tax, same rule as mentioned above for proposed dividend, is applicable for given position. 2. OB (Opening Balance) means previous year's figure and CB (Closing Balance) means current year's figure.		

Contd...

S. No.	**Items**	**Position**	**Rule**
4	Fixed assets without accumulated depreciation	Only in Balance Sheet B/S	Take the difference of both the year's figure: If, CB (Current year's fig.) > OB (Previous year's fig.) ------ Purchase of FA If, CB (Current year's fig.) < OB (Previous year's fig.) ------ Sale of FA. *Note:* • Purchase value of fixed asset calculated above is shown on application of fund side in FFS. Sale value of fixed asset given in additional information is shown on application of fund side in FFS.
5	Fixed Assets (FA) with accumulated depreciation	Only in Balance sheet (B/S)	Calculate purchase of fixed assets during the year using following equation:[2] OB of FA – Current year's dep.* + Purchase of FA = CB of FA (Written down)** (Written down)** *Current year's depreciation is calculated using following equation: OB of dep. (Previous year's fig.) + Current year's dep. = CB of dep. (Current year's fig.) ↓ Added to change in P & L A/c while calculating FPO ** Written down value of FA = Gross value of FA less accumulated depreciation
6	Fixed Assets (FA) without accumulated depreciation is given in Balance Sheet (B/S) and current year's depreciation is given in additional information alongwith part of asset being sold. Calculate BV of part of asset being sold. (BV of part of asset sold = gross value of asset sold less accumulated depreciation on part of asset sold) **If, BV of asset > Sale value of asset -------- Loss on sale** (This amount is added to change in P & L A/c while calculating FPO) **If, BV of asset < Sale value of asset ---- Profit on sale** (This amount is subtracted to change in P & L A/c while calculating FPO)		Calculate purchase of fixed assets during the year using following equation:[3] ↓ OB of FA + (Purchase – current year's dep.*) – BV of part of asset sold =CB of FA (Previous year's fig.) (See column to the left) (Current year's fig.) * Current year's depreciation will be given in additional information. ↓ Added to change in P & L A/c while calculating FPO *Note:* • Purchase value of fixed asset calculated above is shown on application of fund side in FFS. • Sale value of fixed asset given in additional information is shown on application of fund side in FFS. • Abbreviations: BV–Book Value, OB–Opening Balance, CB–Closing Balance, FPO–Fund Provided by Operation, FA–Fixed Asset • Current year's depreciation and provision for depreciation for current year are synonyms.

Contd...

S. No.	*Items*	*Position*	*Rule*
7	Fixed Assets (FA) with accumulated depreciation is given in Balance Sheet (B/S) and current year's depreciation is given in additional information alongwith part of asset being sold. Calculate BV of part of asset being sold. (BV of part of asset sold = gross value of asset sold less accumulated depreciation on part of asset sold) **If, BV of asset > Sale value of asset ---- Loss on sale** (This amount is added to change in P & L A/c while calculating FPO) **If, BV of asset < Sale value of asset ---- Profit on sale** (This amount is subtracted to change in P & L A/c while calculating FPO)		Calculate purchase of fixed assets during the year using following equation:[4] OB of FA + (Purchase – current year's dep.*) – BV of part of asset sold = CB of FA (Written down)** (see column to the left) (Written down)** * Current year's depreciation is calculated using following equation:[5] OB of dep. (Previous year's fig.) + current year's dep. – accumulated dep. on part of asset sold = CB of dep. (Current year's fig.) [Added to change in P & L A/c while calculating FPO] [Given in additional information] ** Written down value of FA = Gross value of FA less accumulated depreciation ***Note:*** • Purchase value of fixed asset calculated above is shown on application of fund side in FFS. • Sale value of fixed asset given in additional information is shown on application of fund side in FFS. • Abbreviations: BV–Book Value, OB–Opening Balance, CB–Closing Balance, FPO–Fund Provided by Operation, FA–Fixed Asset

Remark:

1. The corresponding ledger form of this equation will be as follows:

Proposed Dividend/Provision for tax

Decrease *Increase*

Particulars	*Dr. Amount*	*Particulars*	*Cr. Amount*
To Cash (Amount paid) To Closing Balance (CB) (Current year's figure)	– –	By Opening Balance (OB) (Previous year's figure) By P & L A/c (being provision made for current year) – balancing fig.	– @
Total	**=**	**Total**	**=**

2. The corresponding ledger form of this equation will be as follows:

Fixed Asset A/c (FA A/c)

Increase ***Decrease***

Particulars	***Dr. Amount***	***Particulars***	***Cr. Amount***
To Opening Balance (OB)– written down (Previous year's figure)	–	By Provision for current year's depreciation* – consider balancing fig. of ledger given below	–
To Purchase (balancing fig.)	@	By Closing Balance (CB) – written down (current year's figure)	–
Total	=	**Total**	=

***Provision for depreciation**

Decrease ***Increase***

Particulars	***Dr. Amount***	***Particulars***	***Cr. Amount***
		By Opening Balance (OB) (Previous year's figure)	
To Closing Balance (CB) (Current year's figure)	–	By P & L A/c (being provision for current year's depreciation) – balancing fig.	–@
Total	=	**Total**	=

3. The corresponding ledger form of this equation will be as follows:

Fixed Asset A/c (FA A/c)

Increase ***Decrease***

Particulars	***Dr. Amount***	***Particulars***	***Cr. Amount***
To Opening Balance (OB) (Previous year's figure)	–	By Provision for current year's dep. – being given in additional information	–
To Purchase (balancing fig.)	@	By Book Value (BV) of part of asset sold	–
		By Closing Balance (CB) (Current year's figure)	–
Total	=	**Total**	=

4. The corresponding ledger form of this equation will be as follows:

Fixed Asset A/c (FA A/c)

Increase ***Decrease***

Particulars	***Dr. Amount***	***Particulars***	***Cr. Amount***
To Opening Balance (OB)–written down (Previous year's figure)	–	By Provision for current year's dep.[5]	–
To Purchase (balancing fig.)	@	By Book Value (BV) of part of asset sold	–
		By Closing Balance (CB)–written down (Current year's figure)	–
Total	=	**Total**	=

'Or'

Fixed Asset A/c (FA A/c)

Increase ***Decrease***

Particulars	***Dr. Amount***	***Particulars***	***Cr. Amount***
To Opening Balance (OB)–written down (Previous year's figure)	–	By Provision for current year's dep.[5]	–
		By Sale of Asset	–
		By Loss on sale of asset (in case BV > Sale value)	–
To Purchase (balancing fig.)	@	By Closing Balance (CB) – written down (Current year's figure)	–
Total	=	**Total**	=

'Or'

Fixed Asset A/c (FA A/c)

Increase *Decrease*

Particulars	Dr. Amount	Particulars	Cr. Amount
To Opening Balance (OB)–written down (Previous year's figure)	–	By Provision for current year's dep.[5]	–
To Profit on sale of asset (in case sale value > BV)	–	By Sale of asset	–
To Purchase (balancing fig.)	@	By Closing Balance (CB)–written down (Current year's figure)	–
Total	=	**Total**	=

5. The corresponding ledger form of this equation will be as follows:

Provision for Dep./Accumulated depreciation

Increase *Decrease*

Particulars	Dr. Amount	Particulars	Cr. Amount
To Dep. on part of asset sold (Being given in additional information)	–	By Opening Balance (OB) (Previous year's figure)	–
To Closing Balance (CB) (Current year's figure)	–	By P & L A/c (being provision for current year's depreciation)–balancing fig.	@
Total	=	**Total**	=

Remark:

The general rule for placing Opening Balance (OB) and Closing Balance (CB) in ledger account is as follows:

(a) **For Assets/Expenses:**

Following is the format for ledger:

Assets/Expenses

Increase *Decrease*

Particulars	Dr. Amount	Particulars	Cr. Amount
To Opening Balance (OB) (Previous year's figure)	–	By Closing Balance (CB) (Current year's figure)	–
Total	=	**Total**	=

(b) For Liabilities/Income:

Following is the format for ledger:

Liabilities/Incomes

Increase			*Decrease*
Particulars	***Dr. Amount***	***Particulars***	***Cr. Amount***
		By Opening Balance (OB) (Previous year's figure)	–
To Closing Balance (CB) (Current year's figure)	–		
Total	=	**Total**	=

Exercise Based on Rule No. 1 and Rule No. 4:

Calculate FPO and prepare FFS for Illustration 3:

Illustration 3:

From the following Balance sheets of XYZ Ltd., prepare FFS:

(In Rs.)

Particulars	***2003***	***2004***
Liabilities:		
Equity share capital	4,80,000	7,20,000
Preference share capital (redeemable)	2,40,000	1,20,000
General reserve	48,000	72,000
P & L A/c	43,000	64,800
Proposed dividend	67,200	93,600
Sundry creditors	70,000	1,00,000
Bills payable	14,000	27,200
Outstanding salary	19,200	14,400
Provision for taxation	67,200	76,800
Total	**10,48,800**	**12,88,800**
Assets:		
Discount on issue of shares	1,20,000	96,000
Factory	2,40,000	1,20,000
Machinery	2,16,000	4,58,400
Fixed deposit with Syndicate bank	24,000	84,000
Sundry debtors	1,80,000	2,59,200
Stock	2,04,000	1,87,200
Bank	30,600	50,000
Cash	10,200	17,200
Preliminary expenses	24,000	16,800
Total	**10,48,800**	**12,88,800**

Solution:

Schedule for change in NWC:

Particulars	*Increase*	*Decrease*
Increase in current assets components:		
Sundry debtors	79,200	
Bank	19,400	
Cash	7,000	
Decrease in current assets components:		
Stock		16,800
Increase in current liabilities components:		
Sundry creditors		30,000
Bills payable		13,200
Decrease in current liabilities components:		
Outstanding salary	4,800	
Total	**1,10,400**	**60,000**

Increase in NWC = 1,10,400 – 60,000
= Rs. 50,400

Calculation of FPO:

(In Rs.)

Particulars	*Amount*
Change in P & L A/c	21,600
Add:	
Items which do not decrease operating fund:	
• Proposed dividend (Rule no.1)	93,600
• Provision for tax (Rule no.1)	76,800
• Preliminary expenses written off	7,200
• Transfer to general reserve	24,000
• Discount on issue of shares written off	24,000
FPO	**2,47,200**

Fund Flow statement (In Rs.)

Sources of Fund	*Amount*	*Application of Fund*	*Amount*
FPO	2,47,000	Payment of dividend	67,200
Issue of share capital	2,40,000	Payment of tax	67,200
Sale of factory (Rule no.4)	1,20,000	Redemption of preference capital	1,20,000
		Purchase of machinery (Rule no.4)	2,42,400
		Investment in fixed deposits	60,000
		Increase in NWC	50,400
Total	**6,07,200**	**Total**	**6,07,200**

Exercise Based on Rule No. 1 and Rule No. 5

Calculate FPO and Prepare FFS for Illustration 4:

Illustration 4:

From the following balance sheets of Reshma and Co., calculate change in NWC:

(In Rs.)

Particulars	*2004*		*2005*	
Liabilities:				
Equity share capital	60,000		80,000	
General reserve	34,000		42,000	
P & L A/c	12,000		15,000	
Debentures	40,000		30,000	
Sundry creditors	18,000		21,800	
Bank overdraft	6,000		5,000	
Provision for taxation	18,000		17,000	
Proposed dividend	6,000		7,200	
Total	**1,94,000**		**2,18,000**	
Assets:				
Fixed assets	1,60,000		1,90,000	
Less Depreciation	46,000		58,000	
Net fixed asset		1,14,000		1,32,000
Long-term investment		20,000		16,000
Current assets		51,000		63,500
Preliminary expenses		5,000		4,000
Discount on issue of debentures		4,000		2,500
Total		**1,94,000**		**2,18,000**

Solution:

Schedule for change in NWC:

Particulars	*Increase*	*Decrease*
Increase in current assets components:		
Current assets	12,500	
Decrease in current assets components:		–
Increase in current liabilities components:		
Sundry creditors		3,800
Decrease in current liabilities components:		
Bank overdraft	1000	
Total	**13,500**	**3,800**

Increase in NWC = 13,500 – 3,800
= Rs. 9,700

Calculation of FPO:

(In Rs.)

Particulars	*Amount*
Change in P & L A/c	3,000
Add:	
Items which do not decrease operating fund:	
• Transfer to general reserve	8,000
• Proposed dividend	7,200
• Provision for tax	17,000
• Preliminary expenses written off	1,000
• Discount on issue of shares written off	1,500
• Current year's depreciation*	12,000
FPO	**49,700**

*** Current year's depreciation is calculated using following equation:**

OB of dep. (Previous year's fig.) + current year's dep. = CB of dep. (Current year's fig.)

↓

Added to change in P & L A/c while calculating FPO

46,000 + current year's depreciation = 58,000

Thus, current year's depreciation = 12,000

Fund Flow statement

Sources of Fund	*Amount (Rs.)*	*Application of Fund*	*Amount (Rs.)*
FPO	49,700	Payment of Dividend	6,000
Issue of share capital	20,000	Payment of tax	18,000
Disposal of long-term investment	4,000	Redemption of debentures	10,000
		Purchase of fixed asset (FA)*	30,000
		Increase in NWC	9,700
Total	**73,700**	**Total**	**73,700**

* Purchase of fixed assets (FA) during the year is calculated using following equation:

OB of FA – Current year's dep.* + Purchase of FA = CB of FA
(Written down)** (Written down)**

** Written down value of FA = Gross value of FA less accumulated depreciation
1,14,000 – 12,000 + purchase of FA = 1,32,000
Thus, Purchase of FA = 30,000

Exercise Based on Rule No. 1, Rule No. 2 and Rule No. 4

Illustration 7:

Following are the balance sheets of 'X' Company Ltd., as on 31, March.

(In Rs.)

Particulars	*2004*	*2005*
Liabilities:		
Equity share capital	10,00,000	11,00,000
General reserve	2,00,000	2,00,000
P & L A/c	1,10,000	1,90,000
Debentures	5,00,000	3,00,000
Trade creditors	50,000	40,000
Bills payable	20,000	30,000
Income tax provision	40,000	1,10,000
Provision for doubtful debts	30,000	24,000
Total	**19,50,000**	**19,94,000**
Assets:		
Goodwill	50,000	40,000
L and B	4,20,000	6,60,000
P and M	6,00,000	8,00,000
Closing stock	2,50,000	2,10,000
Debtors	3,00,000	2,40,000
Cash	3,00,000	24,000
Preliminary expenses	30,000	20,000
Total	**19,50,000**	**19,94,000**

Dividend paid during the year ended 31st March 2005 was Rs. 80,000.
Prepare Fund Flow Statement (FFS).

Solution:

Schedule for change in NWC:

Change in NWC = $(NWC)_{current\ year} - (NWC)_{previous\ year}$

Or Change in NWC = $(NWC)_{2005} - (NWC)_{2004}$

Or Change in NWC = $(CA - CL)_{2005} - (CA - CL)_{2004}$

Or Change in NWC = $(4,74,000 - 94,000)_{2005} - (8,50,000 - 1,00,000)_{2004}$

Or Change in NWC = $(3,80,000)_{2005} - (7,50,000)_{2004}$

Since $(NWC)_{2005} < (NWC)_{2004}$

Therefore,

Decrease in NWC = 7,50,000 – 3,80,000

Decrease in NWC = 3,70,000

Calculation of FPO:

(In Rs.)

Particulars	*Amount*
Change in P & L A/c	80,000
Add:	
Items which do not decrease operating fund:	
• Goodwill written off	10,000
• Preliminary expenses written off	10,000
• Provision for dividend (Rule No. 2)	80,000
• Provision for tax (Rule No. 1)	1,10,000
FPO	**2,90,000**

Fund Flow Statement (In Rs.)

Sources of Fund	*Amount Rs.*	*Application of Fund*	*Amount*
FPO	2,90,000	Payment of Dividend (Rule No. 2)	80,000
Issue of share capital	1,00,000	Payment of tax (Rule No. 1)	40,000
Decrease in NWC	3,70,000	Redemption of debentures	2,00,000
		Purchase of L and B (Rule No. 4)	2,40,000
		Purchase of P and M (Rule No. 4)	2,00,000
Total	**7,60,000**	**Total**	**7,60,000**

Exercise Based on Rule No. 2, Rule No. 3 and Rule No. 6

Illustration 8:

Following are the balance sheets of 'X' Company Ltd. as on 31, March.

(In Rs.)

Particulars	*2004*	*2005*
Liabilities:		
Equity share capital	10,00,000	11,00,000
General reserve	2,00,000	2,00,000
P & L A/c	1,10,000	1,90,000
Debentures	5,00,000	3,00,000
Trade creditors	50,000	40,000
Bills payable	20,000	30,000
Income tax provision	40,000	1,10,000
Provision for doubtful debts	30,000	24,000
Total	**19,50,000**	**19,94,000**
Assets:		
Goodwill	50,000	40,000
L and B	4,20,000	6,60,000
P and M	6,00,000	8,00,000
Closing stock	2,50,000	2,10,000
Debtors	3,00,000	2,40,000
Cash	3,00,000	24,000
Preliminary expenses	30,000	20,000
Total	**19,50,000**	**19,94,000**

Additional information:

1. Dividend paid during the year ended 31st March 2005 was Rs. 80,000.
2. Income tax actually paid during the year ended 31st March 2005 was Rs. 60,000.
3. During the year 2005 a part of machinery costing Rs. 7,500 (accumulated depreciation thereon being Rs. 2,500) was sold for Rs. 3000.
4. Depreciation for the year 2005 was provided as follows:
   - P and M : Rs. 50,000
   - L and B : Rs. 30,000

Solutions:

Schedule for change in NWC:

Change in NWC = $(\text{NWC})_{\text{current year}} - (\text{NWC})_{\text{previous year}}$

Or Change in NWC = $(\text{NWC})_{2005} - (\text{NWC})_{2004}$

Or Change in NWC = $(\text{CA} - \text{CL})_{2005} - (\text{CA} - \text{CL})_{2004}$

Or Change in NWC = $(4{,}74{,}000 - 94{,}000)_{2005} - (8{,}50{,}000 - 1{,}00{,}000)_{2004}$

Or Change in NWC = $(3{,}80{,}000)_{2005} - (7{,}50{,}000)_{2004}$

Since $(NWC)_{2005} < (NWC)_{2004}$

Therefore,

Decrease in NWC = 7,50,000 – 3,80,000

Decrease in NWC = 3,70,000

Calculation of FPO:

(In Rs.)

Particulars	***Amount***
Change in P & L A/c	80,000
Add:	
Items which do not decrease Operating fund:	
• Goodwill written off	10,000
• Preliminary expenses written off	10,000
• Provision for dividend (Rule No. 2)	80,000
• Provision for tax (Rule No. 3)[1]	1,30,000
• Current year's depreciation (Rule No. 6)	
□ P and M	50,000
□ L and B	30,000
• Loss on sale of machinery (Rule No. 6)[2]	2000
FPO	**3,92,000**

1. Provision for tax and amount of tax paid during the year is calculated using following equation:
   OB (Previous year's fig.) + Provision – Amount paid = CB (Current year's fig.)

   Provision ↓ → Added to change in P & L A/c while calculating FPO

   Amount paid ↓ → Shown as application of fund in FFS (given in additional information)

   40,000 + Provision for tax – 60,000 = 1,10,000

   Provision for tax = 1,30,000

2. Profit/Loss on sale of machinery is calculated as follows (Rule No. 6):
   Book value of part of asset being sold = gross value less accumulated depreciation
   = 7,500 – 2,500
   = 5,000

   Market value of part of asset being sold = 3,000

   Loss on sale of machinery = 5,000 – 3,000 = Rs. 2000

Fund Flow Statement

Sources of Fund	*Amount (Rs.)*	*Application of Fund*	*Amount (Rs.)*
FPO	3,92,000	Payment of dividend (Rule No. 2)	80,000
Issue of share capital	1,00,000		
Sale of machinery	3,000	Payment of tax (Rule No. 3)	60,000
Decrease in NWC	3,70,000	Redemption of debentures	2,00,000
		Purchase of L and B (Rule No. 6)*	2,70,000
		Purchase of P and M (Rule No. 6)**	2,55,000
Total	**7,60,000**	**Total**	**7,60,000**

* Calculation of Purchase of L and B (Rule No. 6)

Calculate purchase of L and B during the year using following equation:

OB of L and B + (Purchase of L and B – current year's dep.*) – BV of part of asset sold = CB of L and B
(Previous year's fig.) (Current year's fig.)

* Current year's depreciation will be given in additional information.

↓

Added to change in P & L A/c
while calculating FPO

Given,

4,20,000 + (Purchase of L and B – 30,000) – 0 = 6,60,000

Thus,

Purchase of L and B = 2,70,000

** Calculation of Purchase of P and M (Rule No. 6)

Calculate purchase of P and M during the year using following equation:

OB of P and M + (Purchase of P and M – current year's dep.*) – BV of part of asset (P and M) sold = CB of P and M
(Previous year's fig.) (Current year's fig.)

* Current year's depreciation will be given in additional information.

↓

Added to change in P & L A/c
while calculating FPO

Given,

6,00,000 + (Purchase of P and M – 50,000) – 5000 = 8,00,000

Thus,

Purchase of P and M = 2,55,000

Exercise Based on Rule No. 2, Rule No. 4, Rule No. 5 and Rule No. 7

Illustration 9:

Following are the balance sheets of YP and Co. as on 31, March.

(In Rs.)

Particulars	***2004 (Previous Year)***		***2005 (Current Year)***	
Liabilities:				
Equity share capital	10,00,000		10,00,000	
P & L A/c	60,000		80,000	
Bank overdraft	1,60,000		6,00,000	
Sundry creditors	20,00,000		6,00,000	
Total	**14,20,000**		**22,80,000**	
Assets:				
L and B		3,00,000		5,00,000
P and M	5,00,000		6,00,000	
Less depreciation	1,20,000		1,80,000	
Net P and M		3,80,000		4,20,000
Vehicle	1,16,000		1,24,000	
Less depreciation	56,000		84,000	
Net Vehicle		60,000		40,000
Stock		2,20,000		7,20,000
Debtors		4,60,000		6,00,000
Total		**14,20,000**		**22,80,000**

Additional information

1. During the year a dividend of 10% was distributed to the shareholders.
2. On 1st Jan of the current year, a motor car (vehicle), which originally cost Rs. 20,000, showing a book value of Rs. 10,000, was sold for Rs.16,000.

You are required to prepare FFS.

Solution:

Schedule for change in NWC:

Particulars	*Increase*	*Decrease*
Increase in current assets components:		
• Debtors	1,40,000	
• Stock	5,00,000	
Decrease in current assets components:		–
Increase in current liabilities components:		
• Bank overdraft		4,40,000
• Sundry creditors		4,00,000
Decrease in current liabilities components:		
Total	**6,40,000**	**8,40,000**

Decrease in NWC = 8,40,000 – 6,40,000
= Rs. 2,00,000

L and B: (Rule No. 4):

Take the difference of both the year's figure:

If, CB (Current year's fig.) > OB (Previous year's fig.) —— Purchase of FA

Given,

CB (Current year's fig.) = 5,00,000

OB (Previous year's fig.) = 3,00,000

Thus,

Purchase of FA (L and B) = 5,00,000 – 3,00,000 = Rs. 2,00,000

P and M (Rule No. 5):

Current year's depreciation is calculated using following equation:

OB of dep. (Previous year's fig.) + current year's dep. = CB of dep. (Current year's fig.)

↓

Added to change in P & L A/c while calculating FPO

1,20,000 + current year's depreciation = 1,80,000

Thus,

Current year's depreciation = 60,000

Purchase of fixed assets (P and M) during the year is calculated using following equation:

OB of P and M (Written down)** – Current year's dep. + Purchase of P and M = CB of P and M (Written down)**

** Written down value of P and M = Gross value of P and M less accumulated depreciation

3,80,000 – 60,000 + purchase of P and M = 4,20,000

Thus,

Purchase of P and M = 1,00,000

Vehicle (Motor car) (Rule No. 7):

Current year's depreciation is calculated using following equation:

OB of dep. + Current year's dep.– accumulated dep. on part of asset sold = CB of dep.

(Previous year's fig.) (Current year's fig.)

Current year's dep. → Added to change in P & L A/c while calculating FPO

Accumulated dep. on part of asset sold → Given in additional information

56,000 + Current year's depreciation – 10,000* = 84,000

Current year's depreciation = 38,000

(* Given gross value = 20,000 and book value = 10,000, therefore depreciation on part of vehicle sold = Rs. 10,000)

Calculate purchase of Vehicle during the year using following equation:

OB of Vehicle + (Purchase of Vehicle – current year's dep.) – BV of part of Vehicle sold = CB of Vehicle

(Written down)** (Written down)**

60,000+ (Purchase of Vehicle – 38,000) – 10,000 = 40,000

Thus,

Purchase of Vehicle = 28,000

Profit/Loss on sale of Vehicle

BV of part of vehicle sold = Rs. 10,000

Sale value of part of vehicle sold = Rs. 16,000

Profit on sale of part of vehicle sold = 16,000 – 10,000 = Rs. 6,000

Calculation of FPO

(In Rs.)

Particulars	***Amount***
Change in P & L A/c	20,000
Add:	
Items which do not decrease Operating fund:	
• Current year's depreciation on P and M	60,000
• Current year's depreciation on Vehicle	38,000
• Provision for dividend (Rule No. 2) – at 10%	1,00,000
Less:	
Items which do not increase Operating fund:	
• Profit on sale of Vehicle	6,000
FPO	**2,12,000**

Fund Flow Statement

Sources of fund	*Amount (Rs.)*	*Application of fund*	*Amount (Rs.)*
FPO	2,12,000	Payment of dividend (Rule No. 2)	1,00,000
Issue of share capital	–		
Sale of vehicle	16,000	Purchase of L and B (Rule No. 4)	2,00,000
Decrease in NWC	2,00,000	Purchase of P and M (Rule No. 5)	1,00,000
		Purchase of vehicle (Rule No. 7)	28,000
Total	**4,28,000**	**Total**	**4,28,000**

5.2.3 Preparation of Fund Flow Statement (FFS) on the Basis of Cash and Bank Balance or {Cash Flow Statement (CFS)}

The format for the preparation of CFS is as follows:

Sources of cash	*Amount*	*Application of fund*	*Amount*
7. Cash Provided by Operation (CPO)	–	6. Payment of dividend	–
		7. Payment of tax	–
8. Issue of shares	–	8. Redemption of debenture/ repayment of borrowings	–
9. Issue of debentures/borrowings	–		
10. Sale of non-current assets	–	9. Purchase of non-current assets	–
11. Non-operational receipts	–		
12. Decrease in cash and bank balance*	–	10. Increase in cash and bank balance*	–
Total	=	**Total**	=

*** Only one will occur.**

Note:

- The mechanism involved in preparation of items of Cash Flow Statement except CPO is exactly same as that of Fund Flow Statement.
- In Cash Flow Statement as compared with Fund Flow Statement, FPO is being replaced by CPO whereas increase/decrease in NWC is replaced by increase/decrease in cash and bank balance.
- The format for preparation of Cash Provided by Operation (CPO) is as follows —

Calculation of CPO

CPO is FPO adjusted with Current Asset (CA) components except cash and bank balance and Current Liability (CL) components as per schedule given below:

(In Rs.)

Particulars	*Amount*
FPO (As per FFS)	–
***Add:**	
• Decrease in Current Asset (CA) components	–
• Increase in Current Liabilities (CL) components	–
****Less:**	
• Increase in Current Asset (CA) components	(–)
• Decrease in Current Liabilities (CL) components	(–)
CPO	–

Note:

*In FFS decrease in NWC acts as source of fund. Decrease in NWC means either decrease in CA components and/or increase in CL components. That is why these items are added to FPO while calculating CPO.

**Similarly in FFS increase in NWC acts as application of fund. Increase in NWC means either increase in CA components and/or decrease in CL components. That is why these items are subtracted to FPO while calculating CPO.

Illustration: (Illustration 3 of FFS)

From the following balance sheets of XYZ Ltd., prepare CFS:

(In Rs.)

Particulars	*2003*	*2004*
Liabilities:		
Equity share capital	4,80,000	7,20,000
Preference share capital (redeemable)	2,40,000	1,20,000
General reserve	48,000	72,000
P & L A/c	43,000	64,800
Proposed dividend	67,200	93,600
Sundry creditors	70,000	1,00,000
Bills payable	14,000	27,200
Outstanding salary	19,200	14,400
Provision for taxation	67,200	76,800
Total	**10,48,800**	**12,88,800**
Assets:		
Discount on issue of shares	1,20,000	96,000
Factory	2,40,000	1,20,000
Machinery	2,16,000	4,58,400

Contd...

(In Rs.)

Particulars	***2003***	***2004***
Fixed deposit with Syndicate bank	24,000	84,000
Sundry debtors	1,80,000	2,59,200
Stock	2,04,000	1,87,200
Bank	30,600	50,000
Cash	10,200	17,200
Preliminary expenses	24,000	16,800
Total	**10,48,800**	**12,88,800**

Solution:

Calculation of CPO:

(In Rs.)

Particulars		***Amount***
Change in P & L A/c	21,600	
Add:		
Items which do not decrease operating fund:		
• Proposed dividend (Rule no.1)		93,600
• Provision for tax (Rule no.1)		76,800
• Preliminary expenses written off		7,200
• Transfer to general reserve		24,000
• Discount on issue of shares written off		24,000
FPO		**2,47,200**
Add:		
Decrease in current assets components except cash and bank balance:		
• Stock		16,800
Increase in current liabilities components:		
• Sundry creditors		30,000
• Bills payable		13,200
Less:		
Increase in current assets components except cash and bank balance:		
• Sundry debtors		(79,200)
Decrease in current liabilities components:		
• Outstanding salary		(4,800)
CPO		**2,23,200**

Cash Flow Statement (CFS)

Sources of cash	*Amount (Rs.)*	*Application of cash*	*Amount (Rs.)*
CPO	2,23,200	Payment of dividend	67,200
Issue of share capital	2,40,000	Payment of tax	67,200
Sale of factory (Rule no.4)	1,20,000	Redemption of preference capital	1,20,000
		Purchase of machinery (Rule no.4)	2,42,400
		Investment in fixed deposits	60,000
		Increase in cash and bank balance	26,400
Total	**5,83,200**	**Total**	**5,83,200**

5.3 DIFFERENCE BETWEEN FUND FLOW STATEMENT (FFS) AND CASH FLOW STATEMENT (CFS)

Point of difference	*Fund Flow Statement (FFS)*	*Cash Flow Statement (CFS)*
Interpretation	FFS depicts fund position measured in terms of Net Working Capital (NWC) *i.e.* fund inflow and fund outflow between two successive balance sheets.	CFS depicts cash* position measured in terms of cash *i.e.* cash inflow and cash outflow between two successive balance sheets.
Schedule for change in working capital	Required	Not required
Basis of analysis	It discloses cause of changes in working capital during financial year.	It discloses cause of changes in cash balance during financial year.
Accounting principle	FFS is prepared on 'accrual basis' of accounting e.g. sales whether cash or credit generate funds from operation.	CFS is prepared on 'cash basis' of accounting e.g. only cash sales generate fund in terms of cash from operation.
Major source of fund	Fund provided by operation (FPO) is a major source of fund.	Cash provided by operation (CPO) is a major source of fund.

*** Cash means cash in hand and cash at bank *i.e.* cash and bank balance.**

5.4 DIFFERENCE BETWEEN FUND FLOW STATEMENT (FFS) AND INCOME STATEMENT

Point of difference	*Fund Flow Statement (FFS)*	*Income Statement (P & L A/c)*
Interpretation	FFS depicts fund position measured in terms of Networking Capital (NWC) *i.e.* fund inflow and fund outflow between two successive balance sheets.	Income Statement depicts summary of all expenses and incomes during financial year.
Requirements	All items whether capital or revenue are considered in preparing this statement.	Only revenue items are considered in preparing this statement.
Basis of analysis	It discloses cause of changes in working capital during financial year.	It discloses the result of business operation *i.e.* net profit/net loss.
Statutory information	Preparation of FFS is optional and if it is prepared, it can be done so in any manner.	Preparation of income statement is compulsory and is prepared according to law.
Inter-relationship	FFS is dependent on income statement as Fund Provided by Operation (FPO) is calculated from income statement.	FFS does not help in preparation of income statement.

5.5 DIFFERENCE BETWEEN FUND FLOW STATEMENT (FFS) AND BALANCE SHEET (B/S)

Point of difference	*Fund Flow Statement (FFS)*	*Balance Sheet (B/S)*
Interpretation	FFS shows changes in financial position *i.e.* changes in assets and liabilities between two successive balance sheets.	Balance Sheet (B/S) shows financial position *i.e.* picture of assets and liabilities at a given point of time usually as on 31st March.
Nature	FFS is dynamic in nature as it shows changes in assets and liabilities.	Balance Sheet (B/S) is static in nature at it shows position of assets and liabilities at a particular point of time.
Requirements	All items whether capital or revenue are considered in preparing this statement.	Only items, which are of long-term nature, are considered in preparing this statement.
Statutory information	Preparation of FFS is optional and if it is prepared, it can be done so in any manner.	Preparation of Balance Sheet is compulsory and is prepared according to law.
Inter-relationship	To prepare FFS, two successive balance sheets are required.	To prepare balance sheet, FFS is not required.

Exercises

Q. 1. What is fund flow statement? Discuss the significance of fund flow statement as a tool of financial analysis.

Q. 2. Discuss the methodology of preparing fund flow statement.

Q. 3. What are the major sources and uses of networking capital?

Q. 4. What do you understand by working capital concept of term fund? How is fund flow prepared under this concept?

Q. 5. The balance sheets of ABC Ltd., as on December 31, 2001 and December 31, 2002 are as under:

	Dec.31, 2001 (Rs.)	***Dec. 31,2002 (Rs.)***
Assets		
Cash	10,000	12,000
Sundry Debtors	28,000	28,000
Stock	44,000	16,000
Prepaid Insurance	400	500
Prepaid Rent	300	200
Prepaid Property Tax	600	800
Land and Buildings	8,000	16,000
Machinery and Truck	60,000	96,000
TOTAL ASSETS	**1,51,300**	**1,69,500**
Liabilities and Capital		
Sundry Creditors	40,000	36,000
Accrued Expenses	4,000	8,000
Income Tax Payable	2,000	2,200
Share Capital	60,000	74,000
General Reserve	25,300	27,300
Depreciation Fund	20,000	22,000
TOTAL LIABILITIES	**1,51,300**	**1,69,500**

Sales for the Year 2002 were Rs. 4,20,000. Net income after taxes was Rs. 14,000. In arriving at the net profit, items deducted from sales included among others: cost of good sold Rs. 3,30,000; depreciation of Rs. 10,000, wages and salaries Rs. 40,000 and a gain of Rs. 2,000 on the sale of a truck. The truck had cost Rs. 12,000, depreciation of Rs. 8,000 had been accumulated for it and it was old for Rs. 6,000. This was the only asset written off during the year. The company declared and paid Rs. 12,000 in dividends during the year.

Prepare a schedule of changes in working capital and a statement showing the source and application of funds for the year 2002.

Chapter–6

Cost Accounting

LEARNING OBJECTIVES

In this chapter we will study:

Fundamentals of Cost

Cost Accounting

- Objective of Cost Accounting
- Cost-Volume-Profit (CVP) Analysis/Break-even Analysis
- Advantages and Limitations of CVP Analysis

Absorption Costing and Marginal Costing

Inventory Management

- Inventory/Types of inventory
- Inventory Management
- Need of Inventory Management
- Objective of Inventory Management
- Approach of Inventory Management
- Techniques/Models used for Inventory Control
  - ❑ EOQ Model
  - ❑ A-B-C Analysis

6.1 FUNDAMENTALS OF COST

Meaning of Cost

Cost means sacrificing resources to receive benefits. Benefits may be anything tangible or intangible. On the other hand, an expired cost is expense. Depreciation (amortization of asset), maintenance charges, telephone bill etc. are examples of expenses.

Basic Elements of Cost

There are three basic elements of cost of product/services *viz.* material cost, labour cost and overhead cost. Overhead cost includes expenses other than material and labour. It might happen that as compared to one basic element other elements are negligible/insignificant.

Classification of Cost

Classification of cost is done on the basis of purpose of management. Following are some important classification:

- **Direct cost and indirect cost**

  Direct costs are those costs which affects Cost of Goods Sold (COGS) *e.g.* material cost, labour cost, manufacturing expenses are direct costs. Here the purpose of management is to know the gross profit, net profit etc.
- **Controllable and uncontrollable cost**

  Controllable costs are those costs, which remain under jurisdiction of concerned manager. Here the purpose of management is to set accountability. *e.g.* consumption of material is controllable cost for production manager whereas it is uncontrollable cost for purchase manager who is responsible for purchasing of material and hence material prices.
- **Shut down cost and sunk cost**

  Shut down costs are those costs, which incur at the time of shut down of the production *e.g.* rent, minimum taxes, salaries or permanent labour. Shut down cost are important for continue or shut down decision.

  Sunk costs on the other hand are historical or past costs. These costs cannot be altered by later decisions and hence are irrelevant for decision-making.
- **Conversion cost**

  Conversion cost is the cost incurred in converting Raw Material (R/M) into Finished Goods (FG).
- **Explicit cost and implicit cost**

  All those costs, which incur exclusively like material cost, labour cost and overhead costs are explicit costs.

  Whereas all the implied costs like opportunity cost, depreciation, loss on sale are implicit costs.
- **Out of pocket costs, traceable costs and untraceable costs**

  All the explicit costs are out of pocket costs whereas implicit costs are not out of pocket costs.

  Traceable costs are those, which can be traced. Whereas those, which cannot be traceable, *e.g.* scam, suspense account etc. are untraceable costs.
- **Fixed cost, semi variable cost and variable cost**
  - Fixed costs are those costs, which remain unchanged with change in level of activity up to the capacity level *e.g.* interest cost, fixed salary, depreciation etc. are fixed costs.
  - Semi variable costs are those costs part of which changes with change in level of activity *e.g.* telephone bill is semi variable cost as after free calls every additional call increases bill amount.
  - Variable costs are those costs which changes with change in level of activity *e.g.* material cost, labour cost etc. are variable costs.

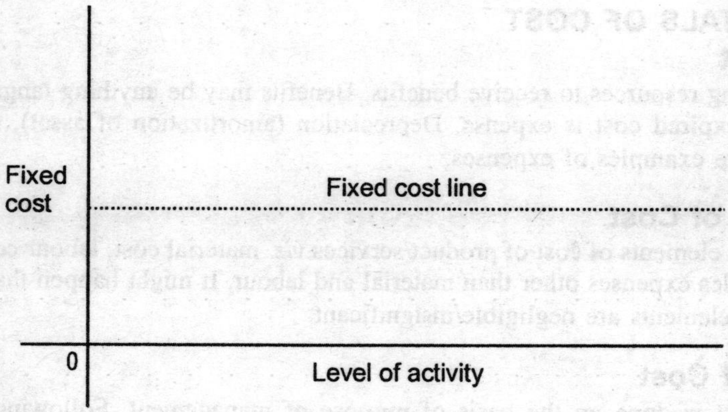

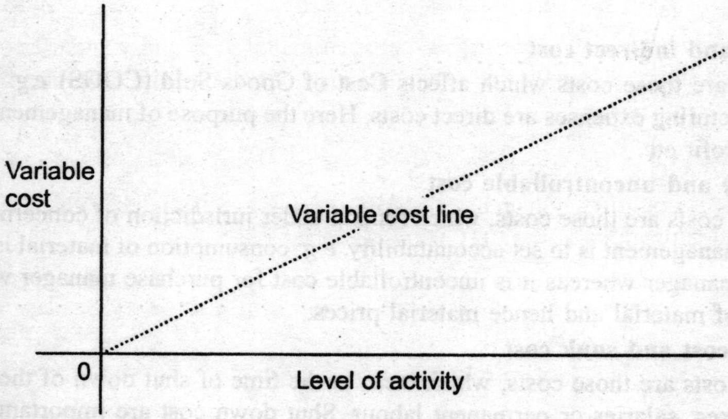

Remark: Total fixed cost remains fixed whereas fixed cost per unit changes with change in level of activity. Similarly, total variable cost changes whereas variable cost per unit remains fixed with change in level of activity.

6.2 COST ACCOUNTING

Cost accounting is the process of maintaining cost records and controlling cost. Cost accounting process includes:

1. Cost determination/costing
2. Cost analysis
3. Cost control

Cost Determination/Costing

- Costing is a technique used to determine cost of product/services at different levels of ongoing operation.
- Costing is done through process of accumulation.
- Preparation of cost sheet is a method of costing.
- Cost sheet helps in knowing unit cost at different levels (known as cost centres) of ongoing operation.
- Costing helps in cost control because costing estimates cost incurred at departments/sub-departments level and cost can be controlled only at the point of incurrence *i.e.* at department/sub-department levels popularly known as cost centers.

Cost analysis

- Cost analysis means analyzing cost.
- The most popular technique used for cost analysis is Cost-Volume-Profit analysis (CVP analysis).
- CVP analysis refers to study of behaviour of profit with respect to cost and volume.
- CVP analysis is also referred as Break-Even Analysis (BE-Analysis)
- CVP analysis helps in profit planning and therefore recognized as important tool of management accounting.

Cost control

- Cost control means comparison of actual cost with predetermined cost (known as standard cost) and if there is deviation, taking corrective action.
- The most popular technique for cost control is standard costing.
- Standard costing leads to variance analysis.
- Variance exists when there is deviation between actual cost and standard cost. Variance may be favourable (when Actual Cost is less than Standard Cost) or Unfavourable/Adverse (when Actual Cost is more than Standard Cost).

6.2.1 Objective of Cost Accounting

The objective of cost accounting is to maintain cost records and to control cost in order to accomplish ultimate goal of an organization *i.e.* wealth maximization.

6.2.2 Cost-Volume-Profit (CVP) Analysis

- CVP analysis is study of behaviour of profit with respect to cost and volume *i.e.* level of activity.
- CVP analysis is also referred as Break-Even Analysis (BE-Analysis).
- Thus under CVP analysis we try to find out Break-Even Point (BEP).
- BEP is that level of activity at which there is no profit no loss.
- For the purpose of CVP analysis cost is divided into two parts—Fixed cost and Variable cost.
- Fixed cost is that cost which remains unchanged with change in level of activity *e.g.* depreciation, interest cost, fixed salary, monthly rent etc.
- Variable costs are those cost which changes with change in level of activity *e.g.* raw material cost, productive labour, manufacturing expenses etc.

Thus at BEP,

$$\text{Profit/Loss} = 0$$

$$\text{Revenue} - \text{Cost} = 0$$

$$\text{Revenue} = \text{Fixed cost} + \text{Variable cost} \qquad ...(i)$$

Let at BEP, 'n' units is the level of activity. Let S.P. is the selling price per unit and V.C. is the variable cost per unit.

Then, According to equation (*i*),

$$n \times \text{S.P.} = \text{Fixed cost} + n \times \text{V.C.}$$

$$n\,(\text{S.P.} - \text{V.C.}) = \text{Fixed cost}$$

$$n = \text{BEP (Units)} = \frac{\text{Fixed cost}}{(\text{S.P.} - \text{V.C.})}$$

$$\boxed{\text{BEP (units)} = \frac{\text{Fixed cost (FC)}}{\text{Contribution Margin per unit (CM)}}}$$

Again, $\text{BEP (Sales or Rs.)} = \text{BEP (units)} \times \text{S.P.} = \frac{\text{Fixed Cost (FC)}}{\text{Contribution Margin per unit (CM)}} \times \text{S.P.}$

Or, $\text{BEP (Sales or Rs.)} = \frac{\text{Fixed Cost (FC)}}{\text{(CM) per unit/SP per unit)}}$

Or, $$\boxed{\text{BEP (Sales or Rs.)} = \frac{\text{Fixed Cost (FC)}}{\text{P/V ratio}}}$$

Where P/V ratio is also referred as Profit-Volume ratio and

$$\text{P/V ratio} = \text{(CM per unit/SP per unit)}$$

$$\text{P/V ratio} = \frac{\text{CM per unit} \times n}{\text{SP per unit} \times n}$$

$$\text{P/V ratio} = \frac{\text{Total Contribution}}{\text{Total Sales Revenue}}$$

$$\text{P/V ratio} = \frac{\text{(Total Sales Revenue – Total Variable Cost)}}{\text{Total Sales Revenue}}$$

$$\text{P/V ratio} = \frac{(S-V)}{S}$$

$$\boxed{\text{P/V ratio} = 1 - \frac{V}{S}}$$

Thus,

$$\text{P/V ratio} = f\,(V, S)$$

P/V ratio is function of variable cost and selling price. It is independent of fixed cost.

- P/V ratio is very important ratio for multi-product organization.
- Multi-product organizations choose that product for maximum operation whose P/V ratio is maximum because this will lower the BEP as,

  $\text{BEP} \propto 1/\text{PV ratio}$

Relationship between Actual units/Target units and Actual profit/Desired profit

$$\boxed{\text{Actual units or Target units} = \text{BEP (units)} + \frac{\text{Acutal profit or Desired profit}}{\text{Contribution Margin per unit (CM)}}}$$

Or,

$$\boxed{\text{Actual units or Target units} = \frac{\text{(Fixed cost + Acutal profit or Desired profit)}}{\text{Contribution Margin per unit (CM)}}}$$

Relationship between Actual Sales/Target Sales and Actual profit/Desired profit

$$\text{Actual sales or Target sales} = \text{BEP (sales)} + \frac{\text{Actual profit or Desired profit}}{\text{P/V ratio}}$$

Or,

$$\text{Actual sales or Target sales} = \frac{(\text{Fixed cost} + \text{Actual profit or Desired profit})}{\text{P/V ratio}}$$

Margin of safety

It measures the extent up to which the level of operation may go down for no profit, no loss.

Thus,

Margin of safety in Rs. = Actual sales – BEP (sales)

Or, Margin of safety in units = Actual units – BEP (units)

Or, $$\text{Margin of safety in units} = \frac{\text{Actual profit or Desired profit}}{\text{Contribution Margin per unit (CM)}}$$

Break-Even (BE) Chart

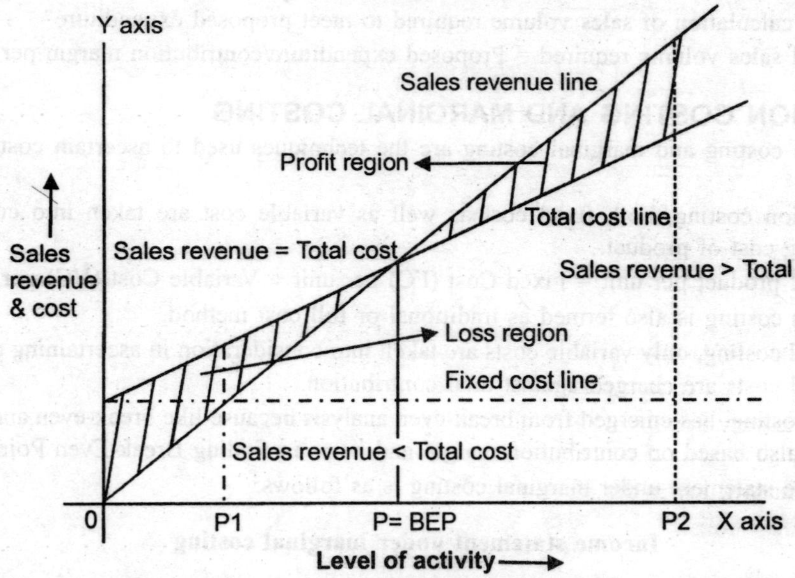

- BE chart depicts graphical presentation of BEP (Break-even point).
- As shown in above chart, at P = BEP there is no profit no loss *i.e.,* Sales revenue = Total cost.
- Beyond BEP *i.e.,* at P2 there is profit region, means sales revenue > total cost.
- Before BEP *i.e.,* at P1 there is loss region, means sales revenue < total cost.

6.2.3 Advantages and Limitations of CVP Analysis/Break-Even Analysis

Limitations

1. For the purpose of break-even analysis, cost is divided into fixed cost and variable cost. It becomes difficult to separate fixed cost and variable cost because most costs remain semi variable in nature. This leads to difficulty in break-even analysis.

2. Break-even analysis do not incorporate those costs which are semi variable in nature.
3. In break-even analysis total sales revenue and total variable cost increase in rigid proportion with the increase in level of activity whereas practically total sales revenue and total variable cost do not increase in rigid proportion. At higher level of activity they are less proportionate than what they should be. This is due to trade discounts, economies of bulk buying, concession for higher sales etc.
4. In controlling costs, marginal costing is not useful in concerns where fixed costs are huge as compared to variable costs.
5. Since variable overheads are apportioned on estimated basis, problem of under or over recovery cannot be eliminated.

Advantages

1. It is an important tool of profit planning as it refers to analyzing the behaviour of profit with respect to cost and volume.
2. It is simple to calculate and understand.
3. It helps in calculation of profits for different sales volume.
4. It helps in fixing selling price for a particular break-even point.
5. It helps in determination of BEP. The level of activity at which there is no profit no loss.
6. It helps in calculation of additional sales volume to offset price reduction.
7. It helps in calculation of sales volume required to meet proposed expenditure (Additional sales volume required = Proposed expenditure/contribution margin per unit).

6.3 ABSORPTION COSTING AND MARGINAL COSTING

- Absorption costing and marginal costing are the techniques used to ascertain cost of product or services.
- In absorption costing, both fixed cost as well as variable cost are taken into consideration in ascertaining cost of product.

  i.e. Cost of product per unit = Fixed Cost (FC) per unit + Variable Cost (VC) per unit
- Absorption costing is also termed as traditional or full cost method.
- In marginal costing, only variable costs are taken into consideration in ascertaining cost of product while fixed costs are charged against total contribution.
- Marginal costing, has emerged from break-even analysis because like break-even analysis marginal costing is also based on contribution margin and helps in finding Break-Even Point (BEP).

  The income statement under marginal costing is as follows:

Income statement under marginal costing

Selling price per unit	______
Less Variable cost per unit	______
Contribution margin per unit	______
Let, the level of activity is 'n' units,	
Then, Total contribution = n × CM per unit ('n' units at CM per unit)	______
Less Total Fixed Assets	______
Profit/Loss	______

At BEP,

Profit/Loss = 0

Total contribution = Total fixed assets

n × CM per unit = Total fixed assets

$$n = \text{BEP (units)} = \frac{\text{Total fixed assets}}{\text{CM per unit}}$$

Thus, we can conclude that marginal costing is a part of break-even analysis.

Why only variable cost is taken into consideration in marginal costing?

Actually marginal costing is concerned with marginal cost where marginal cost refers to cost of producing one additional unit.

Thus,

$$\begin{aligned}\text{Marginal Cost (MC) per unit} &= \text{Cost of } (n + 1) \text{ units} - \text{Cost of } n \text{ units}\\ &= [FC + (n + 1) \times VC/\text{unit}] - [FC + n \times VC/\text{unit}]\\ &= FC + n \times VC/\text{unit} + VC/\text{unit} - n \times VC/\text{unit} - FC\end{aligned}$$

$$\boxed{\text{MC per unit} = \text{VC per unit}}$$

This is the reason why marginal costing considers only variable cost and that is why marginal costing is also termed as **variable costing**.

Note:

Marginal costing is a better technique than absorption costing as it helps in short-term decision-making. This can be seen from the following illustration.

Illustration:

You are the CEO of Anuja Automobiles Ltd. and have received a special offer for the supply of 200 components at Rs. 60 per piece from a motor manufacturer. Your company has a capacity to produce 1000 components. You are at present working at 80% capacity. The present selling price per component is Rs. 100. The cost details as supplied by your cost accountant, are as follows:

Variable cost per unit	Rs. 40
Fixed overhead cost per unit	Rs. 30
(Total fixed cost is Rs. 24000)	
Total cost per unit	Rs. 70

Your cost accountant advises you to reject the order since you will be getting less than the total cost of the component. How would you react?

Solution:

The advice given by the cost accountant is not correct since it is based on absorption costing.

On the basis of marginal costing we see that by accepting additional (special) offer the profit increases by Rs. 4000, therefore we will accept the proposal. The profit under marginal costing is as follows:

In existing case:

	Selling price per unit	Rs. 100
Less	Variable cost per unit	Rs. 40
	Contribution margin per unit	Rs. 60
Then, Total contribution = 800 units @ Rs. 60 per unit ('n' units @ CM per unit)		Rs. 48000
Less	Total Fixed Assets	Rs. 24000
Profit		Rs. 24000

For additional offer:

	Selling price per unit	Rs. 60
Less	Variable cost per unit	Rs. 40
	Contribution margin per unit	Rs. 20
Then, Total contribution = 200 units @ Rs. 20 per unit ('n' units @ CM per unit)		Rs. 4000
Less	Increase in Fixed Assets	NIL (As additional production is within capacity)
Additional Profit		Rs. 4000

Total Profit = 24000 + 4000 = Rs. 28000

6.4 INVENTORY MANAGEMENT

- Inventory/types of inventory
- Inventory management
- Need of inventory management
- Objective of inventory management
- Approach of inventory management
- Techniques/models used for inventory control
  - ❑ EOQ Model
  - ❑ A-B-C analysis

6.4.1 Inventory/Types of Inventory

Inventory is list of items (materials), which an organization needs to maintain. There are 3 types of inventory:

1. **Raw material is the input materials. It is maintained to carry on the production.**
2. **Work in progress/semi-finished goods.**
3. **Finished goods: It is maintained to meet the demand whenever it arises.**
4. **Spare parts/consumable stores.**

Note: **The finished good of one organization may act as raw material for another organization. Raw materials are the integral part of finished goods.**

6.4.2 Inventory Management

Inventory management is a process of procuring, holding, and distributing the inventories at minimum cost.

6.4.3 Need for Inventory Management

Maintaining various components of current asset are essential for smooth operation of the organization and inventory being an essential component of current asset (generally 50% of the current assets remain in the form of inventory) is required to be maintained. Since, holding inventory involves substantial cost and there is time lag between ordering and receiving inventory a proper inventory management system is needed.

6.4.4 Objective of Inventory Management

The objective of inventory management system is to find out the trade-off between cost of having inventory and cost of not having inventory. Cost of having inventory includes item cost, ordering cost, holding cost and distribution cost etc.

Cost of not having inventory includes—(1) Monetary cost *e.g.* additional labor cost, higher material cost due to scarcity of material. (2) Non-monetary cost *e.g.* goodwill loss due to delay in supply.

6.4.5 Approach of Inventory Management

The approach of inventory management lies in developing proper inventory control system *i.e.* to assess what and how much inventory is to be maintained.

Again, the basic purpose of inventory control is to reduce the investment in inventory in such a way that it does not affect the production process at any time. In other words, inventory control is concerned with finding out the solution of:

1. What quantity of inventory is required?
2. When to place the order for inventory?
3. What quantity should be ordered?

6.4.6 Techniques/Models used for Inventory Control

For the efficient inventory control system, different models and techniques were proposed from time to time. They are Economic Order Quantity model (EOQ model) and Always Better Control (ABC) analysis.

6.4.6.1 EOQ Model

- EOQ is that optimum size at which total inventory cost is minimum.
- Total inventory cost is equal to total ordering cost + total carrying (holding) cost.
- Ordering cost is associated with placement of an order for the procurement of inventories. It includes:
  1. Cost related to finalizing orders and placing orders.
  2. Manpower cost.
  3. Money spent in sending enquiries, receiving quotations, inspection cost and cost of settlement.
- Carrying cost is associated with the level of inventories. It includes storage space cost including rent, electricity etc., handling cost, insurance cost, cost of maintaining inventory records etc.

6.4.6.1.1 EOQ model without inventory shortage

According to this model:

1. $Q^* = EOQ = \sqrt{\dfrac{2DC_0}{C_h}}$

Where: D = Annual demand (units).

C_0 = Ordering cost per order.

C_h = Carrying cost per unit.

2. Optimal number of orders placed per year $(N^*) = \dfrac{D}{Q^*}$

3. Optimal time between orders $(T^*) = \dfrac{\text{No. of working days in a year}}{N^*}$

(T^* is also known as inventory cycle time.)

4. Total annual variable cost $TC\ (Q^*) = \sqrt{2DC_0C_h}$

6.4.6.1.2 EOQ model with inventory shortage

According to this model:

1. Optimal or economic order quantity

$$Q^* = \sqrt{\frac{2DC_0(C_h + C_0)}{C_h(C_b)}}$$

Where C_b = shortage cost/stock out cost per unit per period

D = Annual demand

C_0 = Ordering cost per order per time

C_h = Holding cost per order per time

Q^* = Economic number of units per order

2. Maximum number of back orders/planned shortages

$$S^* = Q^* \frac{(C_h)}{(C_h + C_b)}$$

3. Number of order per year

$$D^* = \frac{D}{Q^*} \text{ units}$$

4. Time between orders

$$T^* = \frac{Q^*}{D} \text{ years}$$

5. Maximum inventory level

$$I_{Max} = Q^* \frac{C_b}{(C_b + C_h)}$$

6. Total annual variable cost

$$TC\ (Q^*) = \sqrt{2DC_0C_h}\sqrt{\frac{C_b}{C_h + C_b}}$$

6.4.6.2 A-B-C Analysis

Under this technique, material are divided into different categories on the basis of value to control it. Generally in manufacturing concern a small percentage of items contribute a large percentage of value of consumption and a large percentage of items of materials contribute a small percentage of value. In between these two limits there are some items, which have almost equal percentage of value of materials.

Under A-B-C analysis, the materials are divided into three categories *viz.* A, B and C. Past experience has shown that almost 10% of the items contribute 70% of value consumption and this category is called

'A' category. About 20% of the items contribute about 20% of value of consumption and this is known as category 'B' materials. Category 'C' covers about 70% of items of materials, which contribute only 10% of value of consumption. There may be some variations in different organizations and an adjustment can be made in these percentages.

The information is shown in following diagram:

Class	No. of items (%)	Value of items (%)
A	10	70
B	20	20
C	70	10

A-B-C analysis helps to concentrate more efforts on category A since greatest monetary advantage will come by controlling these items. Attention should be paid in estimating requirements, purchasing and maintaining safety stocks and properly storing of 'A' category materials. These items are kept under a constant review so that a substantial material cost may be controlled. The control of 'C' items may be relaxed and these stocks may be purchased for the year. A little more attention should be given towards 'B' category items and their purchase should be undertaken at quarterly or half yearly intervals.

Exercises

Q. 1. What is cost and what are basic elements of cost? Also describe different classification of cost.

Q. 2. Briefly describe different steps involved in cost accounting process.

Q. 3. Write short note on Cost-Volume-Profit (CVP) analysis and explain how CVP analysis helps in profit planning.

Q. 4. Break-even-analysis is a tool for profit planning. Discuss.

Q. 5. What do you mean by margin of safety?

Q. 6. Briefly describe limitations and advantages of Break-Even analysis.

Q. 7. Differentiate between absorption costing and marginal costing.

Q. 8. Through illustration, show how break-even analysis helps in short-term decision-making.

Q. 9. Define inventory and types of inventory.

Q. 10. Write short note on Inventory management.

Q. 11. Describe Economic Order Quantity (EOQ) and its usefulness in the context of Inventory Management.

Q. 12. X Ltd. and Y Ltd. manufacture and sell the same type of product in the same market. The following figures have been obtained from their account for the year ending 31st Dec. 2005.

	X Ltd. Rs.	Y Ltd. Rs.
Sales	1,50,000	1,50,000
Variables costs	1,20,000	1,00,000
Fixed costs	15,000	35,000

Calculate

1. Contribution
2. P/V Ratio
3. Break-Even Point
4. Margin of Safety

Q. 13. The Rashu & Co.'s income statement for the preceding year is presented below. Except as noted, the cost–revenue relationship for the coming year is expected to follow the same pattern as in the preceding year.

Income Statement for the year 31st Dec.2005	**Rs.**
Sales (20,00,000 bottles @ 25 Paise)	5,00,000
Variable Costs	3,00,000
Fixed Costs	1,00,000
Total	**4,00,000**
Pre-tax profit	Rs. 1,00,000
Income Tax	50,000
Profit after Income Tax	Rs. 50,000

You are required to calculate:

(*i*) What is the break-even point in sales and units?

(*ii*) Suppose that a plant expansion will add Rs. 50,000 to fixed costs and increase capacity by 60%, how many bottles would have to be sold after the addition, to break-even?

(*iii*) At what level of sales, will the company be able to maintain its present pre-tax profit position even after expansion?

(*iv*) The company's management feels that it should earn at least Rs. 10,000 (pre-tax per annum) on the new investment. What sales volume is required to enable the company to maintain existing profits and earn the minimum required on the new investment?

(*v*) Suppose the plant operates at full capacity after the expansion, what profit will be earned?

Q. 14. The ABC Ltd. furnishes you the following income information:

		Year 1976	
		First half Rs.	***Second half*** Rs.
Sales	....	8,10,000	10,26,000
Profit earned	....	21,600	64,800

From the above you are required to compute the following, assuming that the fixed cost remains the same in both periods:

1. Profit/Volume ratio.
2. Sales at break-even point.
3. Fixed cost.

4. The amount of profit or loss where sales are Rs. 6,48,000.
5. The amount of sales required to earn a profit of Rs. 1,08,000.
6. Variable expenses during the second half

Q. 15. A firm sells 7000 units at Rs. 2 per unit. Its fixed cost amounts to Rs. 44,000 and variable cost to Rs. 16 per unit. Calculate margin of safety.

Q. 16. The fixed cost of stock hold company for the year 1999 are Rs. 80000. Variable cost per unit for the single product being made is Rs. 4. Estimated sales for the period are valued at Rs. 2,00,000. The number of units invoked coincides with the expected volume of output. Units are sold at Rs. 20 each. You are required to calculate the break-even point.

Q. 17. Total fixed cost of a firm are Rs. 9,000, total variable cost are Rs. 15,000, total sales are Rs. 30,000 and units sold are 10,000. The margin of safety is

(*a*) 5,000 units
(*b*) 8,000 units
(*c*) 4,000 units
(*d*) 6,500 units
(*e*) None of the above.

Q. 18. If the variable cost per unit is Rs. 10, fixed costs are Rs. 1,00,000 and selling price per unit is Rs. 20 and if the break-even point is lowered to 8,000 units, the selling price would be

(*a*) Rs. 25.00
(*b*) Rs. 30.00
(*c*) Rs. 27.50
(*d*) Rs. 22.50
(*e*) None of the above

Q. 19. Where total costs are Rs. 60,000, fixed costs are Rs. 30,000 and sales are Rs. 1,00,000, the break-even point in rupees would be

(*a*) Rs. 50,450
(*b*) Rs. 42,857
(*c*) Rs. 45,332
(*d*) Rs. 60,000
(*e*) None of the above

Q. 20. Total fixed costs remain constant but per unit fixed costs decline with increase in volume of activity. Explain with the help of suitable diagrams. Also give five examples of fixed costs.

Q. 21. "Break-even analysis considers variable costs while fixed costs are adjusted against the revenue from the period." Discuss

Q. 22. 'Profit will occur only once break-even point is reached. There[illegible], it is desirable to reduce the break-even level'. Discuss and suggest three ways of reducing break-even level.

Q. 23. Explain the calculation of break-even point in terms of rupees and also in units. Al[illegible]aw the profit graph to show break-even point.

Part – III

Financial Management

Chapter–7

Financial Management

LEARNING OBJECTIVES

In this chapter we will study:

Defining Financial Management

Functions of Financial Management or Role of Finance Manager

Financial Management and Management Accounting

Objective of Financial Management

Scope of Financial Management

Basic Financial Concepts

- Indian Financial System
- Difference Between Short-term Decision and Long-term Decision
- Time Value of Money Concept along with some practical application

Capital Budgeting Decision

- Introduction
- Characteristics of Capital Budgeting Decision
- Difficulties Associated with Capital Budgeting Decision
- Sources of Financing Capital Budgeting Decision
- Capital Budgeting Evaluation Techniques
- Application of Evaluation Techniques in the Context of Information Technology

7.1 DEFINING FINANCIAL MANAGEMENT

Financial management is concerned with management of fund. It may be defined as "acquisition of fund at optimum cost and its utilization with minimum financial risk."

7.2 FUNCTIONS OF FINANCIAL MANAGEMENT OR ROLE OF FINANCE MANAGER

Finance function has three broad categories:

1. Financial planning followed by implementation of financial decisions *viz.*
   - Financing decision
   - Investment decision
   - Dividend decision
2. Financial Analysis
3. Financial Control

1. Financial Planning

- Planning means deciding in advance. Thus financial planning is the act of deciding in advance the activities related to financial decisions necessary to achieve the objectives of financial management.
- In other words, financial planning is the process of determining the financial objectives, procedures and strategies, programmes and policies and budgets to deal with the activities related to financial decisions of an organization.
- Thus financial planning provides framework within which financial decisions take place.
- Financial decisions refer to financing decision (procurement of fund), investment decision (utilization of fund) and dividend decision (distribution of fund).
- Financial planning *i.e.* planning for financing, investment and dividend decision must confront with (*i.e.* take into account) external environment (industry level and country level factors) and internal environment (organizational level factors). Factors like risk or uncertainty, inflation, liquidity, taxation etc. are some examples in this regard.
- Capitalization, financial forecasting and budgeting are important tools for financial planning which helps in planning financing and investment decisions.
- Capitalization refers to planning of financing decision, which means estimation of total fund requirement to run the concerned organization.
- Financial forecasting includes preparation of projected income statement, projected balance sheet, projected fund flow statement etc.
- Budgeting includes preparation of budgets and installation of proper budgetary control system.
- Financial planning leads to implementation of financial decisions *viz.* financing decision, investment decision and dividend decision.

Financial planning as framework for financial decisions confront with external and internal factors

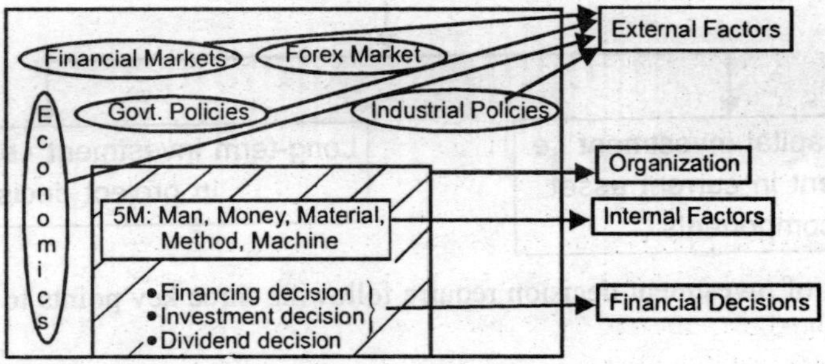

- **Financial Decisions**

Business decisions are of two types *viz.* short-term decision, also known as working capital decision and long-term decision, also known as capital budgeting decision/project decision capital expenditure decision and therefore financing decision and investment must be viewed in the light of these decisions.

Following is a brief description of financial decisions *viz.* Financing decision, Investment decision and Dividend decision:

❑ **Financing decision: (procurement of fund)**

Financing decision is categorized into two parts:

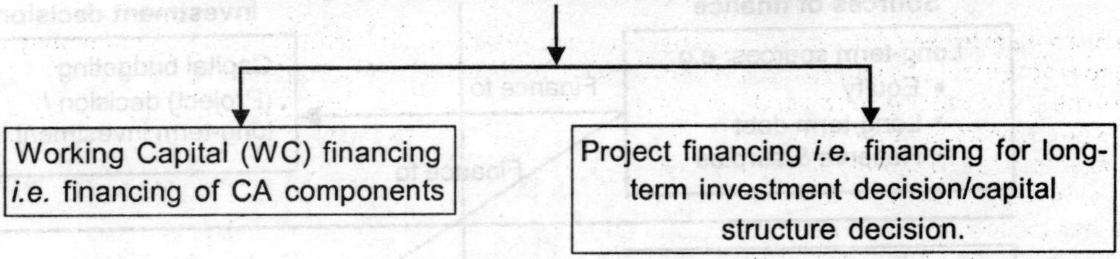

Both category of financing decision require following three key points to take into consideration:

(*i*) Sources

(*ii*) Sources mix

(*iii*) Cost and other consequences

Sources: A finance manager has to identify the various sources available to him through which he can raise the fund. It is the financial system which facilitates financing decision in identifying/procuring short-term as well as long-term sources of finance (for details refer to Financial Market/Financial System).

Sources mix: He has to decide the composition of each source in total capital.

Cost and other consequences: A finance manager while raising fund must take into consideration the cost and other consequences associated with each source.

❑ **Investment decision: (Application of fund)**

Investment decision is also categorized into two parts:

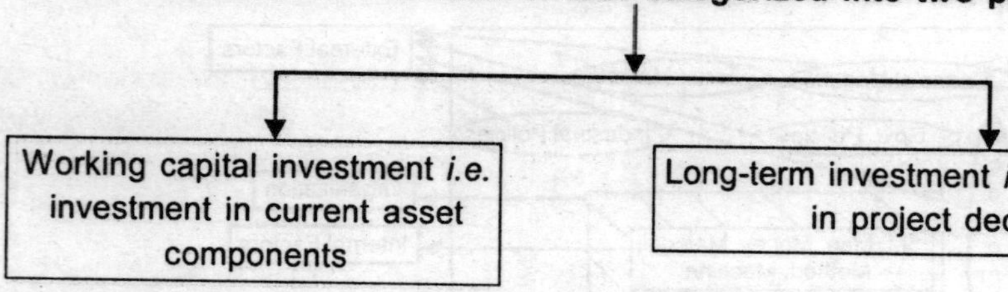

Both categories of investment decision require following three key points to take into consideration:

(*i*) Assets

(*ii*) Assets mix

(*iii*) Profitability

Assets: Assets means resources to the organization. A finance manager has to identify what are the various assets required to maintain for smooth functioning of concerned organization.

Assets mix: He has to decide the composition of each asset in total assets.

Profitability: A finance manager while investing fund must take into consideration the profitability associated with each asset. Profitability means ability to earn profit.

Note: **Financing of Investment Decision**

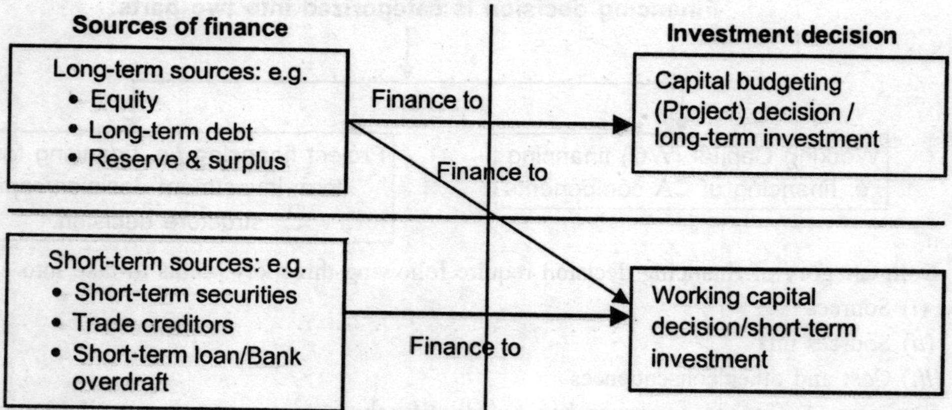

Thus project decision is always financed through only long-term sources whereas working capital decision is financed through long-term as well as short-term sources.

❑ **Dividend decision: (Distribution of fund)**

A finance manager has to decide what percentage of profit he has to distribute as dividend among shareholders and how much to retain for further requirement. This aspect of financial management is dealt under dividend policy.

2. Financial Analysis

- Financial analysis refers to study of financial health from different interested groups' (management, employee, government, suppliers, lenders, investors etc.) point of view.

- Financial health means ability to serve above-mentioned groups.
- Ratio Analysis, Cost-Volume-Profit (CVP), Fund Flow/Cash Flow Analysis are popular tools for financial analysis which in turn further helps in financial planning for subsequent periods.

3. Financial Control

- Financial control refers to comparison of actual activities related to financial decisions with planned activities.
- In other words, it is reviewing financial performances as per planning schedule in order to meet the set financial objective.
- Budgetary control system, variance analysis are some popular tools, which help in controlling activities related to financial decisions.

Apart from above-mentioned categories of finance function, finance department is also responsible for support services. They are,

- Finance department has to make available the fund to other functional departments whenever they need money in time.
- Finance department under financing activity has to negotiate with the lenders to acquire the fund at optimum cost.
- Finance department keeps an eye on stock market as stock market prices reflects performance of the concerned organization.

7.3 FINANCIAL MANAGEMENT AND MANAGEMENT ACCOUNTING

Management accounting provides tools for financial planning, analysis and control mentioned above and hence management accountant is of great help to financial management for financial decisions *viz.* Financing, Investment and Dividend decisions.

7.4 OBJECTIVE OF FINANCIAL MANAGEMENT

Traditional approach

Traditionally the basic objective of financial management was profit maximization but later on this was overruled by shareholders' (owners) wealth maximization. Presently wealth maximization is the real objective of financial management. Profit maximization was overruled by wealth maximization because of following limitations:

- **It is vague:** Objective of profit maximization does not clarify what exactly it means *e.g.* which profits are to be maximized—short run or long run, rate of profit or the amount of profit.
- **It ignores timing:** The concept of profit maximization does not help in making a choice between projects giving different benefits spread over a period of time.

Illustration:

Project A

Project B

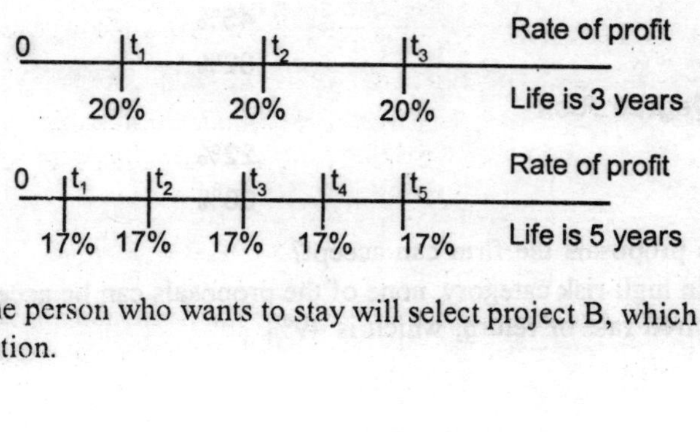

Clearly the person who wants to stay will select project B, which is contrary to the concept of profit maximization.

- **It ignores qualitative aspect:** The person who wants to expand his market will procure qualitative input material which will incur substantial cost, which in turn will bring down margin and hence profit. Thus the quality aspect is contrary to the concept of profit maximization.

Wealth maximization

- Shareholders' wealth maximization is the real objective of financial management because it helps the management in financial decisions *viz.* Financing decision, Investment management and dividend decision.
- Shareholders' wealth maximization is also referred as firm's value maximization.
- Shareholders' wealth maximization *i.e.* value maximization is also goal of the firm.

There are two approaches to accomplish wealth maximization:

(*i*) Risk vs Return Approach

(*ii*) Liquidity vs Profitability Approach

Risk vs Return Approach:

Logically, Risk $\propto$ Return

According to this approach –

(*a*) A finance manager has to minimize risk for given level of return.

(*b*) A finance manager has to maximize return for given degree of risk.

In other words, in order to maximize shareholders' wealth a finance manager has to find out trade-off point between risk and return (which means level of operation at which risk and return are optimized) while taking financial decisions.

Illustration:

A firm has determined the following expected rate of return keeping in view the degree of risk involved in the proposals under consideration.

Degree of Risk	Expected return
Low	25%
Medium low	29%
Medium	33%
Medium high	41%
High	49%

The firm has the following proposal with it,

High Degree Risk	Expected rate of return
X	45%
Y	32%
Medium Degree Risk	
P	22%
Q	36%

Question: Which of the above proposals the firm can accept?

Answer: Out of the proposals in high-risk category, none of the proposals can be accepted since they are all giving return below the required rate of return, which is 49%.

Out of the medium degree risk proposals, the firm can accept only proposal Q, which is giving 36% return. Proposal P has to be rejected since it is giving only 22% return as compared to 29% which is minimum return required from such category of proposals.

Liquidity vs Profitability Approach:

Logically,

$$\text{Liquidity} \propto \frac{1}{\text{Profitability}}$$

i.e. increase in liquidity results in decrease in profitability.

Thus, according to this approach,

A finance manager has to manage conflict between liquidity and profitability in order to maximize 'shareholders' wealth while taking financial decisions *viz.* Financing, Investment and Dividend decision.

In other words, he has to make financial decisions in such a manner that the liquidity should be just adequate *i.e.* neither more nor less to enhance profitability, which in turn will increase value of the firm.

Illustration:

In case the management in anticipation of increase in raw material prices, decides to purchase raw material more than the requirement then this decision will certainly lead to profitability but this may endanger the liquidity (because fund will get blocked in the form of excess raw material stock) and therefore a very careful estimate of liquidity and profitability is required to manage the conflict between the two.

Similarly, the firm by allowing liberal credit policy may be in a position to push up its sales and hence profitability but this may endanger liquidity (because funds will get blocked in form of receivables), which may lower the value of the firm.

Summarizing above two approaches, we conclude,

$$\text{Risk} \propto \text{Profitability} \propto \frac{1}{\text{Liquidity}}$$

Thus the objective of finance manager is to manage risk, return (profitability) and liquidity while taking financial decisions in order to maximize shareholders' wealth/value of the firm. This can be done through proper Assets and Funds management.

7.5 SCOPE OF FINANCIAL MANAGEMENT

The major activity of financial management is to take financial decisions *viz.* Financing decision (Procurement of fund), Investment decision (Application of fund) and Dividend decision (Distribution of fund) in order to accomplish goal of the firm *i.e.* to maximize shareholder's (owner's) wealth.

Again, since financial decisions especially financing and investment decisions are very necessary and crucial activities of every aspect of life, it therefore, can be concluded that the scope (area) of financial management is very wide and is spread over all the entities of society *viz.* individuals, organizations and government to carry on their activities. A brief description of Financing and Investment decisions are as follows:

□ **Financing decision: (procurement of fund)**

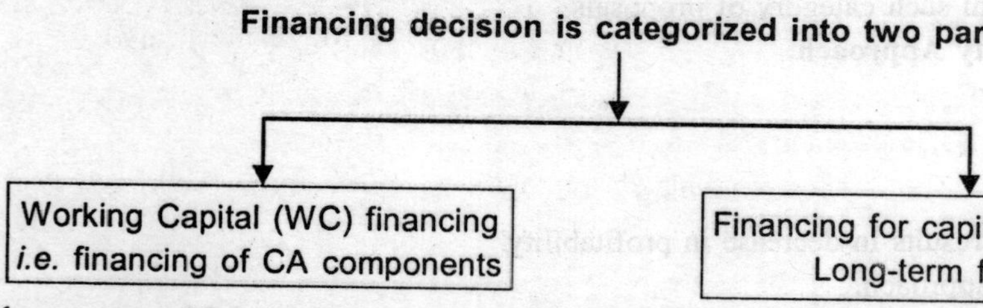

Both category of financing decision require the following three key points to take into consideration:

(*i*) Sources

(*ii*) Sources mix

(*iii*) Cost and other consequences

Sources: One has to identify what are the various sources available to him through which he can raise the fund.

Sources mix: He has to decide the composition of each source in total capital.

Cost and other consequences: Cost and other consequences associated with each source must be taken into consideration while raising fund.

□ **Investment decision: (Application of fund)**

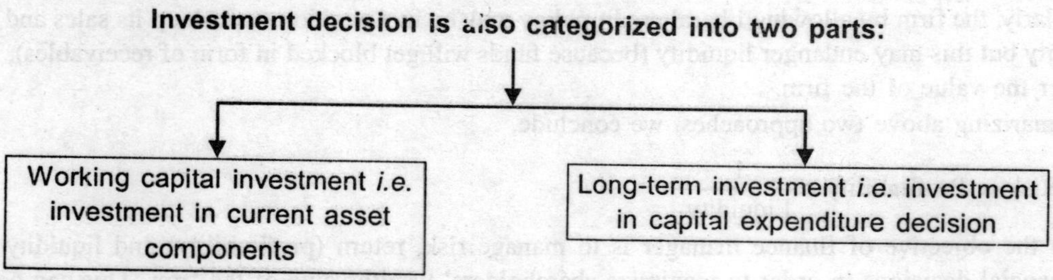

Both category of investment decisions require following three key points to take into consideration:

(*i*) Assets

(*ii*) Assets mix

(*iii*) Profitability

Assets: Assets means resources to the organization. One has to identify what are various assets required to maintain for the smooth functioning of concerned entity.

Assets mix: He has to decide the composition of each asset in total assets.

Profitability: The profitability associated with each asset must be taken into consideration while investing fund. Profitability means ability to earn profit.

7.6 BASIC FINANCIAL CONCEPTS

7.6.1 Indian Financial System

- **Financial system** of any country represents the organizational setup for financial market.

PLAYERS OF FINANCIAL MARKET
(Components of Financial System)

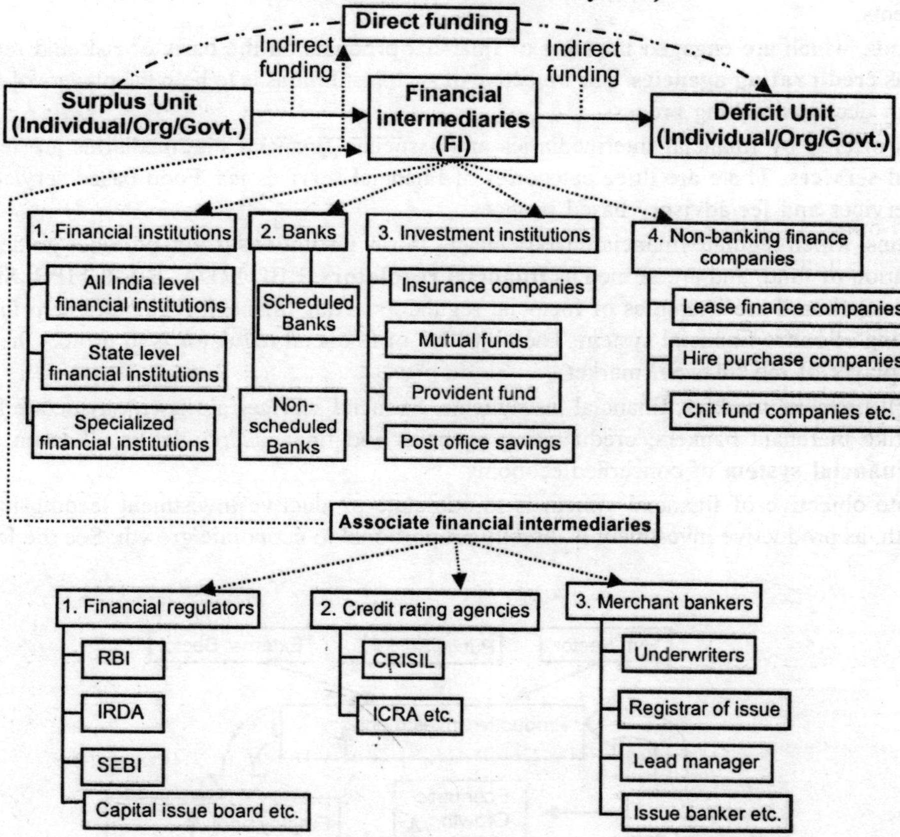

- **Financial market** like any other market is the market, which facilitates mobilization of fund between buyer of the fund (Deficit unit) and seller of the fund (Surplus unit) either directly with the help of associate financial intermediaries or indirectly *i.e.* through Financial Intermediaries (FI) alongwith associate financial intermediaries using financial products or fund itself. In other words, financial market facilitates funding requirement of deficit unit.
- **Associate financial intermediaries** are those intermediaries, which advise/assist financial intermediaries, buyer of the fund (deficit unit) and seller of the fund (surplus unit) in mobilization of fund on the basis of fee/commission.
- Merchant bankers, credit rating agencies and financial regulators are examples of associate financial intermediaries.
- **Merchant bankers** provide a blend of financial services on the basis of fee/commission. Underwriter, Lead manager/Co-manager, registrar, book building runner, issue banker are some roles performed by merchant bankers.

- Thus deficit unit, surplus unit and financial intermediaries alongwith associate financial intermediaries are **players of financial market**.
- Products offered in financial market are known as **financial products/instruments**. Broadly, there are two categories of products *viz.* long-term instruments or capital market instruments and short-term instruments or money market instruments. For the purpose of liquidity, financial instruments are traded at secondary markets *e.g.* stock exchanges are secondary market for capital market instruments.
- Institutions, which are engaged in rating of financial products on the basis of risk and return, are termed as **credit rating agencies**. The objective of such institutions is to help the players of financial market in decision-making process.
- Services offered by financial intermediaries and associate financial intermediaries are termed as **financial services**. There are three categories of financial services *viz.* Fund based services, asset based services and fee/advisory based services.
- Institutions, which regulate financial market means, those institutions which provides guidelines for mobilization of fund, and are termed as **financial regulators**. RBI, IRDA, BIFR, FIPB, SEBI and Capital issue board are examples of financial regulators. Thus financial regulators help in smooth functioning of entire financial system. The objective of financial regulator is to protect the interest of each player of the financial market.

In a nutshell financial markets, financial instruments, financial services alongwith associate financial intermediaries like merchant bankers, credit rating agencies and financial regulators all taken together constitute the **financial system** of concerned economy.

The ultimate objective of financial system is to stimulate productive investment leading to overall economic growth, as productive investment is directly proportional to economic growth. See the following diagram.

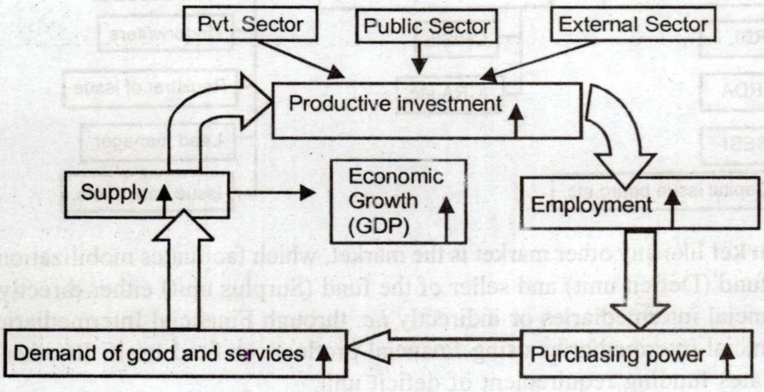

7.6.2 Difference Between S.T. Decision and L.T. Decision

Difference between S.T. decision and L.T. decision are as follows:

S.T. Decision (W.C. decision)	*L.T. Decision (Capital Budgeting decision)*
(i) Does not involve substantial capital outlay.	(i) Involve substantial capital outlay.
(ii) W.C. decision is financed through short-term sources as well as long-term sources *e.g.* operating profit, which is part of reserve and surplus (internal fund).	(ii) Capital Budgeting Decision is financed through only long-term sources.
(iii) Reversible in nature.	(iii) Irreversible in nature.
S.T. Decision (W.C. decision)	*L.T. Decision (Capital Budgeting decision)*
(iv) Short-term effect *i.e.* benefits are realized immediately/within short-period (Revenue nature).	(iv) Long-term effect *i.e.* benefits are realized over a period of time *i.e.* up to the life of the project (Capital nature).
(v) S.T. decisions involve no time lag between cost and benefits and hence time value of money concept is not required for Cost-Benefit analysis.	(v) L.T. decisions involve time lag between cost and benefits and hence time value of money concept is required for Cost-Benefit analysis.

7.6.3 Time Value of Money Concept Along with Some Practical Applications

- According to this concept, the value of money changes with change in time. In other words, a rupee received today is more valuable than a rupee received one year hence
- There are two aspects of time value of money concept:
  1. Present Value concept (PV concept)
  2. Future or Compounding Value concept (FV concept)

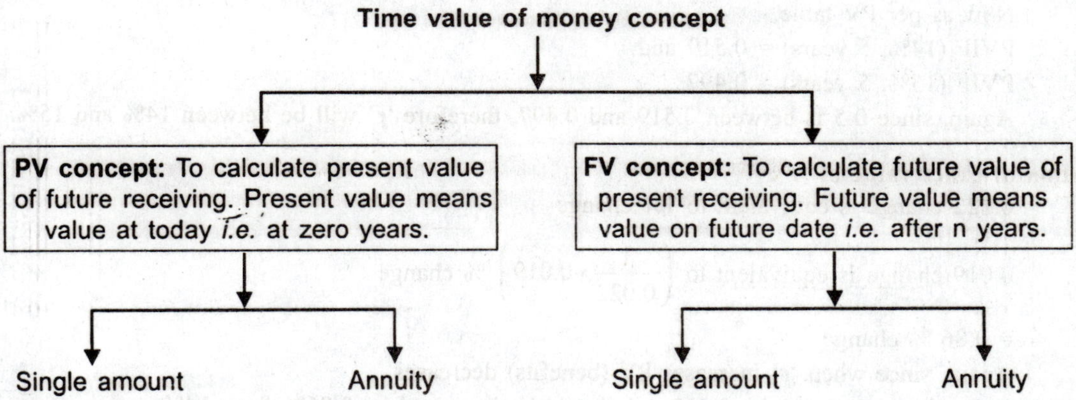

Note: Annuity means series of constant cash flows starting from first year to n^{th} year (say up to 5th year, 10 years etc.).

Present Value (PV) of single amount

Let the single amount 'A' is due to receive after n^{th} year and the required rate of return/rate of interest/ discount rate is r%, then

PV of single amount will be: $\boxed{PV\ (A) = A \times PVIF\ (r\%, n^{th}\ year)}$

Where, PVIF (r%, n^{th} year) is present value interest factor at r%, n^{th} year. It can be taken from present value interest factor table.

Mathematically, $\boxed{PVIF\ (r\%, n^{th}\ year) = 1/(1 + r)^{n}}$

Illustration 1:

Suppose Mr. X deposits Rs. 10000 in Syndicate bank. Calculate in how many years it will become double, in case the rate of interest offered by Syndicate bank is 8%.

Solution: According to question,

Let in 'n' years Rs. 10000 grows to Rs. 20000 at 8% interest rate.

Then it can be presented as,

PV (20000) = 10000

⇒ 20000 × PVIF (8%, n years) = 100000

⇒ PVIF (8%, n years) = 0.5

⇒ n = 9 years (approx.)

(Because as per PV table PVIF (8%, 9 years) = 0.5)

Illustration 2:

Suppose Mr. X deposits Rs. 10000 in Syndicate bank. Calculate rate of interest offered by Syndicate bank in case deposit becomes double in just five years.

Solution: According to question,

Let at r% interest rate Rs. 10000 grows to Rs. 20000 in 5 years.

Then it can be presented as,

PV (20000) = 10000

⇒ 20000 × PVIF (r%, 5 years) = 100000

⇒ PVIF (r%, 5 years) = 0.5

Now as per PV table,

PVIF (14%, 5 years) = 0.519 and

PVIF (15%, 5 years) = 0.497

Again, since 0.5 is between 0.519 and 0.497, therefore 'r' will be between 14% and 15%.

Calculation of exact value of 'r':

0.022 change is equivalent to 1% change

$\therefore$ 0.019 change is equivalent to $\left(\frac{1}{0.022} \times 0.019\right)$ % change

= 0.86 % change

Again, since when 'r' increases PV (benefits) decreases.

$\therefore$ To decrease 0.519 by 0.019, 'r' should be increased by 0.86% from 14%

Thus r = 14% + 0.86%

$\therefore$ $\boxed{r = 14.86\%}$

Present Value (PV) of single amount for shorter discounting period:
Let the single amount 'A' is due to receive after n^{th} year and the required rate of return/rate of interest/ discount rate is r% and 'm' is number of times per year discounting is done, then

PV of single amount will be: $\boxed{PV (A) = A \times PVIF \{(r/m)\%, (m*n)^{th} \text{ year}\}}$

Where, PVIF $\{(r/m)\%, (m*n)^{th}$ year$\}$ is present value interest factor at $(r/m)\%,(m*n)^{th}$ year. It can be taken from present value interest factor table.

Mathematically, $\boxed{PVIF \{(r/m)\%, (m*n)^{th} \text{ year}\} = 1/(1 + r/m)^{mn}}$

Note:

- **When discounting is done monthly, value of 'm' will be 12**
- **When discounting is done quarterly, value of 'm' will be 4**
- **When discounting is done six monthly (*i.e.* semi-annually), value of 'm' will be 2**

Illustration:
Consider a cash flow of Rs. 10000 is to be received by Mr. X at the end of four years. Determine present value in case discount rate is 12% and discounting is done quarterly (m = 4).

Solution:

$PV (A) = A \times PVIF \{(r/m)\%, (m*n)^{th} \text{ year}\}$

$\Rightarrow$ PV (10000) = 10000 × PVIF $\{(12/4)\%, (4*4)^{th}$ year$\}$

$\Rightarrow$ PV (10000) = 10000 × PVIF (3%,16 years)

$\Rightarrow$ PV (10000) = 10000 × 0.623

$\Rightarrow$ PV (10000) = Rs. 6,230

Present Value (PV) of Annuity
Let the amount of annuity is 'A' and it is receivable up to n^{th} year. Again let the required rate of return/ rate of interest/discount rate is r%, then

PV of Annuity will be: $\boxed{PV (Annuity) = A \times PVIFA (r\%, n^{th} \text{ year})}$

Where, PVIFA (r%, n^{th} year) is present value interest factor for annuity at r%, n^{th} year. It can be taken from present value interest factor for annuity table.

Mathematically, $\boxed{PVIFA (r\%, n^{th} \text{ year}) = \sum_{t=1}^{n} 1/(1+r)^t}$

Illustration:
Mr. X received Rs. 5,00,000 as gratuity after retirement. He deposited the same with State Bank of India (SBI). How much money can he withdraw each year upto 30 years so that the amount at the end of 30 years becomes zero. The rate of interest offered by SBI is 7%.

Solution:
Let the amount withdrawn each year is 'A'

∴ According to question,

PV (annuity) = 500000

$\Rightarrow$ A × PVIFA (7%, 30 years) = 500000

$\Rightarrow$ A × 12.409 = 500000 (As per present value interest factor for annuity table, PVIFA, PVIFA (7%,30 years) = 12.409)

$$\therefore \quad A = \frac{500000}{12.409}$$

$\therefore$ A = Rs. 40293.335

Thus Mr. X can withdraw Rs. 40293.335 annually up to next 30 years.

Future Value (FV) of Single Amount

Let the single amount 'A' is received today and the required rate of return/rate of interest/discount rate is r% then,

FV of single amount after n years will be: FV (A) = A × FVIF (r%, n^{th} year)

Where, FVIF (r%, n^{th} year) is future value interest factor at r%, n^{th} year. It can be taken from future value interest factor table.

Mathematically, FVIF (r%, n^{th} year) = $(1 + r)^n$

Illustration:

Suppose an insurance company offers Rs. 10000 after 8 years against a deposit of Rs. 5000 made today. Would you accept the offer in case rate of return required by you is a minimum 12%?

Solution:

Compare the future value of Rs. 5000 at required rate with Rs. 10000.

If FV (5000) < 10000 then accept the offer otherwise reject it.

Again FV(5000) = 5000 × FVIF (12%, 8 years)

= 5000 × 2.476 (As per FV table, FVIF (12%, 8 years) = 2.476)

= 12380 > 10000

Thus since the amount offered by insurance company after 8 years is less than the expected future value, it therefore, can not be accepted.

Future Value (FV) of single amount for shorter compounding period

Let the single amount 'A' is received today and the required rate of return/rate of interest/discount rate is r% and 'm' is number of times per year compounding is done then,

FV of single amount after n years will be: FV (A) = A × FVIF {(r/m)%, $(m*n)^{th}$ year}

Where, FVIF {(r/m)%, $(m*n)^{th}$ year} is future value interest factor at (r/m)%,$(m*n)^{th}$ year. It can be taken from future value interest factor table.

Mathematically, FVIF {(r/m)%, $(m*n)^{th}$ year} = $(1 + r/m)^{mn}$

Illustration:

Consider a cash flow of Rs. 10000 is received today by Mr. X. Determine future value at the end of four years in case required rate of return is 12% and compounding is done quarterly (m = 4).

Solution:

FV (A) = A × FVIF {(r/m)%, $(m*n)^{th}$ year}

⇒ FV (10000) = 10000 × FVIF {(12/4)%, (4*4)th year}
⇒ FV (10000) = 10000 × FVIF (3%,16 years)
⇒ FV (10000) = 10000 × 1.605
⇒ FV (10000) = Rs. 16050

Note:

- **When compounding is done monthly, value of 'm' will be 12**
- **When compounding is done quarterly, value of 'm' will be 4**
- **When compounding is done six monthly (*i.e.* semi-annually), value of 'm' will be 2**

Future Value (FV) of Annuity

Let the amount of annuity is 'A' and it is receivable up to nth year. Again let the required rate of return/rate of interest/discount rate is r% then,

FV of annuity after n years will be: FV (Annuity) = A × FVIFA (r%, nth year)

Where, FVIFA (r%, nth year) is future value interest factor for annuity at r%, nth year. It can be taken from future value interest factor for annuity table.

Mathematically, $\text{FVIFA}(r\%, n^{th}\text{ year}) = \sum_{t=1}^{n} (1+r)^t$

Illustration:

Suppose you deposit Rs. 5000 every year up to 10 years in PPF account then what would be the value after 15 years if the current rate of interest on PPF account is 8% and it is expected to continue for next 15 years.

Solution:

The regular deposited money will grow by future value annuity factor for first 10 years and thereafter up to next 5 years it will grow by future value interest factor.

Thus,

Terminal value at the end of 15th year *i.e.* Future Value at the end of 15 years

= FV of {FV of Rs. 5000 deposited each year for first 10 years} for next 5 years
= FV {FV (Annuity) for 10 years} for 5 years
= {5000 × FVIFA (8%, 10 years)} × FVIF (8%, 5 years)
= {5000 × 14.487} × 1.469 (As per future value interest factor for annuity table, FVIFA (8%, 10 years) = 14.487 and as per future value interest factor table, FVIF (8%, 5 years) = 1.469)
= {72435} × 1.469
= 106407.015

Thus terminal value at the end of 15th year = Rs. 106407.015

7.7 CAPITAL BUDGETING DECISION

7.7.1 Introduction

1. Capital budgeting is the process of planning for purchases of long-term assets.
2. In other words, Capital Budgeting is a process of undertaking Project Decision/Capital Investment Decision/Long-term Investment Decision or Capital Expenditure Decision.

3. Capital Budgeting process includes following stages:
   - Planning
   - Analysis
     - ❑ Market Analysis
     - ❑ Technical Analysis
     - ❑ Financial Analysis
     - ❑ Economic Analysis and
     - ❑ Ecological Analysis
   - Selection
   - Implementation
   - Review
4. Capital budgeting decision is very complex decision among all the financial decisions undertaken by an organization because of following characteristics and difficulties associated with it.

7.7.2 Characteristics of Capital Budgeting Decision

Following are important characteristics of Capital Budgeting Decision:

- **Substantial investment:** As compared to working capital decision, Capital Budgeting Decision requires substantial investment.
- **Long-term effect:** Capital budgeting decision provides long-term effect *i.e.* up to the life of the project.
- **Irreversibility:** Capital Budgeting Decision once taken cannot be reversed otherwise it will involve substantial cost.

7.7.3 Difficulties associated with Capital Budgeting Decision

Following are difficulties associated with capital budgeting decision:

- **Uncertainty regarding expected benefits:** In capital budgeting decision, investment is made today whereas benefits are received in future and since future is always uncertain, expected benefits therefore remain in uncertainty.
- **Measurement problem:** Because of uncertainties associated with future due to change in external factors like technological, political, social and economical etc., it becomes difficult to measure cost and benefits associated with capital budgeting decision.
- **Problems in equating Cost and Benefits:** In capital budgeting decisions, cost and benefits are spread over a long period of time. This creates difficulty in estimating discount rates and hence in equating cost and benefits.

5. There are two aspects of Capital Budgeting Decision *viz.* Financing Decision and Investment Decision.

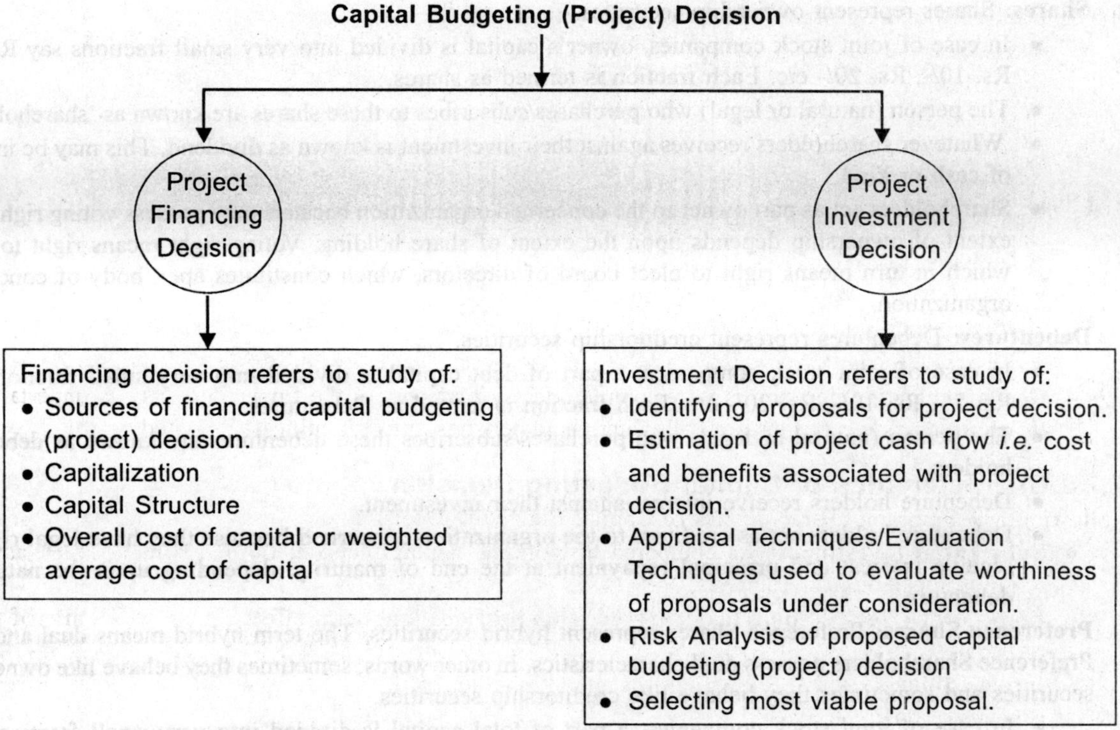

- Financing decision results into cost of capital (denoted by Ko) whereas investment decision results into Internal Rate of Return (IRR).
- Cost of capital of Financing decision acts as benchmark for investment decision. In other words, for capital budgeting decision to be financially viable cost of capital (Ko) must be lesser than Internal Rate of Return (IRR).
- Financing decision and Investment decision both go side by side, without one other is meaningless.
- After selecting most viable proposal among those under appraisal (evaluation), fund is raised according to planning of financing decision and thereafter project implementation starts.

7.7.4 Sources of financing Capital Budgeting Decision/Project Finance

Capital budgeting decisions are financed using long-term sources. The various types of long-term sources are categorized into:

- Equity Capital
- Hybrid Capital
- Debt Capital

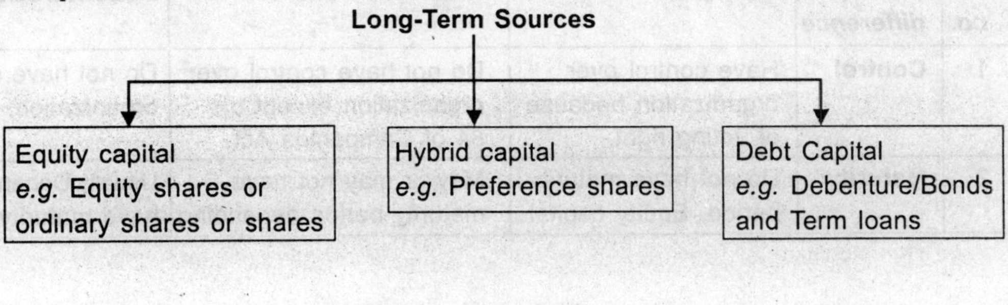

Shares: Shares represent ownership securities.

- In case of joint stock companies, owner's capital is divided into very small fractions say Rs. 5/-, Rs. 10/-, Rs. 20/- etc. Each fraction is termed as shares.
- The person (natural or legal) who purchases/subscribes to these shares are known as 'shareholders'.
- Whatever shareholders receives against their investment is known as dividend. This may be in form of cash or kind.
- Shareholders act as part owner to the concerned organization because they possess voting right. The extent of ownership depends upon the extent of share holding. Voting right means right to vote, which in turn means right to elect board of directors, which constitutes apex body of concerned organization.

Debentures: Debentures represent creditorship securities.

- In case of joint stock companies, a part of debt capital is divided into very small fractions say Rs. 5/-, Rs. 10/-, Rs. 20/- etc. Each fraction is termed as Debentures.
- The person (natural or legal) who purchases/subscribes these debentures are known as debenture holders.
- Debenture holders receive interest against their investment.
- Debenture holders act as creditors to the organization concerned because they have legal right to receive interest and principal repayment at the end of maturity, depending upon the nature of debenture.

Preference Shares: Preference Shares represent hybrid securities. The term hybrid means dual and thus Preference Shareholders possess dual characteristics. In other words, sometimes they behave like ownership securities and sometimes they behave like creditorship securities.

- In case of joint stock companies, a part of total capital is divided into very small fractions say Rs. 5/-, Rs. 10/-, Rs. 20/- etc. Each fraction is termed as Preference shares.
- The person (natural or legal) who purchases/subscribes these Preference shares are known as Preference shareholders.
- Whatever Preference shareholders receives against their investment is known as Preference dividend. The rate of preference dividend remains fixed and thus Preference share behaves like debt (creditorship) securities. The term preference means preference over equity shareholder.
- Unlike equity shareholders, preference shareholders do not act as part owner to the concerned organization because they do not possess voting right. However, under section 84 of Companies Act, in case the organization defaults in paying preference dividend up to three years, then Preference Shareholders will automatically get voting right and hence will interfere in the controlling of concerned organization and thus Preference Shareholders start behaving like equity (ownership) shareholders.

Difference between Equity shares, Preference shares and Debentures/Bonds

S. no.	*Point of difference*	*Equity shares*	*Preference shares*	*Debentures/Bonds*
1	Control	Have control over organization because of voting right.	Do not have control over organization except u/s 84 of Companies Act.	Do not have control over organization.
2	Maturity	Do not have maturity period. Equity capital	May or may not have maturity period depending	Usually Debentures/Bonds have maturity period.

Contd...

S. no.	Point of difference	Equity shares	Preference shares	Debentures/Bonds
		permanently remains with the organization.	upon type of preference share (redeemable or irredeemable).	
3	Claim on Income	Have residual claim. Thus all the risk is borne by equity shareholders.	Have preference over equity shares.	Have first claim on income.
4	Claim on Asset	Have residual claim. Thus all the risk is borne by equity shareholders.	Have preference over equity shares.	Have first claim on Asset.

Difference between Debentures and Bonds

Technically there is no difference between Debentures and Bonds as both are debt instruments. However the difference between two is due to practice in the financial market. They are,

- Generally, public sector organizations issue their debt instruments in the name of bonds whereas private sector organizations issue their debt instruments in the name of debentures. *e.g.* Railway Bonds, RBI bonds etc.
- Generally the unit size of bonds is very high as compared to debentures and therefore bonds are normally secured whereas debentures are unsecured. *e.g.* the unit size of bonds come in lakhs but again there are bonds of Rs. 100 prevailing in market but again Rs. 5 or Rs. 10 sized bonds do not exist.
- Generally bonds are not convertible whereas debentures are convertible. Convertible debentures are those debentures, which convert into pre-specified number of shares after certain time.

7.8 ADVANTAGES AND DISADVANTAGES OF EQUITY SHARES, PREFERENCE SHARES AND DEBENTURES

7.8.1 Advantages of Equity Shares

Company's Point of View

- **No legal obligation:** In case of equity shares, there is no legal obligation regarding payment of dividend.
- **Permanent source of finance:** Equity capital permanently remains with the organization. It is never paid except under liquidation.
- **Suitable source of finance:** A company whose expected future earnings are not stable or which deals in products with highly elastic demand or which does not have sufficient fixed assets to offer as security to debenture holders can use this source of raising funds to its benefit because of risk sharing capabilities.

Investor's or Shareholder's Point of View

- **Ownership:** Equity shareholders are the real owners of the organization (company) because they have voting rights. In other words, only equity shareholders have right to elect board of directors alongwith Managing Director, which is the apex body of any organization.

- **Risk-return trade off:** Since all the risk is borne by equity shareholders, they get the rewards by way of increased dividends (in case of huge residual income) leading to appreciation in the value of shares.

7.8.2 Disadvantages of Equity Shares

Company's Point of View

- **Trading on equity:** In case only equity shares are issued, the company cannot take the advantage of trading of equity, which is against the firm's objective of maximizing shareholder's wealth.
- **No maturity:** Equity shares do not have maturity period. In other words, equity capital permanently remains with the organization.
- **Over capitalization:** As equity capital cannot be redeemed, there is a danger of over capitalization.
- **Interference in functioning of management:** Because of voting right, equity shareholders can interfere in the management and hence can put obstacles in fair functioning of management.
- **Speculation:** Possibility of speculation goes up during prosperous periods because of higher dividends to be paid leading to increase in the value of shares in the market.

Investor's or Shareholder's Point of View

- **No fixed/stable income:** Investors, who are risk-averse and wish to earn fixed income, have no attraction for such shares.
- **Residual claim on income:** Equity shareholders have residual claim on income. In other words, they are paid after preference shareholders and debenture holders. Thus all the risk is borne by equity shareholders.
- **Residual claim on Asset:** Equity shareholders have residual claim on asset in case of liquidation. Thus again all the risk is borne by equity shareholders.
- **No maturity:** Equity capital do not have maturity period, they permanently remain with the organization.

7.8.3 Advantages or Merits of Preference Shares

Company's Point of View

- **No legal obligation:** There is no legal obligation regarding payment of preference dividend. Preference dividend is payable only out of distributable profits at the discretion of the management. Hence, a company does not face legal action if it does not pay dividend.
- **Long-term source:** Preference shares provide a long-term capital for the company.
- **No interference in management:** Preference shareholders do not carry voting power and hence do not interfere in the management of concerned organization except under section 84 of Companies Act.
- **Trading on equity:** In case of preference shares, fixed rate of dividend is paid. This enables a company to adopt trading on equity *i.e.* to increase rate of earnings on equity shares after paying a lower fixed rate of dividend on preference shares.
- **No security:** As no specific assets are pledged against preferred stock, the mortgageable assets of the company are conserved.

Investor's or Shareholder's Point of View

- **Stable income:** It earns a fixed rate of dividend.
- **Preferential right against assets:** It has preference over equity shares regarding claim on assets for repayment of capital at the time of liquidation.

- **Preferential right against income:** It provides preferential rights regarding payment of dividends.
- **Safety of interest:** Preference shares although carry no voting rights, but in case the organization defaults in paying dividend up to three years, then according to section 84 of Companies Act they automatically get voting right and hence behaves like equity shares.

7.8.4 Disadvantages of Preference Shares

Company's Point of View

- **High cost of capital:** It is an expensive source of finance as compared to debt because generally the investors expect a higher rate of dividend on preference shares as compared to the rate of interest on debentures.
- **Fixed burden:** Cumulative preference shares become a permanent burden so far as the payment of dividend is concerned.
- **Loss of credit worthiness:** Although there is no legal obligation of a company to pay dividend on preference shares, but frequent delays or non-payment of preference dividend adversely affect the credit worthiness of the firm.
- **No tax advantage:** Preference share dividend is not a deductible expense while calculating tax whereas interest on debt capital is a deductible expense.
- **Disadvantage to equity shareholders:** In some cases, *i.e.* in case the organization defaults in paying dividend up to three years, then according to section 84 of Companies Act they automatically get voting right and hence the control of the company in the hands of equity shareholders may get diluted.

Shareholder's Point of view

- **Dependency on management:** As the preference shareholders, ordinarily, do not have any voting rights, they remain at the mercy of the management for the payment of dividend and redemption of their capital.
- **Low income:** The rate of dividend on preference shares is usually lower as compared to the equity shares.
- **Claim on asset:** Preference shareholders do not have any charge on the assets of the company, while debentures usually provide a charge on all the assets of the company.
- **Market price:** The market prices of preference shares fluctuate much more than that of debentures.

7.8.5 Advantages of Debentures

Company's Point of View

- **Long-term source:** Debentures provide long-term funds to a company.
- **Low rate of interest:** The rate of interest payable on debentures is, usually, lower than the rate of dividend paid on share.
- **Tax advantage:** The interest on debentures is a tax-deductible expense. This lowers effective cost of debentures (debt capital) as compared to ownership securities where dividend is not a tax-deductible expense.
- **No interference in management:** Debt financing does not result into dilution of control because debenture holders do not have any voting rights.
- **Trading on equity:** A company can trade on equity by mixing debentures in its capital structure and thereby increase its earnings per share.
- **Remedy for over capitalization:** In the case of over capitalization the company can redeem the debentures to balance its capital structure.

- **Flexibility in capital structure:** Debentures provide flexibility in the capital structure of a company as the same can be redeemed as and when the company has surplus funds and desires to do so.
- **A boon during depression period:** Even during depression, when the stock market sentiment is very low, a company may be able to raise funds through issue of debentures or bonds because of certainty of income and low risk to investors.

Investor's or Shareholder's Point of View

- **Fixed and stable income:** Debentures provide a fixed, regular and stable source of income to its investors.
- **Safe investment:** It is a comparatively safer investment because debenture holders have either a specific or a floating charge on all the assets of the company and enjoy the status of a superior creditor in the event of liquidation of the company.
- **Convertibility**: In case of convertible debentures, debenture holders have option to convert debentures into shares.
- **Liquidity:** A debenture is usually a more liquid investment and an investor can sell or mortgage his instrument to obtain loans from financial institutions.
- **Security:** Various provisions of the debenture trust deed and the guidelines issued by the Securities and Exchange Board of India in this regard protect the interest of debenture holders.

7.8.6 Disadvantage of Debentures

Company's Point of View

- **Fixed obligation:** The fixed interest charges and repayment of principal amount on maturity are legal obligations of the company. These have to be paid even when there are no profits. Hence, it is a permanent burden on the company.
- **Cost of equity capital:** The use of debt financing usually increases the risk perception of investors in the firm. This enhanced financial risk increases the cost of equity capital.
- **Cost of debenture:** Cost of rising finance through debenture is also high because of high stamp duty.
- **Unsuitable source of finance**: A company whose expected future earnings are not stable or which deals in products with highly elastic demand or which does not have sufficient fixed assets to offer as security to debenture holders cannot use this source of raising funds to its benefit.

Investor's or Shareholder's Point of View

- **Control:** Debentures do not carry any voting rights and hence its holders do not have any controlling power over the management of the company.
- **Fixed income:** Debenture holders are merely creditors and not the owners of the company. They do not have any claim on the surplus assets and profits of the company beyond the fixed interest and their principal amount.
- **Tax liability:** Interest on debentures is fully taxable while shareholders may avoid tax by way of stock dividend (bonus shares) in place of cash dividend.
- **Market price:** The prices of debentures in the market fluctuate with the changes in the interest rates.
- **Uncertainty about redemption** also restricts certain investors from investing in such securities.

Capital Budgeting Evaluation Techniques/Project Appraisal Techniques

Evaluation Techniques are used to evaluate worthiness of proposals under consideration.

There are two categories of evaluation techniques *viz.*

1. Non-discounting techniques
2. Discounting techniques

Appraisal criterion (Evaluation Techniques)

Non-discounting techniques (Traditional techniques) do not consider time value of money concept. The different methods of traditional techniques are:

- Average Rate of Return/Accounting Rate of Return (ARR)
- Pay Back Period (PBP)

Discounting techniques (Discounting cash flow techniques) consider time value of money concept. The different methods of discounting techniques are:

- Net Present Value method (NPV)
- Benefit-Cost Ratio (BCR)/ Profitability Index
- Internal Rate of Return (IRR)

The details of above mentioned methods are as follows:

Average Rate of Return/Accounting Rate of Return (ARR)
Average rate of return also known as accounting rate of return is defined as average cash inflows (Benefits) against unit investment.

Thus, $$\text{ARR} = \frac{\text{Average Cash Inflows (Benefits)}}{\text{Initial Investment}} \times 100$$

Decision rule

1. If ARR > Target rate** - Accept the proposal (project)
2. If ARR < Target rate - Reject the proposal (project)
3. If ARR = Target rate - Further analysis is required

(**Target rate is the minimum rate of return targeted by management. It acts as benchmark for those involved in capital budgeting decision.)

Illustration:
Let the cash flows associated with a project under consideration is as follows: (Assuming life of the project is five years)

Year	*Cash-flows (Rs.)*	
0	(1,00,000)	→ Initial investment (cash outflows/cost)
1	20,000	Cash inflows (Benefits)
2	30,000	
3	30,000	
4	20,000	
5	40,000	

Then
Average cash inflows = (20,000 + 30,000 + 30,000 + 20,000 + 40,000)/5 = Rs. 28,000

Therefore $$\text{ARR} = \frac{28{,}000}{1{,}00{,}000} \times 100$$

ARR = 28%

Advantages of Average Rate of Return (ARR) Method

The Average Rate of Return method has the following advantages:

- It is very simple to understand and easy to calculate.
- It uses the entire earnings of a project in calculating rate of return and not only the earnings up to pay-back period and hence gives a better view of profitability as compared to pay-back period method.
- As this method is based upon accounting concept of profits, it can be readily calculated from the data taken from financial statements.

Disadvantage of Average Rate of Return (ARR) Method

In spite of so many advantages, it suffers from the following drawbacks;

- Like pay-back period method this method also ignores the time value of money concept as the profits earned at different points of time are given equal weight by averaging the profits.
- It does not take into consideration the cash flows, which are more important than the accounting profits.
- This method cannot be applied to a situation where investment in a project is to be made in parts.

Pay Back Period (PBP)

It is the time length required to cover initial investment.

Decision rule:

1. If PBP > Target period** - Accept the proposal (project)
2. If PBP < Target period - Reject the proposal (project)
3. If PBP = Target period - Further analysis is required

(**Target period is the minimum period targeted by management to cover initial investment. It acts as benchmark for those involved in capital budgeting decision.)

Illustration:

Let the cash flows associated with a project under consideration be as follows: (Assuming life of the project is five years)

Year	*Cash-flows (Rs.)*	
0	(1,00,000) →	Initial investment (cash outflows/cost)
1	20,000	Cash inflows (Benefits)
2	30,000	
3	30,000	
4	20,000	
5	40,000	

Thus 1,00,000 = (20,000 + 30,000 + 30,000 + 20,000)

= (1 + 1 + 1 + 1) years

Therefore **PBP = 4 years**

Advantages of Pay-Back Period (PBP) method

The Pay-Back Period (PBP) method has the following advantages:

- It is simple to understand and easy to calculate.
- This method is cost effective compared to other methods of capital budgeting, as it requires lesser time and labour.
- This method is effective for short-term projects under consideration because in this method, time value of money concept is usually not taken into consideration.
- In this method, a project with a shorter pay-back period is preferred to the one having a longer pay-back period. It, therefore, reduces the loss through obsolescence and is more suited to developing countries like India, which are in the process of development and have quick obsolescence.
- Due to its short-term approach, this method is particularly suited to a firm which has shortage of cash or whose liquidity position is not particularly good or which has acquired term loan with short maturity (less than five years).

Disadvantage of Pay-Back Period (PBP) Method

In spite of so many advantages, it suffers from the following drawbacks:

- It calculates time period and does not take into account the entire cash inflows and hence this method cannot assess the true profitability of the project.
- It does not take into consideration the time value of money concept. In other words, it treats all cash flows as equal (in terms of unit purchasing power) though they occur in different periods.
- It does not take into consideration the cost of capital, which is a very important factor in making sound investment decisions.
- It may be difficult to determine the minimum acceptable pay-back period; it is usually, a subjective decision.

Net Present Value (NPV)

- It represents residual net benefits in present value term available to owners (shareholders) *i.e.* net benefits after meeting their opportunity cost or Required Rate of Return (RRR).
- NPV is directly linked with the organization's objective of shareholders' wealth maximization. That is why NPV is taken as best appraisal criterion.
- In other words, higher the NPV, higher will be the 'shareholders' wealth maximization.

Thus, **NPV = PV (Benefits) – I (Initial investment)**

Where, PV (Benefits) is the present value of benefits (cash inflows) calculated using weighted average cost of capital (also known as overall cost of capital (Ko) as discount rate (%).

i.e., $$\text{PV (Benefits)} = \sum_{t=1}^{n} \text{Ct} \times \text{PVIF (Ko\%, t}^{\text{th}}\text{year)}$$

Where, PVIF (Ko%, t^{th} year) is Present Value Interest Factor at Ko%, t^{th} year. It can be taken from Present Value Interest Factor (PVIF) table and 'Ct' is the cash inflows (benefits) at the end of tth year.

Mathematically, $$\text{NPV} = \sum_{t=1}^{n} \text{Ct}/(1+\text{Ko})^{t} - \text{I}$$

Decision rule

1. If NPV > 0 - Accept the proposal (project)
2. If NPV < 0 - Reject the proposal (project)
3. If NPV = 0 - Further analysis is required

Illustration:

Let the cash flows associated with a project under consideration is as follows: (Assuming life of the project is five years and weighted average cost of capital, Ko, is 10%)

Year	*Cash-flows (Rs.)*	
0	(1,00,000)	→ Initial investment (cash outflows/cost)
1	20,000 (C_1)	Cash inflows (Benefits)
2	30,000 (C_2)	
3	30,000 (C_3)	
4	20,000 (C_4)	
5	40,000 (C_5)	

Then, $$\text{NPV} = \sum_{t=1}^{n} Ct \times \text{PVIF (Ko\%, t}^{\text{th}}\text{ year)} - 1$$

$$\text{NPV} = \{C_1 \times \text{PVIF (Ko\%, 1}^{\text{st}}\text{ year)} + C_2 \times \text{PVIF (Ko\%, 2}^{\text{nd}}\text{ year)} + C_3 \times \text{PVIF (Ko\%, 3}^{\text{rd}}\text{ year)} + C_4 \times \text{PVIF (Ko\%, 4}^{\text{th}}\text{ year)} + C_5 \times \text{PVIF (Ko\%, 5}^{\text{th}}\text{ year)}\} - \text{I}$$

$$= \{20000 \times \text{PVIF (10\%, 1}^{\text{st}}\text{ year)} + 30000 \times \text{PVIF (10\%, 2}^{\text{nd}}\text{ year)} + 30000 \times \text{PVIF (10\%, 3}^{\text{rd}}\text{ year)} + 20000 \times \text{PVIF (10\%, 4}^{\text{th}}\text{ year)} + 40000 \times \text{PVIF (10\%, 5}^{\text{th}}\text{ year)}\} - 100000$$

$$= \{20000 \times 0.909 + 30000 \times 0.826 + 30000 \times 0.751 + 20000 \times 0.683 + 40000 \times 0.621\} - 100000$$

$$= \{18180 + 24780 + 22530 + 13660 + 24840\} - 100000$$

$$\text{NPV} = \text{Rs. } 3990$$

Advantages of the Net Present Value (NPV) Method

The Net Present Value (NPV) method has the following advantages:

- It takes into consideration time value of money concept and is suitable to be applied for projects under consideration with uniform cash outflows (Investments) and uneven cash inflows (Benefits).
- It takes into account the earnings over the entire life of the project and thus it evaluates true profitability of the investment proposal.
- NPV is directly linked with the organization's objective of 'shareholders' wealth maximization. In other words, higher the NPV, higher will be the 'shareholders' wealth maximization *i.e.* why NPV is taken as best appraisal criterion.

Disadvantages of the Net Present Value (NPV) Method

In spite of so many advantages, it suffers from the following drawbacks:

- As compared to the traditional methods, the net present value method is more difficult to understand and to calculate.

- It may not give good results while comparing projects with unequal lives as the project having higher net present value but realized in a longer life span may not be as desirable as a project having something lesser net present value achieved in a much shorter span of life.
- In the same way as above, it may not give good result while comparing project with unequal investment of funds.
- Because of uncertainty involved in future earning and long-term effect it becomes difficult to determine an appropriate discount rate used to calculate present value and hence NPV.

Benefit–Cost Ratio (BCR)/Profitability Index (PI)

- It represents the present value of residual benefits available to owners (shareholders) against unit investment *i.e.* benefits after meeting their opportunity cost or Required Rate of Return (RRR).
- BCR is directly linked with the organization's profitability *i.e.* (Return on Investment).
- In other words, higher the BCR, higher will be the profitability, which in turn will lead to shareholders' wealth maximization.

Thus, **BCR = PV (Benefits) ÷ I (Initial investment)**

Where, PV (Benefits) is present value of benefits (cash inflows) calculated using weighted average cost of capital (also known as overall cost of capital (Ko) as discount rate (%).

i.e., $$\textbf{PV (Benefits)} = \sum_{t=1}^{n} Ct \times PVIF\,(Ko\%,\ t^{th}\ year)$$

Where, PVIF (Ko%, t^{th} year) is Present Value Interest Factor at Ko%, t^{th} year. It can be taken from Present Value Interest Factor (PVIF) table and 'Ct' is the cash inflows (benefits) at the end of tth year.

Mathematically, $$\textbf{BCR} = \sum_{t=1}^{n} Ct/(1+Ko)^t \div I$$

Decision rule:

1. If BCR > 1 - Accept the proposal (project)
2. If BCR < 1 - Reject the proposal (project)
3. If BCR = 1 - Further analysis is required

Illustration:

Let the cash flows associated with a project under consideration is as follows: (Assuming life of the project is five years and weighted average cost of capital, Ko, is 10%)

Year	*Cash-flows (Rs.)*	
0	(1,00,000)	→ Initial investment (cash outflows/cost)
1	20,000 (C_1)	Cash inflows (Benefits)
2	30,000 (C_2)	
3	30,000 (C_3)	
4	20,000 (C_4)	
5	40,000 (C_5)	

Then, $$\textbf{BCR} = \sum_{t=1}^{n} Ct \times PVIF\,(Ko\%,\ t^{th}\ year) \div I$$

$$BCR = \{C_1 \times PVIF\ (Ko\%,\ 1^{st}\ year) + C_2 \times PVIF\ (Ko\%,\ 2^{nd}\ year) + C_3 \times PVIF\ (Ko\%,\ 3^{rd}\ year) + C_4 \times PVIF\ (Ko\%,\ 4^{th}\ year) + C_5 \times PVIF\ (Ko\%,\ 5^{th}\ year)\} \div I$$

$$= \{20000 \times PVIF\ (10\%,\ 1^{st}\ year) + 30000 \times PVIF\ (10\%,\ 2^{nd}\ year) + 30000 \times PVIF\ (10\%,\ 3^{rd}\ year) + 20000 \times PVIF\ (10\%,\ 4^{th}\ year) + 40000 \times PVIF\ (10\%,\ 5^{th}\ year)\} \div 100000$$

$$= \{20000 \times 0.909 + 30000 \times 0.826 + 30000 \times 0.751 + 20000 \times 0.683 + 40000 \times 0.621\} \div 100000$$

$$= \{18180 + 24780 + 22530 + 13660 + 24840\} \div 100000$$

$$BCR = \frac{103990}{100000},\quad \mathbf{BCR = 1.04\ (Approx.)}$$

7.8.7 Advantages of Benefit–Cost Ratio (BCR) Method

The Benefit–Cost ratio method has the following advantages

- Like the net present value method, it takes into account the time value of money concept and is suitable to be applied for comparing projects with unequal investment of funds as it measures present value of benefits against unit investment.
- It considers the profitability of the project for its entire economic life and hence evaluates true profitability.
- It helps in ranking of various proposals under consideration due to its presentation in terms of present value of benefit per unit investment.
- This method is also compatible with the objective of shareholder's wealth maximization and is considered to be a more reliable technique of capital budgeting.

Disadvantages of Benefit–Cost Ratio (BCR) Method

In spite of so many advantages, it suffers from the following drawbacks:

- It is difficult to understand and is the most difficult method of evaluation of investment proposals.
- Because of uncertainty involved in future earnings and long-term effect it becomes difficult to determine an appropriate discount rate used to calculate present value of benefits and hence BCR.
- The results of BCR method and IRR method may differ when the projects under evaluation differ in their size (initial investment), life and timings of each cash flow.

Internal Rate of Return (IRR)

- It is that rate at which present value of benefits equals the initial investment. In other words, it is that discount rate at which NPV equals zero.
- IRR represents Return on Investment in terms of percentage.
- IRR is popular appraisal criterion for capital budgeting decision.
- IRR is calculated through hit and trial method.

Let at r%, **NPV = 0 *i.e.* PV (Benefits) = I (Initial investment)**

Then, **IRR = r%**

Thus, at IRR = r%,

$$\mathbf{PV\ (Benefits)} = \sum_{t=1}^{n} Ct \times PVIF(r\%, t^{th}\ year) = I\ (Initial\ investment)$$

Where, PVIF (r%, t^{th} year) is Present Value Interest Factor at r%, t^{th} year. It can be taken from Present Value Interest Factor (PVIF) table and 'Ct' is the cash inflows (benefits) at the end of tth year.

Decision rule

1. If IRR > Ko - Accept the proposal (project)
2. If IRR < Ko - Reject the proposal (project)
3. If IRR = Ko - Further analysis is required

Illustration:

Let the cash flows associated with a project under consideration is as follows: (Assuming life of the project is five years and weighted average cost of capital, Ko, is 10%)

Year	*Cash-flows (Rs.)*	
0	(1,00,000)	→ Initial investment (cash outflows/cost)
1	20,000 (C_1)	Cash inflows (Benefits)
2	30,000 (C_2)	
3	30,000 (C_3)	
4	20,000 (C_4)	
5	40,000 (C_5)	

Then, at IRR = r%,

$$\textbf{NPV} = 0 \quad \textit{i.e.}\ \textbf{PV (Benefits)} \left\{ \sum_{t=1}^{n} \textbf{Ct} \times \textbf{PVIF}(\textbf{r}\%, \textbf{t}^{th}\ \textbf{year}) \right\} = \textbf{I}$$

At r = 15%,

PV (Benefits) = {C_1 × PVIF (r%, 1st year) + C_2 × PVIF (r%, 2nd year) + C_3 × PVIF (r%, 3rd year) + C_4 × PVIF (r%, 4th year) + C_5 × PVIF (r%, 5th year)}

= {20000 × PVIF (15%, 1st year) + 30000 × PVIF (15%, 2nd year) + 30000 × PVIF (15%, 3rd year) + 20000 × PVIF (15%, 4th year) + 40000 × PVIF (15%, 5th year)}

= {20000 × 0.870 + 30000 × 0.756 + 30000 × 0.658 + 20000 × 0.572 + 40000 × 0.497}

= 17400 + 22680 + 19740 + 11440 + 19880

PV (Benefits) = 91140

At r = 10%,

PV (Benefits) = {C_1 × PVIF (Ko%, 1st year) + C_2 × PVIF (Ko%, 2nd year) + C_3 × PVIF (Ko%, 3rd year) + C_4 × PVIF (Ko%, 4th year) + C_5 × PVIF (Ko%, 5th year)}

= {20000 × PVIF (10%, 1st year) + 30000 × PVIF (10%, 2nd year) + 30000 × PVIF (10%, 3rd year) + 20000 × PVIF (10%, 4th year) + 40000 × PVIF (10%, 5th year)}

= {20000 × 0.909 + 30000 × 0.826 + 30000 × 0.751 + 20000 × 0.683 + 40000 × 0.621}

= {18180 + 24780 + 22530 + 13660 + 24840}

PV (Benefits) = 103990

Thus 'r' lies between 10% and 15%. Following is the calculation of exact value of 'r':

Rs. 12850 change is equivalent to 5% change.

$\therefore$ Rs. 1 change is equivalent to $\left(\frac{5}{12850}\right)$ % change

$\therefore$ Rs. 3990 change is equivalent to $\left(\frac{5}{12850}\times 3990\right)$ % change

= 1.55 % change

Again, since when 'r' increases PV (benefits) decreases.

$\therefore$ To decrease 103990 by 3990, 'r' should be increased by 1.55% from 10%

Thus r = 10% + 1.55%

i.e. **r = IRR = 11.55%**

Thus according to definition of IRR,

At IRR = 11.55%, PV(Benefits) = I = Rs. 1,00,000

Advantages of Internal Rate of Return (IRR) Method

The internal rate of return method has the following advantages:

- Like the net present value method, it takes into account the time value of money concept and is suitable to be applied for comparing projects with unequal investment of funds.
- It considers the profitability of the project for its entire economic life and hence evaluates true profitability.
- The determination of cost of capital is not a pre-requisite for the use of this method and hence it is better than net present value method where the cost of capital cannot be determined easily.
- It helps in ranking of various proposals under consideration due to its presentation in terms of percentage rate of return.
- This method is also compatible with the objective of shareholder's wealth maximization and is considered to be a more reliable technique of capital budgeting.

Disadvantages of Internal Rate of Return (IRR) Method

In spite of so many advantages, it suffers from the following drawbacks:

- It is difficult to understand and is the most difficult method of evaluation of investment proposals.
- This method is based upon the assumption that the earning are reinvested at the internal rate of return for the remaining life of the project, which is not a justified assumption particularly when the average rate of return earned by the firm is not close to the internal rate of return, In this sense, net present value method seems to be better as it assumes that the earnings are reinvested at the rate of firm's cost of capital (Ko).
- The results of NPV method and IRR method may differ when the projects under evaluation differ in their size (initial investment), life and timings of each cash flow.
- This method is not useful if investment (cash outflows) occurs at different points of time as in that situation IRR takes more than one value misleading sound investment decision.

Application of Evaluation Techniques in the Context of Information Technology (IT)

- IT professionals are supposed to deliver IT solutions. Developing software is a part of IT solution *i.e.* proposed automation.
- The IT solution team comprises of following members:

Team member	*Job profile*
Director (Project)	His main job is to deal with customer and to convince the customer on the basis of feasibility analysis of proposed automation.
Project leaders/managers	Their job is to critically evaluate the system designed by system analyst taking into account the requirements/expectations of customer from proposed automation.
System analyst	The job of system analyst is to analyse the existing system and designing of automated system for customer in terms of DFD* and ER** diagram taking into account the requirements of customer.
Senior programmer	The job of senior programmer is to design the structure using appropriate language/package.
Junior programmer	Jr. Programmer is concerned with the coding aspect using appropriate language/package

* Data Flow Diagram
** Entity Relation

- In the process of automation *i.e.* providing IT solution the different types of cost and benefits associated with proposed automation are as follows:

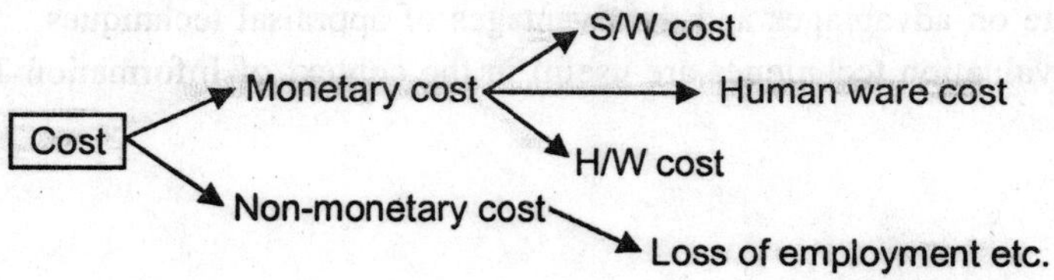

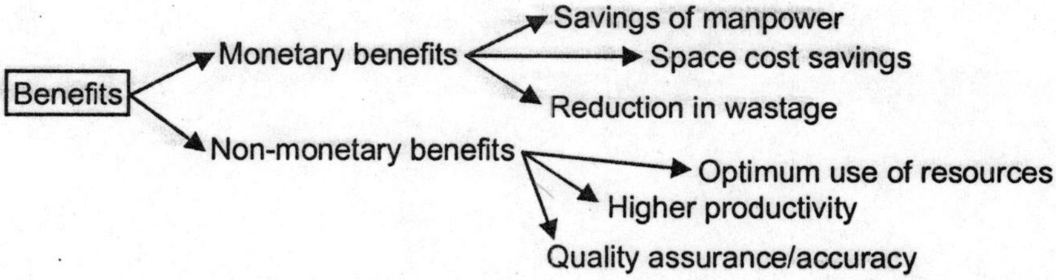

- Feasibility analysis refers to Cost and Benefits analysis associated with proposed automation.
- Social Cost and Benefits analysis refers to study of non-monetary cost and benefits analysis.
- The techniques used for cost and benefit analysis are termed as appraisal/evaluation techniques also referred as appraisal criterion.

Exercises

Q. 1. Define Financial Management. Briefly describe functions of Financial Management.

Q. 2. Describe role of finance manager.

Q. 3. "Profit maximization vs. Wealth maximization". Comment

Q. 4. Wealth maximization is the real objective of Financial Management as it helps in financial decisions. Explain this statement.

Q. 5. Describe scope of Financial Management.

Q. 6. Briefly describe Indian Financial System.

Q. 7. Differentiate between short-term investment decision and long-term investment decision.

Q. 8. Explain time value of money concept with suitable example.

Q. 9. Through illustration show how present value concept or future value concept helps in long-term investment decision.

Q. 10. The present age of Mr. X is 30 years. Mr. X will retire at the age of 60 years. Calculate how much amount Mr. X should deposit in his PPF Account, maintained continuously for two terms so that he can withdraw Rs. 20,000 per month (or Rs. 2,40,000 per annum) for next 30 years after retirement. Assume that the rate of interest offered on PPF account is 8% during service period; also assume that Mr. X will invest the entire sum of post retirement in fixed income scheme offering 8% rate of interest. Currently the term for PPF account is 15 years.

Q. 11. Define capital budgeting and write down steps involved in capital budgeting process.

Q. 12. What are characteristics and difficulties associated with capital budgeting decision?

Q. 13. Briefly describe sources of financing capital budgeting decision.

Q. 14. Differentiate between equity shares, preference shares and debentures/bonds.

Q. 15. Briefly describe advantages and disadvantages of equity shares, preference shares and debentures.

Q. 16. Differentiate between non-discounting and discounting techniques. Also describe examples of non-discounting and discounting techniques.

Q. 17. Write short note on advantages and disadvantages of appraisal techniques.

Q. 18. Explain how evaluation techniques are useful in the context of Information Technology (IT).

Appendix

Table A.1

Future Value Interest Factor (FVIF)

$$FVIF\ (k, n) = (1 + k)^n$$

Period n	1%	2%	3%	4%	5%	6%	7%	8%	9%	10%	11%	12%	13%
0	1.000	1.000	1.000	1.000	1.000	1.000	1.000	1.000	1.000	1.000	1.000	1.000	1.000
1	1.010	1.020	1.030	1.040	1.050	1.060	1.070	1.080	1.090	1.100	1.110	1.120	1.130
2	1.020	1.040	1.061	1.082	1.102	1.124	1.145	1.166	1.188	1.210	1.232	1.254	1.277
3	1.030	1.061	1.093	1.125	1.158	1.191	1.225	1.260	1.295	1.331	1.368	1.405	1.443
4	1.041	1.082	1.126	1.170	1.216	1.262	1.311	1.360	1.412	1.464	1.518	1.574	1.630
5	1.051	1.104	1.159	1.217	1.276	1.338	1.403	1.469	1.539	1.611	1.685	1.762	1.842
6	1.062	1.126	1.194	1.265	1.340	1.419	1.501	1.587	1.677	1.772	1.870	1.974	2.082
7	1.072	1.149	1.230	1.316	1.407	1.504	1.606	1.714	1.828	1.949	2.076	2.211	2.353
8	1.083	1.172	1.267	1.369	1.477	1.594	1.718	1.851	1.993	2.144	2.305	2.476	2.658
9	1.094	1.195	1.305	1.423	1.551	1.689	1.838	1.999	2.172	2.358	2.558	2.773	3.004
10	1.105	1.219	1.344	1.480	1.629	1.791	1.967	2.159	2.367	2.594	2.839	3.106	3.395
11	1.116	1.243	1.384	1.539	1.710	1.898	2.105	2.332	2.580	2.853	3.152	3.479	3.836
12	1.127	1.268	1.426	1.601	1.796	2.012	2.252	2.518	2.813	3.138	3.498	3.896	4.335
13	1.138	1.294	1.469	1.665	1.886	2.133	2.410	2.720	3.056	3.452	3.883	4.363	4.898
14	1.149	1.319	1.513	1.732	1.930	2.261	2.579	2.937	3.342	3.797	4.310	4.887	5.535
15	1.161	1.346	1.558	1.801	2.079	2.397	2.759	3.172	3.642	4.177	4.785	5.474	6.254
16	1.173	1.373	1.605	1.873	2.183	2.540	2.952	3.426	3.970	4.595	5.311	6.130	7.067
17	1.184	1.400	1.653	1.948	2.292	2.693	3.159	3.700	4.328	5.054	5.895	6.866	7.986
18	1.196	1.428	1.702	2.026	2.407	2.854	3.380	3.996	4.717	5.560	6.544	7.690	9.024
19	1.208	1.457	1.754	2.107	2.527	3.026	3.617	4.316	5.142	6.116	7.263	8.613	10.197
20	1.220	1.486	1.806	2.191	2.653	3.207	3.870	4.661	5.604	6.728	8.062	9.646	11.523
25	1.282	1.641	2.094	2.666	3.386	4.292	5.427	6.848	8.623	10.835	13.585	17.000	21.231
30	1.348	1.811	2.427	3.243	4.322	5.743	7.612	10.063	13.268	17.449	22.892	29.960	39.116

Period n	14%	15%	16%	17%	18%	19%	20%	24%	28%	32%	36%	40%
0	1.000	1.000	1.000	1.000	1.000	1.000	1.000	1.000	1.000	1.000	1.000	1.000
1	1.140	1.150	1.160	1.170	1.180	1.190	1.200	1.240	1.280	1.320	1.360	1.400
2	1.300	1.322	1.346	1.369	1.392	1.416	1.440	1.538	1.638	1.742	1.850	1.960
3	1.482	1.521	1.561	1.602	1.643	1.685	1.728	1.907	2.097	2.300	2.515	2.744
4	1.689	1.749	1.811	1.874	1.939	2.005	2.074	2.364	2.684	3.036	3.421	3.842
5	1.925	2.011	2.100	2.192	2.288	2.386	2.488	2.392	3.436	4.007	4.653	5.378
6	2.195	2.313	2.436	2.565	2.700	2.840	2.986	3.635	4.398	5.290	6.328	7.530
7	2.502	2.660	2.826	3.001	3.185	3.379	3.583	4.508	5.629	6.983	8.605	10.541
8	2.853	3.059	3.278	3.511	3.759	4.021	4.300	5.590	7.206	9.217	11.703	14.758
9	3.252	3.518	3.803	4.108	4.435	4.785	5.160	6.931	9.223	12.166	15.917	20.661

Contd...

Period n	14%	15%	16%	17%	18%	19%	20%	24%	28%	32%	36%	40%
10	3.707	4.046	4.411	4.807	5.234	5.695	6.192	8.594	11.806	16.060	21.647	28.925
11	4.226	4.652	5.117	5.624	6.176	6.777	7.430	10.657	15.112	21.199	29.439	40.496
12	4.818	5.350	5.936	6.580	7.288	8.064	8.916	13.215	19.343	27.983	40.037	56.694
13	5.492	6.153	6.886	7.699	8.599	9.596	10.699	16.386	24.759	36.937	54.451	79.372
14	6.261	7.076	7.988	9.007	10.147	11.420	12.839	20.319	31.961	48.757	74.053	111.120
15	7.138	8.137	9.266	10.539	11.974	13.590	15.407	25.196	40.565	64.359	100.712	155.568
16	8.137	9.358	10.748	12.330	14.129	16.172	18.488	31.243	51.923	84.954	136.969	217.795
17	9.276	10.761	12.468	14.426	16.672	19.244	22.186	38.741	66.461	112.139	186.278	304.914
18	10.575	12.375	14.463	16.879	19.673	22.901	26.623	48.039	85.071	148.023	253.338	426.879
19	12.056	14.232	16.777	19.748	23.214	27.252	31.948	59.568	108.890	195.391	344.540	597.630
20	13.743	16.367	19.461	23.106	27.393	32.429	38.338	73.864	139.380	257.916	468.574	836.683
25	26.462	32.919	40.874	50.658	62.669	77.388	95.396	216.542	478.905	1033.590	2180.081	4499.880
30	50.950	66.212	85.850	111.065	143.371	184.675	237.376	634.820	1645.504	4142.075	10143.019	24201.432

Tables A.2

Future Value Interest Factor for an Annuity

$$FVIFA\ (k,\ n) = \frac{(1+k)^n - 1}{k}$$

Period n	1%	2%	3%	4%	5%	6%	7%	8%	9%	10%	11%	12%	13%
1	1.000	1.000	1.000	1.000	1.000	1.000	1.000	1.000	1.000	1.000	1.000	1.000	1.000
2	2.010	2.020	2.030	2.040	2.050	2.060	2.070	2.080	2.090	2.100	2.110	2.120	2.130
3	3.030	3.060	3.091	3.122	3.152	3.184	3.215	3.246	3.278	3.310	3.342	3.374	3.407
4	4.060	4.122	4.184	4.246	4.310	4.375	4.440	4.506	4.573	4.641	4.710	4.779	4.850
5	5.101	5.204	5.309	5.416	5.526	5.637	5.751	5.867	5.985	6.105	6.228	6.353	6.480
6	6.152	6.308	6.468	6.633	6.802	6.975	7.153	7.336	7.523	7.716	7.913	8.115	8.323
7	7.214	7.434	7.662	7.898	8.142	8.394	8.654	8.923	9.200	9.487	9.783	10.089	10.405
8	8.286	8.583	8.892	9.214	9.549	9.897	10.260	10.637	11.028	11.436	11.859	12.300	12.757
9	9.369	9.755	10.159	10.583	11.027	11.491	11.978	12.488	13.021	13.579	14.164	14.776	15.416
10	10.462	10.950	11.464	12.006	12.578	13.181	13.816	14.487	15.193	15.937	16.722	17.549	18.420
11	11.567	12.169	12.808	13.486	14.207	14.972	15.784	16.645	17.560	18.531	19.561	20.655	21.814
12	12.683	13.412	14.192	15.026	15.917	16.870	17.888	18.977	20.141	21.384	22.713	24.133	25.650
13	13.809	14.680	15.618	16.627	17.713	18.882	20.141	21.495	22.953	24.523	26.212	28.029	29.958
14	14.947	15.974	17.086	18.292	19.599	21.015	22.550	24.215	26.019	27.975	30.095	32.393	34.883
15	16.097	17.293	18.599	20.024	21.579	23.276	25.129	27.152	29.361	31.772	34.405	37.280	40.417
16	17.258	18.639	20.157	21.825	23.657	25.673	27.888	30.324	33.003	35.950	39.190	42.753	46.672
17	18.430	20.012	21.762	23.698	25.840	28.213	30.840	33.750	36.974	40.545	44.501	48.884	53.739
18	19.615	21.412	23.414	25.645	28.132	30.906	33.999	37.450	41.301	45.599	50.396	55.750	61.725
19	20.811	22.841	25.117	27.671	30.539	33.760	37.379	41.446	46.018	51.159	56.939	63.440	70.749
20	22.019	24.297	26.870	29.778	33.066	36.786	40.995	45.762	51.160	57.275	64.203	72.052	80.947
25	28.243	32.030	36.459	41.646	47.727	54.865	63.249	73.106	84.701	98.347	114.413	133.334	155.620
30	34.785	40.568	45.575	56.805	66.439	79.058	94.461	113.283	136.308	164.494	199.021	241.333	293.199

Period n	14%	15%	16%	17%	18%	19%	20%	24%	.28%	32%	36%	40%
1	1.000	1.000	1.000	1.000	1.000	1.000	1.000	1.000	1.000	1.000	1.000	1.000
2	2.140	2.150	2.160	2.170	2.180	2.190	2.200	2.240	2.280	2.320	2.360	2.400
3	3.440	3.473	3.506	3.539	3.572	3.606	3.640	3.778	3.918	4.062	4.210	4.360
4	4.921	4.993	5.066	5.141	5.215	5.291	5.368	5.684	6.016	6.362	6.725	7.104
5	6.610	6.742	6.877	7.014	7.154	7.297	7.442	8.048	8.700	9.398	10.146	10.946
6	8.536	8.754	8.977	9.207	9.442	9.683	9.930	10.980	12.136	13.406	14.799	16.324
7	10.730	11.067	11.414	11.772	12.142	12.523	12.916	14.615	16.534	18.696	21.126	23.853
8	13.233	13.727	14.240	14.773	15.327	15.902	16.499	19.123	22.163	25.678	29.732	34.395
9	16.085	16.786	17.518	18.285	19.086	19.923	20.799	24.712	29.369	34.895	41.435	49.153
10	19.337	20.304	21.321	22.393	23.521	24.709	25.959	31.643	38.592	47.062	57.352	69.814
11	23.044	24.349	25.733	27.200	28.755	30.404	32.150	40.238	50.399	63.122	78.998	98.739
12	27.271	29.002	30.850	32.824	34.931	37.180	39.580	50.958	65.510	84.320	108.437	139.235
13	32.089	34.352	36.786	39.404	42.219	45.244	48.497	64.110	84.853	112.303	148.475	195.929
14	37.581	40.505	43.672	47.103	50.818	54.841	59.196	80.496	109.612	149.240	202.926	275.300
15	43.842	27.580	51.660	56.110	60.965	66.261	72.035	100.815	141.303	197.997	276.979	386.420
16	50.980	55.717	60.925	66.649	72.939	79.850	87.442	126.011	181.868	262.356	377.692	541.988
17	59.118	65.075	71.673	78.979	87.068	96.022	105.931	157.253	233.791	347.310	514.661	759.784
18	68.394	75.836	84.141	93.406	103.740	115.266	128.117	195.994	300.252	459.449	700.939	1064.697
19	78.969	88.212	98.603	110.285	123.414	138.166	154.740	244.033	385.323	607.472	954.277	1491.376
20	91.025	102.44	115.380	130.033	146.628	165.418	186.688	303.601	494.213	802.863	1298.817	2089.206
25	181.871	212.793	249.214	292.105	342.603	402.042	471.981	898.092	1706.803	3226.844	6053.004	11247.199
30	356.787	434.745	530.321	647.439	790.948	966.712	1181.882	2640.916	5873.231	12940.859	28172.276	60501.081

Table A.3

Present Value Interest Factor

PVIF (k, n) = $(1 + k)^{-n}$

Period n	1%	2%.	3%	4%	5%	6%	7%	8%	9%	10%	11%	12%	13%
0	1.000	1.000	1.000	1.000	1.000	1.000	1.000	1.000	1.000	1.000	1.000	1.000	1.000
1	0.990	0.980	0.971	0.962	0.952	0.943	0.935	0.926	0.917	0.909	0.901	0.893	0.885
2	0.980	0.961	0.943	0.925	0.907	0.890	0.873	0.857	0.842	0.826	0.812	0.797	0.783
3	0.971	0.942	0.915	0.889	0.864	0.840	0.816	0.794	0.772	0.751	0.731	0.712	0.693
4	0.961	0.924	0.889	0.855	0.823	0.792	0.763	0.735	0.708	0.683	0.659	0.636	0.613
5	0.951	0.906	0.863	0.822	0.784	0.747	0.713	0.681	0.650	0.621	0.593	0.567	0.543
6	0.942	0.888	0.838	0.790	0.746	0.705	0.666	0.630	0.596	0.564	0.535	0.507	0.480
7	0.933	0.871	0.813	0.760	0.711	0.665	0.623	0.583	0.547	0.513	0.482	0.452	0.425
8	0.923	0.853	0.789	0.731	0.677	0.627	0.582	0.540	0.502	0.467	0.434	0.404	0.376
9	0.914	0.837	0.766	0.703	0.645	0.592	0.544	0.500	0.460	0.424	0.391	0.361	0.333
10	0.905	0.820	0.744	0.676	0.614	0.558	0.508	0.463	0.422	0.386	0.352	0.322	0.295
11	0.896	0.804	0.722	0.650	0.585	0.527	0.475	0.429	0.388	0.350	0.317	0.287	0.261
12	0.887	0.788	0.701	0.625	0.557	0.497	0.444	0.397	0.356	0.319	0.286	0.257	0.231

Contd...

Period n	1%	2%	3%	4%	5%	6%	7%	8%	9%	10%	11%	12%	13%
13	0.879	0.773	0.681	0.601	0.530	0.469	0.415	0.368	0.326	0.290	0.258	0.229	0.204
14	0.870	0.758	0.661	0.577	0.505	0.442	0.388	0.340	0.299	0.263	0.232	0.205	0.181
15	0.861	0.743	0.642	0.555	0.481	0.417	0.362	0.315	0.275	0.239	0.209	0.183	0.160
16	0.853	0.728	0.623	0.534	0.458	0.394	0.339	0.292	0.252	0.218	0.188	0.163	0.141
17	0.844	0.714	0.605	0.513	0.436	0.371	0.317	0.270	0.231	0.198	0.170	0.146	0.125
18	0.836	0.700	0.587	0.494	0.416	0.350	0.296	0.250	0.212	0.180	0.153	0.130	0.111
19	0.828	0.686	0.570	0.475	0.396	0.331	0.276	0.232	0.194	0.164	0.138	0.116	0.098
20	0.820	0.673	0.554	0.456	0.377	0.312	0.258	0.215	0.178	0.149	0.124	0.104	0.087
25	0.780	0.610	0.478	0.375	0.295	0.233	0.184	0.146	0.116	0.092	0.074	0.059	0.047
30	0.742	0.552	0.412	0.308	0.231	0.174	0.131	0.099	0.075	0.057	0.044	0.033	0.026

Period n	14%	15%	16%	17%	18%	19%	20%	24%	28%	32%	36%	40%
0	1.000	1.000	1.000	1.000	1.000	1.000	1.000	1.000	1.000	1.000	1.000	1.000
1	0.877	0.870	0.862	0.855	0.847	0.840	0.833	0.806	0.781	0.758	0.735	0.714
2	0.769	0.756	0.743	0.731	0.718	0.706	0.694	0.650	0.610	0.574	0.541	0.510
3	0.675	0.658	0.641	0.624	0.609	0.593	0.579	0.524	0.477	0.435	0.398	0.364
4	0.592	0.572	0.552	0.534	0.516	0.499	0.482	0.423	0.373	0.329	0.292	0.260
5	0.519	0.497	0.476	0.456	0.437	0.419	0.402	0.341	0.291	0.250	0.215	0.186
6	0.456	0.432	0.410	0.390	0.370	0.352	0.335	0.275	0.227	0.189	0.158	0.133
7	0.400	0.376	0.354	0.333	0.314	0.296	0.279	0.222	0.178	0.143	0.116	0.095
8	0.351	0.327	0.305	0.285	0.266	0.249	0.233	0.179	0.139	0.108	0.085	0.068
9	0.308	0.284	0.263	0.243	0.226	0.209	0.194	0.144	0.108	0.082	0.063	0.048
10	0.270	0.247	0.227	0.208	0.191	0.176	0.162	0.116	0.085	0.062	0.046	0.035
11	0.237	0.215	0.195	0.178	0.162	0.148	0.135	0.094	0.066	0.047	0.034	0.025
12	0.208	0.187	0.168	0.152	0.137	0.124	0.112	0.076	0.052	0.036	0.025	0.018
13	0.182	0.163	0.145	0.130	0.116	0.104	0.093	0.061	0.040	0.027	0.018	0.013
14	0.160	0.141	0.125	0.111	0.099	0.088	0.078	0.049	0.032	0.021	0.014	0.009
15	0.140	0.123	0.108	0.095	0.084	0.074	0.065	0.040	0.025	0.016	0.010	0.006
16	0.123	0.107	0.093	0.081	0.071	0.062	0.054	0.032	0.019	0.012	0.007	0.005
17	0.108	0.093	0.080	0.069	0.060	0.052	0.045	0.026	0.015	0.009	0.005	0.003
18	0.095	0.081	0.069	0.059	0.051	0.044	0.038	0.021	0.012	0.007	0.004	0.002
19	0.083	0.070	0.060	0.051	0.043	0.037	0.031	0.017	0.009	0.005	0.003	0.002
20	0.073	0.061	0.051	0.043	0.037	0.031	0.026	0.014	0.007	0.004	0.002	0.001
25	0.038	0.030	0.024	0.020	0.016	0.013	0.010	0.005	0.002	0.001	0.000	0.000
30	0.020	0.015	0.012	0.009	0.007	0.005	0.004	0.002	0.001	0.000	0.000	0.000